Confucius's *Analects*

學而第一
論語

Confucius's *Analects*

AN ADVANCED READER OF CHINESE LANGUAGE AND CULTURE

读论语学中文

Zu-yan Chen

GEORGETOWN UNIVERSITY PRESS
Washington, D.C.

Georgetown University Press
Washington, D.C. www.press.georgetown.edu

Library of Congress Cataloging-in-Publication Data
Confucius.
Confucius's Analects : an advanced reader of Chinese
language and culture / Zu-yan Chen. — 1st ed.
p. cm.
Chinese and English.
Includes indexes.
ISBN 978-1-58901-635-4 (pbk. : alk. paper)
1. Chinese language—Readers. 2. Chinese language—
Textbooks for foreign speakers—English. I. Chen, Zu-yan. II. Title.
PL1117.C68 2010
495.1'82421—dc22
2009024527

∞ This book is printed on acid-free paper meeting the
requirements of the American National Standard for
Permanence in Paper for Printed Library Materials.

15 14 13 12 11 10 9 8 7 6 5 4 3 2
First printing

Printed in the United States of America

Contents

Preface

The *Analects* (*Lunyu* 论语), a collection of sayings by Confucius (551–479 BCE) and his disciples, is one of the most influential texts in East Asian intellectual history. It is within this work that most of the basic framework regarding Confucian values such as humanity (*ren* 仁), righteousness (*yi* 义), filial piety (*xiao* 孝), and propriety (*li* 礼) is developed. The *Analects* served as a fundamental course of study for all scholars in China, as well as a textbook of literacy, for over two millennia. This textbook, *Confucius's* Analects*: An Advanced Reader of Chinese Language and Culture,* is thus essentially a return to this tradition. Pedagogically, however, it presents an innovative approach to teaching Chinese language and culture at the advanced level, featuring three integrations: those of classical and modern Chinese, of language and culture, and of expository and narrative writing.

These three integrations are mainly achieved through this book's "quadruple text" system. First and foremost are, of course, the quotations from the *Analects*. Of its 492 passages, 82 are presented herein; the selections are both educational and practical for present-day students. These passages are grouped thematically into twenty chapters and are further organized into four parts: Knowledge (*zhixue* 治学), Morality (*xiushen* 修身), Wisdom (*chushi* 处世), and Government (*weizheng* 为政). These subjects cover Confucian teachings on matters ranging from personal cultivation to social contribution.

The other three texts, all in modern Chinese, are designed as interpretations of the *Analects* passages in different forms. The modern Chinese translation, literal in nature, aims at an intelligible modern rendering of the Master's words. The short exegetical essays discuss the major points of the quotations, elaborating upon their richness and subtleties. The historical stories, all well known in China, illustrate the theme of each chapter. Together, these four texts provide an effective and interesting learning process, allowing students to improve their skills in both classical and modern Chinese.

This new approach is intended to correct the view that classical and modern Chinese belong in separate domains. On the contrary, not only is classical Chinese the source of modern Chinese, but it also permeates the vital stream of present-day communications. This linguistic continuity provides the foundation for the two pedagogical strategies that are employed throughout the chapters: vocabulary expansion and idiom acquisition.

The vocabulary expansion section and corresponding exercises are created based on the fact that most classical Chinese words are monosyllabic (e.g., *xue* 学), whereas the majority of modern Chinese words comprise two characters (e.g., *xuexi* 学习). A monosyllabic classical word may have a range of possible meanings (its specific meaning to be determined by context), whereas the corresponding modern disyllabic word—or each of several corresponding modern words—will carry a specific meaning. This practice of expanding one classical word into a number of modern words helps students better understand the classical words' facets of meaning and speeds the development of their modern Chinese vocabulary.

The distinction between the classical and the modern blurs once idioms are introduced. These traditional bits of wit, mostly comprising four characters, have played and still play a major role in everyday oral and written communication. Unfortunately, the rhetorical value of idioms has not attracted due notice in Chinese classrooms. This book flavors its chapters with 279 idioms, a collection of tags that will enable thoughts to be communicated and exchanged with minimal effort in formulation. An idiom section in each chapter, the corresponding exercises, and an index of idioms attest to a high regard for the positive pedagogical implications of this formulaic wisdom in classical antiquity.

By engaging with the old gems of Chinese language and culture, students learn to express themselves in a more sophisticated and idiomatic way. At the elementary level students talk about issues of daily life (shopping, restaurants, etc.). At the intermediate level students discuss social issues (population, employment, etc.). At the advanced level they need to be able to discuss personal and social issues using historical and philosophical perspectives; they also need to arrange their trains of thought, justify their opinions, defend their statements, and cite examples from the classics and history to support their arguments. This textbook attempts to use the *Analects* as a means to carry learners toward this goal.

前言

《论语》记述孔子和他的弟子的言行，为东亚文明中影响最深远的典籍之一。儒家的核心思想如仁、义、孝、礼等皆由此而生发。《论语》既是两千年中学子研读之经典，也是童蒙之课本。因此，这本《读论语学中文》实为对此悠久传统之回归。然而在教学法上，本书却又代表高级中文教学中的一种创新，标举三个结合：文言文和白话文的结合、语言和文化的结合以及论说文和记叙文的结合。

这三个结合主要是通过本书的“四合一”的课文体系来实现，即每一章有四篇课文。首先当然是《论语》章句。本书从《论语》的492段语录中选用了82段对当今学生既有陶冶作用又能切问近思的段落，按主题分为二十章，并进而集结成《治学》、《修身》、《处世》、《为政》四篇。这四篇二十章涵盖了儒家学说中从个人修养到社会贡献的诸多方面。

每课后续的三篇课文都是用白话文写的，可视为对《论语》的不同形式的阐发。以信达为原则的白话文翻译旨在使圣人之言明白通晓。解读的短文揭示每章的荦荦大端，并进而探幽发微。事例则以在中国家喻户晓的历史故事形象地说明各章语录的主旨。四篇课文环环相扣，为学生提供一条有效并有趣的学习途径，同时提高他们的文言文和白话文的水平。

这种新的教学方法将有助于纠正将文言文和白话文截然割裂的悖论。与此相反，本书表明文言文是白话文的源头活水，并继续流动在现代交际的长河之中。此种语言的延续和演进为本书各章采用的词汇扩展和成语练习两种教学法提供了坚实的基础。

词汇扩展部分和相应的练习是基于一个事实，即文言文基本上是单音词（如“学”）而白话词语大多是双音节（如“学习”）。一个单音节的文言字常一字多义，其所指须在上下文中方能判断；但其相应之白话双音节词却各具特定的意思。这种把一个文言词扩展成多个白话词语的练习既有助于学生理解文言词的丰富涵义，也使学生能迅速扩大白话文的词汇量。

在介绍成语时，就更显出文言文和白话文之交融。这些多半由四个字组成的古代智慧的结晶在当代书面和口头的交流中仍然作用至巨。可惜成语的语言教学功能尚未在中文教育中引起足够重视。成语的意义及结构都是现成的，无需组织，故便于使用、利于表达。此书共收成语279句，在各章中列有专节。加上相应的练习及附录的成语索引，此语言宝库之精华在本书中应能引起足够的重视。

古为今用是为了让学生表达得更典雅细致。在初级中文阶段，学生谈论日常生活（如购物、上饭馆儿等）。在中级中文阶段，学生讨论社会问题（如人口、就业等）。在高级中文阶段，他们应能在历史和哲学的背景上来讨论问题，他们也应能用中文整理思路、说明观点、引经据典、收放自如。本书意在借助学习《论语》达到此目的。

Acknowledgments

What better time for writing acknowledgments than New Year's Eve? The white snow outside the windows and the red flames in the fireplace afford me the best setting in which to reflect upon the legion of people to whom I am indebted for making this book possible.

This textbook is an extension of my teaching at Binghamton University. I created Confucius's Analects as an advanced course in Chinese language and culture in Spring 2007 and taught it again the following year. Students in these two classes downloaded the chapters from the university Blackboard™ system. I appreciated their tolerance for the inconvenience of the virtual textbook, and more important, for the interest and enthusiasm they had for the subject.

The *Analects* has been a focus of study for over two millennia and was first translated into English by James Legge (1815–1897), the first professor of Chinese at Oxford University. Accordingly, my modern Chinese translations of the eighty-two *Analects* passages—and their English counterparts in the appendix—have benefited from the works of previous scholars and translators. To my predecessors I owe much for the accuracy, fluency, and style of these translations.

I am greatly obliged to the four anonymous reviewers of my manuscript for their insightful comments and suggestions. They shed light on many pedagogical and stylistic oversights. I acknowledge with gratitude the beautiful illustrations created by Qianghua Wang. My deep gratitude also goes to my editor, Gail Grella at Georgetown University Press, who has guided me through the many stages of publication with her expertise and enthusiasm. My work with her has turned out to be a richly rewarding experience.

Finally, there are no words adequate to thank my wife and colleague, Hong Zhang, who assisted me with a multitude of tasks. As the first reader of the manuscript, she gave me feedback with perceptive comments and critical reactions. She also made an excellent recording of her recitation of the passages from the *Analects* for the book. Above all, she has accompanied me through the long journey in the profession of education as described by Confucius's dictum, "to learn insatiably and to teach indefatigably" 学而不厌，诲人不倦.

User's Guide

1. This textbook is designed for students who have studied Chinese for three years in college, or the equivalent. Knowledge of classical Chinese is not a prerequisite. This book is targeted for use in such courses as "Advanced Modern Chinese," "Classical Chinese," and "Readings of Traditional Chinese Culture."

2. The sequences of the *Analects* passages. The numbers preceding a passage denote its sequence in this book. For example, 2-1 refers to chapter 2, passage 1. The numbers that appear in parentheses after each passage indicate the passage's position in the original *Analects*. For example, (5.28) refers to the twenty-eighth paragraph of chapter 5 in the *Analects*. The source text used in this book is He Yan 何晏 (d. 249), *Lunyu zhushu* 论语注疏, Shisanjing zhushu 十三经注疏 edition.

3. Translations. Modern Chinese translations of the *Analects* passages follow the original texts. English translations are included in the appendix.

4. Function Words 虚词. The key to understanding classical Chinese is the function words. Each function word is listed by its first appearance in each different function in the function words section of each chapter. An index of function words 虚词索引 includes the sixty-one function words used in this book along with their various usages, as well as a concordance.

5. Idioms 成语. There are three sections relating to the 279 idioms in this book: the idioms section in each chapter, the corresponding exercises, and the index of idioms 成语索引.

6. Vocabulary Expansion 词汇扩展. A total of 145 words from the *Analects*—7 or 8 in each chapter—are treated in this volume. For each selected word, a sampling of 10 "expanded" modern words or idioms is provided. This sampling is far from exhaustive, of course, and there is much room for further expansion.

7. Using dictionaries. The exercises in each chapter comprise ten sections with different functions. In doing some of these exercises, students may often need to use a Chinese-English dictionary or a Chinese dictionary. In those exercises

requiring translation from Chinese into English 中译英, interpretations are supplied only for those words likely to confuse students.

8. Research on the internet. Section 10 of the exercises varies in form in different chapters, including debate, composition, storytelling, and topical research; however, they all require students to do research on the internet. These research projects, although brief in length and limited in scope, will challenge students to check information and resources in Chinese and English, and to report on their findings in Chinese.

9. Companion audio files of the recitation of the *Analects* passages by Hong Zhang, a vocal expert, are available online at www.press.georgetown.edu.

使用说明

1. 本书为学过三年大学中文或同等程度的学生而设计。文言文基础并非必要之前提。“高级中文”、“文言文”和“中国传统文化阅读”等课程均可用本书为教材。

2.《论语》章句序列。每段语录前的数字表明本书的序列，如2-1为第二章第一段。每段语录后的数字表明《论语》原著中的位置，如5.28即《论语》第五章第二十八段。本书采用何晏《论语注疏》（《十三经注疏》本）为底本。

3. 翻译。《论语》章句的白话文翻译排在原文之下，英文翻译收在附录之中。

4. 虚词。读通文言文的关键在虚词。本书共收61个虚词。每个虚词在其不同功用的首次出现时列在该章的虚词表中。附录中的虚词索引列有每个虚词的不同功用及在各课出现的所有例句。

5. 成语。本书收有279句成语。每章有成语专栏及相应的成语练习。附录有成语索引。

6. 词汇扩展。每章列举七、八个《论语》中的文言词（全书总共145个），并为每个词列举十个由此扩展而成的白话词语或成语。此表并不完全，大多数文言词仍可继续扩展。

7. 辞典使用。每章有十种功用不同的练习。有些练习学生需要使用中英或中文词典。在中译英部分，只对有些容易造成误解的词提供注释。

8. 网上研究。练习的第十部分每章形式有所不同，有辩论、作文、讲故事和专题研究等。学生都要在网上做研究才能完成。这些研究大都简单易行，要求学生寻找中文或英文的资料，然后用中文作口头或书面报告。

9. 录音。由声乐专家张泓录制的《论语》章句朗读可在以下网址收听：
www.press.georgetown.edu.

Confucius and the *Analects* 孔子与《论语》

孔子(前551-479)，名丘，字仲尼，伟大的思想家、教育家，儒家的创始人。

孔子的家乡在今山东曲阜，当时是鲁国的首都。孔子早年生活艰辛，但他勤奋好学，遍访名师。成年后，孔子聚徒讲学，相传有弟子三千，其中贤人七十二。孔子五十岁左右在鲁国从政，政绩很好，做到代理宰相。后来因与鲁国国君有分歧，孔子在五十五岁时率弟子周游列国，然而都没获得重用。其间，孔子一行多次遇到困难和危险。十四年后，孔子返回鲁国，专注于教育和古籍整理。

孔子编订的古代文献有《诗经》、《书经》、《易经》、《礼记》和《春秋》。这五部书被后世尊为“五经”。孔子的言行记载在他的弟子编的《论语》一书中。南宋时，朱熹(1130-1200)把它和《大学》、《中庸》和《孟子》合称为“四书”。从此，“四书五经”成为儒家的核心经典。

这九本书中，《论语》是经中之经。它是孔子思想的宝库，因此古人有“半部《论语》治天下”的说法。《论语》涉及哲学、政治、经济、教育、文艺等各方面，内容非常丰富。在表达上，《论语》语言精练而形象生动，是古代散文的典范。

自从汉武帝(前140-87在位)确立儒家为中国的正统思想，孔子学说成为两千年来中华文化的主流。孔子被尊为“万世师表”及“圣人”，对中国、亚洲以至全世界都有深远的影响。

VOCABULARY 词汇

1.	字	zì	style (name)
2.	儒家	rújiā	Confucianism
3.	创始人	chuàngshǐ rén	founder
4.	艰辛	jiānxīn	arduous and difficult
5.	遍	biàn	all over, everywhere
6.	聚	jù	to assemble, to gather
7.	徒	tú	disciple
8.	相传	xiāngchuán	according to legend
9.	弟子	dìzǐ	disciple
10.	贤人	xiánrén	a person of virtue
11.	从政	cóngzhèng	to have a political career
12.	政绩	zhèngjī	achievements in one's official career

13.	代理宰相	dàilǐ zǎixiàng	acting chief minister
14.	国君	guójūn	monarch, king
15.	分歧	fēnqí	difference, divergence
16.	率	shuài	带领
17.	周游列国	zhōuyóu lièguó	to travel to many states
18.	然而	rán'ér	但是
19.	一行	yīxíng	a group traveling together
20.	返	fǎn	to return
21.	专注	zhuānzhù	to concentrate on, to devote one's mind to
22.	古籍	gǔjí	ancient books
23.	编订	biāndìng	to edit, to compile
24.	文献	wénxiàn	documents
25.	后世	hòushì	later generations
26.	核心	héxīn	core
27.	宝库	bǎokù	treasure house
28.	说法	shuōfa	statement, argument
29.	涉及	shèjí	to involve, to relate to, to touch upon
30.	精练	jīngliàn	concise, succinct
31.	典范	diǎnfàn	model, example
32.	确立	quèlì	to establish
33.	正统	zhèngtǒng	legitimate, orthodox
34.	学说	xuéshuō	theory, doctrine
35.	以至	yǐzhì	up to, to such an extent as to
36.	表（率）	biǎo (shuài)	example, model
37.	圣人	shèngrén	sage

PROPER NAMES 专名

1.	丘	Qiū	孔子的名字
2.	仲尼	Zhòngní	孔子的字
3.	山东	Shāndōng	Shandong Province
4.	曲阜	Qūfù	a city in Shandong Province
5.	鲁国	Lǔguó	State of Lu, from the eleventh century to 256 BCE
6.	诗经	Shījīng	*Classic of Poetry*
7.	书经	Shūjīng	*Book of History*
8.	易经	Yìjīng	*Book of Changes*
9.	礼记	Lǐjì	*Book of Rites*
10.	春秋	Chūnqiū	*Spring and Autumn Annals*
11.	南宋	Nán Sòng	Southern Song dynasty (1127–1276)

12.	朱熹	Zhū Xī	a Confucian scholar and educator (1130–1200)
13.	大学	Dàxué	*The Great Learning*
14.	中庸	Zhōngyōng	*The Doctrine of the Mean*
15.	孟子	Mèngzǐ	a Confucian thinker and educator (ca. 372–289 BCE)
16.	汉武帝	Hàn Wǔdì	Emperor Wu of the Han (r. 140–87 BCE)

PART I

Knowledge 治学篇

1. Learning the Way 学以致道

《论语》选段 *Analects* Passages 🎧

1-1. 子曰："学而时习之，不亦说乎？有朋自远方来，不亦乐乎？人不知而不愠，不亦君子乎？" (1.1)

孔子说："学了而能时时练习，不也是很愉快的吗？有朋友从远方来，不也是很快乐的吗？别人不了解你，你也不怨恨，不也是君子吗？"

1-2. 子夏曰："百工居肆以成其事，君子学以致其道。" (19.7)

子夏说："各行各业的工匠在作坊里完成自己的工作，君子通过学习来认识真理。"

1-3. 子夏曰："博学而笃志，切问而近思，仁在其中矣。" (19.6)

子夏说："广博地学习并坚持自己的志向，恳切地发问并思考切近的问题，仁就在其中了。"

词汇一 VOCABULARY I

1.	治学	zhìxué	学习，做学问
2.	篇	piān	chapter, section
3.	子	zǐ	master; used in the *Analects* to refer to Confucius
4.	曰	yuē	说
5.	时	shí	按时, on schedule
6.	习	xí	复习、练习、实习
7.	说	yuè	悦，愉快
8.	愠	yùn	angry, resentful
9.	君子	jūnzǐ	道德高尚的人, virtuous man
10.	实践	shíjiàn	practice
11.	怨恨	yuànhèn	to have a grudge against, to hate
12.	居	jū	住
13.	肆	sì	shop, workshop
14.	致	zhì	to achieve, to attain
15.	道	dào	真理, the Way, the ultimate principle of the universe
16.	各行各业	gèháng gèyè	all trades and professions
17.	行	háng	trade, profession

18. 工匠 gōngjiàng craftsman, artisan
19. 作坊 zuòfáng workshop
20. 笃 dǔ sincere, earnest
21. 志 zhì 志向, aspiration, ambition
22. 切 qiè earnestly, specifically
23. 仁 rén humanity, benevolence
24. 恳切 kěnqiè earnest, sincere
25. 切近 qièjìn 近

虚词 FUNCTION WORDS

1. 而 ér 而且（学而时习之，不亦说乎）
2. 之 zhī 他（们）、它（们）（同上）
3. 亦 yì 也（同上）
4. 乎 hū 吗、呢（同上）
5. 自 zì 从（有朋自远方来）
6. 而 ér 但是（人不知而不愠）
7. 其 qí 他（们）的、它（们）的（百工居肆以成其事）
8. 以 yǐ 用（同上）
9. 而 ér 又（博学而笃志，仁在其中矣）
10. 在 zài 在（同上）
11. 矣 yǐ 了（同上）

专名 PROPER NAMES

1. 子夏 Zǐxià 姓卜名商，字子夏 (b. 507)，孔子的学生

解读 Exegeses

《论语》中论学的章节很多，“学”字共出现了六十六次。我们现在用的“学习”这个词，就是从《论语》的第一句“学而时习之”中来的。《论语》的第一段虽然妇孺皆知，但很多人理解得比较肤浅。其实，这段话揭示了学习的三重境界及其根本目的。

《论语》中的“学”和“习”的含义非常丰富。“学”的内容可以概括为知识、技能和道理三个方面。“习”也有三层意思。首先是“复习”、“温习”。第二层意思是“练习”或“演习”。孔子所讲的功课，一般都和当时的社会生活有密切的关系。像礼、乐、射、御这些内容，都需要练习或演习。第三层意思为“实习”、“实践”。知识要复习，技能要练习，而思想伦理与政治理念则非实践不可。总之，“学而时习之”是学习的第一重境界。

"有朋自远方来"中的"朋"在这儿不是一般的朋友，而是志同道合的人。为什么"朋"会从远方来呢？他来做什么呢？就是来跟你一起探讨人生的道理。这是第二重境界。

"人不知而不愠"是学习的第三重境界。你之所以不怨恨，是因为你学习的目的不是为了博取别人的赞扬，而是要学到道，要做到仁。道和仁是儒家的两个很大也很重要的概念。道是这个世界最大的道理，仁是做人的最高标准。简单来说，学习首先是要学做人。这是孔子教学的成功之处，也是我们学《论语》第一课。

词汇二 VOCABULARY II

1.	妇孺	fùrú	妇女和孩子
2.	皆	jiē	都
3.	肤浅	fūqiǎn	superficial, shallow
4.	揭示	jiēshì	to reveal, to bring to light
5.	重	chóng	layer
6.	境界	jìngjiè	state, realm
7.	含义	hányì	meaning, implication
8.	概括	gàikuò	to summarize, to generalize
9.	技能	jìnéng	skill
10.	礼	lǐ	proprieties, rituals
11.	射	shè	archery
12.	御	yù	to drive (a carriage)
13.	演习	yǎnxí	to exercise, to practice
14.	伦理	lúnlǐ	ethics, moral principles
15.	理念	lǐniàn	ideas, concepts
16.	则	zé	就
17.	非...不可	fēi . . . bùkě	必须、一定要、一定得
18.	志同道合	zhìtóng dàohé	to cherish the same aspirations and take the same course; to have a common goal
19.	探讨	tàntǎo	to explore, to discuss
20.	博取	bóqǔ	to seek, to try to win
21.	概念	gàiniàn	concept

事例 An Illustrative Story

PORRIDGE CAKES 范仲淹断齑画粥

范仲淹是宋代著名的文学家、政治家和军事家。他两岁丧父，家境衰落。十几岁时，住在一个佛寺里，昼夜苦读。每天煮一锅粥，凉了以后，划成四块，早晚各取两块，再吃一点儿咸菜。这样过了三年。这就是有名的“断齑画粥”的故事。范仲淹的一个同学是个富家子弟，送些美食给他，他竟一口不尝，并说：“我已安于过喝粥的生活，一旦享受美餐，日后怕吃不得苦。”

范仲淹在清苦贫寒中修身立志，精通了儒家的经典。他二十七岁时考中进士，步入仕途。他做过副宰相，推行很多政治改革。即使当了大官，也非常节俭，家中不吃两样荤菜。他也做过将军，有效地抵御了西夏的侵略，连敌人都称赞他“胸中有数万甲兵”。范仲淹也是个杰出的文学家。他写的《岳阳楼记》中“先天下之忧而忧，后天下之乐而乐”两句，成为千古传诵的格言，也是他忧国忧民的一生的写照。

词汇三 VOCABULARY III

1.	事例	shìlì	example, case
2.	齑	jī	chopped pickles
3.	画	huà	划、划分, to divide
4.	粥	zhōu	gruel
5.	丧	sàng	to lose, to be deprived of
6.	家境	jiājìng	family financial situation
7.	衰落	shuāiluò	to decline, to be on the wane
8.	佛寺	fósì	Buddhist temple
9.	昼	zhòu	白天
10.	咸菜	xiáncài	pickles
11.	清苦	qīngkǔ	穷苦
12.	贫寒	pínhán	穷
13.	修身	xiūshēn	to cultivate one's moral character
14.	进士	Jìnshì	one who has passed the highest-level imperial examinations
15.	步入	bùrù	走进，走上
16.	仕途	shìtú	official career
17.	宰相	zǎixiàng	chief minister
18.	节俭	jiéjiǎn	thrifty, frugal

19.	荤菜	hūncài	meat dishes
20.	有效	yǒuxiào	effective
21.	抵御	dǐyù	to resist
22.	数	shù	几
23.	甲兵	jiǎbīng	soldiers in armor
24.	千古	qiāngǔ	through the ages
25.	传诵	chuánsòng	to be widely read about, to be admired
26.	格言	géyán	motto
27.	写照	xiězhào	portrayal

专名 PROPER NAMES

1.	范仲淹	Fàn Zhòngyān	a statesman and writer (989–1052)
2.	西夏	Xī Xià	Western Xia (1038–1227), a state neighboring Song China
3.	岳阳楼	Yuèyánglóu	the Yueyang Tower in Yueyang City, Hunan 湖南 Province

---

成语 Idioms

1. 学以致道
   【课文】君子学以致其道。
2. 各行各业
   【课文】各行各业的工匠在作坊里完成自己的工作。
3. 博学笃志
   【课文】博学而笃志，切问而近思。
4. 切问近思
   【课文】同上。
5. 妇孺皆知
   【课文】《论语》的第一段虽然妇孺皆知，但很多人理解得比较肤浅。
6. 志同道合
   【课文】有志同道合的朋友从远方来，不也是很快乐的吗？
7. 断齑画粥
   【课文】范仲淹断齑画粥。
8. 修身立志
   【课文】范仲淹在清苦贫寒中修身立志，精通了儒家的经典。
9. 先忧后乐
   【课文】先天下之忧而忧，后天下之乐而乐。

10. 千古传诵
【课文】他写的《岳阳楼记》中的两句，成为千古传诵的格言。
11. 忧国忧民
【课文】这也是他忧国忧民的一生的写照。

词汇扩展 Vocabulary Expansion

1. 时
【课文】学而时习之，不亦说乎？
【例词】时机、时光、时代、时差、时局、时事、时尚、时装、时刻表、时不再来
2. 知
【课文】人不知而不愠，不亦君子乎？
【例词】知己、知心、知音、知足长乐、知人之明、知过必改、知难而进、自知之明、知其一不知其二、知人知面不知心
3. 居
【课文】百工居肆以成其事。
【例词】居民、居功、居心、新居、故居、侨居、居高临下、居安思危、居心不良、安居乐业
4. 成
【课文】同上。
【例词】成语、成熟、成就、成败、成家立业、成千上万、成人之美、成竹在胸、成双成对、成名成家
5. 致
【课文】君子学以致其道。
【例词】致敬、致谢、致意、致词、致电、致力、致死、学以致道、学以致用、专心致志
6. 志
【课文】博学而笃志。
【例词】志气、志向、志愿、立志、意志、志士仁人、志同道合、胸怀大志、人各有志、志大才疏
7. 切
【课文】切问而近思。
【例词】切近、切身、切实、密切、迫切、亲切、深切、真切、切磋琢磨、切齿痛恨

8. 仁
【课文】仁在其中矣。
【例词】仁爱、仁慈、仁德、仁厚、仁政、仁兄、仁人君子、仁人志士、仁义道德、仁至义尽

练习 Exercises

一、选择题 MULTIPLE CHOICE

1. 《论语》中的“学”和“习”的 ________ 非常丰富。
   a. 意义　　b. 含义
   c. 意思　　d. 道理
2. 孔子所讲的功课，一般都和当时的社会生活有 ________ 的关系。
   a. 密切　　b. 恳切
   c. 贴切　　d. 关切
3. 思想伦理与政治理念则非 ________ 不可。
   a. 实习　　b. 实践
   c. 实际　　d. 实用
4. 道和仁是儒家的两个很大也很重要的 ________。
   a. 思想　　b. 道理
   c. 理论　　d. 概念
5. 范仲淹做过副 ________。
   a. 市长　　b. 部长
   c. 宰相　　d. 将军
6. 范仲淹是 ________ 代著名的文学家、政治家和军事家。
   a. 唐　　b. 宋
   c. 明　　d. 清
7. 他写的《岳阳楼记》中“先天下之忧而忧，后天下之乐而乐”两句，成为千古传诵的 ________。
   a. 诗句　　b. 语录
   c. 格言　　d. 成语
8. 这两句话也是他忧国忧民的一生的 ________。
   a. 反映　　b. 写照
   c. 照相　　d. 纪录

二、改错 CORRECTING MISTAKES

1. 论语的第一段“学而时习之”妇孺皆知，所以大家都理解得很深刻。
2. 《论语》中的“学”和“习”的含义非常简单明了。

3. 学习的目的是为了博取别人的赞扬。
4. 学习就是为了要学到知识，这是孔子教学的成功之处。
5. 范仲淹十几岁时，住在一个佛寺里，做了和尚。
6. 他每天煮一锅粥，凉了以后，划成四块，早晚各取两块，再吃一点美食。

三、问答题 ANSWERING QUESTIONS

1. 《论语》中论学的章节很多，“学”字共出现了多少次？
2. 我们现在用的“学习”这个词，是从《论语》的哪一句中来的？
3. 孔子所讲的哪些功课都和当时的社会生活有密切的关系？
4. “有朋自远方来”中的“朋”指的是什么样的人？
5. 朋友从远方来做什么？
6. 什么是道？什么是仁？
7. 为什么范仲淹不吃同学送给他的美食？
8. 西夏人是怎么称赞范仲淹的？
9. 《岳阳楼记》中有哪两句名句？

四、讨论题 QUESTIONS FOR DISCUSSION

1. 《论语》的第一段话揭示了学习的哪三重境界？谈谈你的想法和体会。
2. 范仲淹年轻时清苦贫寒的生活和他忧国忧民的一生有什么关系？

五、故事复述 RETELLING THE STORY

《范仲淹断齑画粥》

六、用本课的成语改写句子 REWRITING SENTENCES USING IDIOMS FROM THE CHAPTER

1. 这个国家经济不景气，公司、企业、商店等都在裁员。
2. 你读过杜甫的《春望》吗？这首诗里的“感时花溅泪，恨别鸟惊心”可是多少年来人人都知道的名句啊。
3. 这个总统执政时的丑闻人人都知道，难道你不知道？
4. 小王是“两耳不闻天下事，一心只读圣贤书”，小张却是一副关心国家大事的样子。你呢？

七、选词 WORD CHOICE

1. 老李在国外定居很多年了，去年才有空回国看看（故居、新居、侨居）。
2. 我对四川地震有（切实、切身、切近）体会，现在回想起来还很害怕。
3. 小田有一股（知过必改、知难而进、自知之明）的劲头，所以学得这么好。
4. 一个人想做好一件事就必须（学以致道、学以致用、专心致志）。
5. 白先生是（胸怀大志、志大才疏、人各有志），其实没有什么学问和本领。

八、文译白 TRANSLATION FROM CLASSICAL CHINESE INTO MODERN CHINESE

范仲淹《岳阳楼记》节选

嗟夫①！予尝求古仁人之心，或异二者之为，何哉？不以物喜，不以己悲；居庙堂②之高，则忧其民；处江湖③之远，则忧其君。是进亦忧，退亦忧。然则④何时而乐耶⑤？其必曰“先天下之忧而忧，后天下之乐而乐”乎。噫！微⑥斯人，吾谁与归⑦？

【注释】①嗟夫：唉！②庙堂：朝廷。③江湖：四方各地。④然则：那么。⑤耶，呢？⑥微：没有。⑦归：归依

九、英译中 TRANSLATION FROM ENGLISH INTO CHINESE

1. The *Analects* is a record of the words and acts of the Chinese educator and philosopher Confucius and his disciples.
2. The *Analects* is the representative work of Confucianism and continues to have a tremendous influence on Chinese and East Asian thought and values today.
3. For over two thousand years, the *Analects* has been the fundamental course of study for any Chinese scholar.
4. A man was not considered morally upright or enlightened if he did not study Confucius's *Analects*.
5. The civil service examinations emphasized Confucian studies and expected candidates to quote and apply the words of Confucius in their essays.

十、作文 COMPOSITION

【题目】《风声雨声读书声》

【提示】有一副对联说：“风声雨声读书声，声声入耳；家事国事天下事，事事关心”，意思是读书人要关心天下大事。请说说你的大学生活对你对人生的理解有什么帮助？

2. Love for Learning 敏而好学

《论语》选段 *Analects* Passages

2-1. 子曰："十室之邑，必有忠信如丘者焉，不如丘之好学也。"(5.28)

孔子说"只有十户人家的一个小村里，也一定有像我这样又忠诚又讲信用的人，只是不如我喜欢学习罢了。"

2-2. 哀公问："弟子孰为好学？"孔子对曰："有颜回者好学，不迁怒，不贰过。不幸短命死矣。今也则亡，未闻好学者也。"(6.3)

哀公问："您的学生中，哪个是好学的啊？"孔子答道："有一个叫颜回的很好学。他不把怒气发泄在别人身上，也不再犯同样的过失。不幸短命死了。现在再也没有这样的人了，再也没有听说过好学的人了。"

2-3. 子曰："君子食无求饱，居无求安，敏于事而慎于言，就有道而正焉，可谓好学也已。"(1.14)

孔子说："君子饮食不求饱，居处不求舒适，做事勤快，说话谨慎，到有道的人那儿去辨明是非，这样，可以说是好学的了。"

2-4. 子夏曰："日知其所亡，月无忘其所能，可谓好学也已矣。"(19.5)

子夏说："每天都知道自己缺少什么知识，每月都不忘记已经学会的东西，这就可以叫作好学了。"

2-5. 子曰："温故而知新，可以为师矣。"(2.11)

孔子说："温习旧的知识，而能有新的体会，便可以当老师了。"

词汇一 VOCABULARY I

1.	室	shì	household
2.	邑	yì	town
3.	忠	zhōng	loyal, devoted
4.	信	xìn	faithful, honest
5.	罢了	bàle	merely, only, that's all (used at the end of a sentence)
6.	为	wéi	是
7.	好	hào	喜爱
8.	迁怒	qiānnù	to vent one's anger at somebody else
9.	迁	qiān	to move, to change

10.	贰过	èrguò	to repeat errors
11.	贰	èr	二
12.	过	guò	过错，fault, error
13.	未	wèi	没有
14.	发泄	fāxiè	to give vent to, to let out
15.	犯	fàn	to violate, to offend
16.	过失	guòshī	过错
17.	敏	mǐn	nimble, diligent
18.	慎	shèn	careful, cautious
19.	就	jiù	走近
20.	正	zhèng	to correct, to rectify
21.	可谓	kěwèi	可以说（是）
22.	谨慎	jǐnshèn	prudent, careful
23.	辨	biàn	to differentiate, to distinguish
24.	是非	shìfēi	对和错
25.	温	wēn	温习
26.	故	gù	旧
27.	体会	tǐhuì	to know from experience
28.	便	biàn	就, then, in that case

虚词 FUNCTION WORDS

1.	之	zhī	的（十室之邑）
2.	如	rú	像 （必有忠信如丘者焉）
3.	者	zhě	（的）人（同上）
4.	焉	yān	啊（同上）
5.	如	rú	及、比得上（不如丘之好学也）
6.	也	yě	了、啊（同上）
7.	孰	shú	谁，哪个（弟子孰为好学）
8.	矣	yǐ	了、啊（不幸短命死矣）
9.	也	yě	(used to pause, and for emphasis) （今也则亡）
10.	则	zé	就（同上）
11.	亡	wú	无（同上）
12.	未	wèi	没有、不曾（未闻好学者也）
13.	于	yú	对于（敏于事而慎于言）
14.	而	ér	subsequently（就有道而正焉）
15.	已	yǐ	了、啊（可谓好学也已）
16.	无	wú	不（月无忘其所能）
17.	而	ér	就、能（温故而知新，可以为师矣）
18.	可以	kěyǐ	能（同上）

专名 PROPER NAMES

1.	哀公	Āigōng	Duke Ai of Lu鲁哀公 (r. 494–476 BCE)
2.	颜回	Yán Huí	also known as Yán Yuān 颜渊，孔子的学生 (521–490 BCE)

解读 Exegeses

第一章讲了学习的目的，这一章讲的是学习的态度，就是要好学。孔子很谦虚地说，即使在“忠信”这样重要的美德方面，到处都会有人跟他一样好。但他很自信，没有人会比他更好学。可见，孔子把“好学”看作是自己最重要的特质。好学也是孔子对他的弟子的要求。孔子最好的弟子是颜回，他也是最好学的。

那么，怎样才算是好学呢？这一章中也讲了不少做法。“食无求饱，居无求安”是不讲究物质生活，“敏于事而慎于言”是少说多做，“就有道而正焉”是虚心学习，“温故而知新”是一种有效的学习方法，“日知其所亡，月无忘其所能”则提出了一种检验学习效果的准则。

孔子说颜回的好学表现在“不迁怒，不贰过”。这也很明显地告诉我们孔子说的学习并不只是学习书本知识，而是包括道德修养在内的人生追求。

词汇二 VOCABULARY II

1.	谦虚	qiānxū	modest, humble
2.	特质	tèzhì	special quality
3.	讲究	jiǎngjiu	to be particular about, to stress
4.	检验	jiǎnyàn	to test, to examine, to inspect
5.	准则	zhǔnzé	standard, criterion
6.	修养	xiūyǎng	cultivation, training
7.	追求	zhuīqiú	to seek, to pursue

事例 An Illustrative Story

LAMP OF FIREFLIES 囊萤映雪悬梁刺股

中国有很多好学、勤学、苦学的故事。这里讲几个。

晋代的车胤自幼好学不倦，可是由于家境贫困，没有钱买灯油在晚上读书。在夏天的晚上，他用白绢扎成一个小口袋，并抓了几十只萤火虫放在里面，他就借着这微弱的光读书。

同是晋朝的孙康也是由于贫困而无法点灯夜读。在冬天的晚上，他站在院子里，借着白雪的反光如饥似渴地学习。

东汉的孙敬，年轻时常常夜以继日地读书。古人的头发很长。他找一根绳子，一头扎住头发，另一头绑在房梁上。他读书疲劳时要打盹儿，头一低，绳子就牵住头发，他马上就清醒了。

战国时期的苏秦，年轻时学问不多，大家都看不起他，他就发愤读书。他在晚上疲倦时，用一把锥子往自己的大腿上刺一下。这样，他就不会打瞌睡了。

这四个人后来都学有所成。车胤囊萤、孙康映雪、孙敬悬梁、苏秦刺股，本是四个故事，合在一起，成为两句成语："囊萤映雪"和"悬梁刺股"。

词汇三 VOCABULARY III

1.	囊	náng	bag
2.	萤	yíng	firefly
3.	映	yìng	to reflect
4.	悬	xuán	to hang
5.	梁	liáng	roof beam
6.	刺	cì	to stab, to prick
7.	股	gǔ	thigh
8.	幼	yòu	young, underage
9.	绢	juàn	loosely woven raw silk fabric
10.	扎	zā	to tie, to bind
11.	萤火虫	yínghuǒchóng	firefly
12.	微弱	wēiruò	faint, weak
13.	夜以继日	yèyǐ jìrì	day and night, around the clock
14.	绳子	shéngzi	cord, rope, string
15.	绑	bǎng	to bind, to tie
16.	打盹儿	dǎ dǔnr	to doze off
17.	牵	qiān	to pull, to drag
18.	发愤	fāfèn	to make a determined effort, to strive resolutely
19.	锥子	zhuīzi	awl
20.	打瞌睡	dǎ kēshuì	to doze off, to take a nap

专名 PROPER NAMES

1.	晋	Jìn	the Jin dynasty (265–420)
2.	车胤	Chē Yìn	a scholar and official of the Jin dynasty (d. 400)

3. 孙康 Sūn Kāng a scholar and official of the Jin dynasty
4. 东汉 Dong Han Eastern Han 东汉dynasty (25–220)
5. 孙敬 Sūn Jìng a scholar of the Eastern Han
6. 战国 Zhànguó the Warring States period (475–221 BCE)
7. 苏秦 Sū Qín a strategist of the Warring States period

成语 Idioms

1. 食无求饱，居无求安
   【课文】君子食无求饱，居无求安。
2. 敏事慎言
   【课文】敏于事而慎于言。
3. 囊萤映雪
   【课文】车胤囊萤、孙康映雪。
4. 悬梁刺股
   【课文】孙敬悬梁、苏秦刺股。
5. 好学不倦
   【课文】晋代的车胤自幼好学不倦。
6. 如饥似渴
   【课文】借着白雪的反光如饥似渴地学习。
7. 夜以继日
   【课文】年轻时常常夜以继日地读书。
8. 学有所成
   【课文】这四个人后来都学有所成。

词汇扩展 Vocabulary Expansion

1. 忠
   【课文】十室之邑，必有忠信如丘者焉。
   【例词】忠诚、忠实、忠心、忠厚、忠顺、忠告、效忠、忠臣义士、忠孝两全、忠言逆耳
2. 如
   【课文】同上。
   【例词】如同、如此、如何、如临大敌、如获至宝、如饥似渴、如梦初醒、如日中天、如鱼得水、万事如意
3. 好
   【课文】不如丘之好学也。

【例词】好奇、好客、好强、好斗、好战、好吃懒做、好管闲事、好大喜功、好为人师、好逸恶劳

4. 闻

【课文】今也则亡，未闻好学者也。

【例词】见闻、要闻、丑闻、闻名天下、闻一知十、闻鸡起舞、闻过则喜、闻风而动、闻风丧胆、闻所未闻

5. 安

【课文】君子食无求饱，居无求安。

【例词】安康、安乐、安宁、安家、安危、安眠药、安全带、安居乐业、安贫乐道、安分守己

6. 事

【课文】敏于事而慎于言。

【例词】事件、事务、事故、事假、时事、事在人为、事与愿违、事不宜迟、事半功倍、事出有因

7. 言

【课文】同上。

【例词】言论、言谈、发言、言传身教、言行一致、言而无信、言归于好、言过其实、言听计从、言外之意

练习 Exercises

一、选择题 MULTIPLE CHOICE

1. 孔子很 ________，没有人会比他更好学。
   a. 自豪　　b. 自信
   c. 自满　　d. 自尊
2. 孔子把“好学”看作是自己最重要的 ________。
   a. 特色　　b. 特长
   c. 特征　　d. 特质
3. 车胤借着萤火虫的 ________ 的光读书。
   a. 微小　　b. 微薄
   c. 微细　　d. 微弱
4. 孙敬找一根绳子，一头扎住头发，另一头 ________ 在房梁上。
   a. 挂　　b. 吊
   c. 绑　　d. 钉

二、改错 CORRECTING MISTAKES

1. 孔子说在忠信方面，没有人会跟他一样好。
2. 孔子最好的弟子是孟子。

3. 车胤家境贫困，没有钱买蜡烛在晚上读书。
4. 孙康站在院子里，借着月光如饥似渴地学习。
5. 孙敬找一根绳子，一头扎住头发，另一头绑在树枝上。
6. 苏秦在晚上疲倦时，用一把刀子往自己的大腿上刺一下。

三、问答题 ANSWERING QUESTIONS

1. 孔子把什么看作是自己最重要的特质？
2. 谁是孔子最好的弟子？
3. 君子是怎么对待物质生活的？
4. 子夏说什么样的人可以算是好学的？
5. 孔子提出了哪一种有效的学习方法？
6. 子夏说要怎样来检验学习的效果？
7. 孔子说颜回的好学表现在什么地方？
8. 孔子说的学习包括什么？

四、讨论题 QUESTIONS FOR DISCUSSION

1. 这一章中讲了哪些好学的做法？
2. 用颜回好学的例子来说明孔子说的学习包括道德修养在内的人生追求。
3. 把本章中的四个小故事按照年代先后排列一下。

五、故事复述 RETELLING THE STORY

"囊萤映雪"和"悬梁刺股"

六、用本课的成语改写句子 REWRITING SENTENCES USING IDIOMS FROM THE CHAPTER

1. 李小姐是个秘书，她平时少说话、多做事，很得上司的赞赏。
2. 大考来临了，很多学生都"住"在图书馆里，成天成夜地学习。
3. 我也常常开夜车，但至少不需要用古人的法子来提神，多喝点咖啡来就行了。
4. 唐先生和唐太太教子有方，所以唐家的几个孩子都成绩优秀并找到了好工作。

七、选词 WORD CHOICE

1. 中国人喜欢在新年的时候跟人说（如日中天、万事如意、如鱼得水）。
2. 今天报上的头条新闻真是（闻所未闻、闻过则喜、闻风而动），我活了二十年还是第一次听到这样的怪事呢。
3. 老张为了省钱，喜欢自己动手修车，结果常常是（事出有因、事在人为、事倍功半）。
4. 黄太太对自己的家庭和事业都很满意，（安贫乐道、安分守己、安居乐业），真令人羡慕。
5. 你怎么老是（言而无信、言行一致、言过其实）？你看看表，现在都几点了？

八、文译白 TRANSLATION FROM CLASSICAL CHINESE INTO MODERN CHINESE

宋濂①《送东阳马生序》节选

余幼时即嗜学。家贫，无从致书以观，每假借②于藏书之家,手自笔录，计日以还。天大寒，砚冰坚，手指不可屈伸，弗之怠。录毕，走③送之，不敢稍逾约。以是人多以书假余，余因得遍观群书。

【注释】①宋濂(1310–1381)：明朝学者。②假借：借。③走：跑。

九、英译中 TRANSLATION FROM ENGLISH INTO CHINESE

1. Wang Xizhi 王羲之 of the Jin dynasty practiced calligraphy by a pond so he could wash his brushes there. He wrote day and night and the water in the pond turned black.
2. Kuang Heng 匡衡 of the Han dynasty was poor when he was young, so he drilled a small hole in the wall and read by the light of a neighboring home.
3. When Li Mi 李密 of the Sui dynasty rode an ox to visit his friend, he hung a bag of books from the ox's horn so he could read along the way.
4. There was a garden behind the study room of Dong Zhongshu 董仲舒 of the Han dynasty, but he concentrated on his studies and did not enter the garden for three years.

十、作文 COMPOSITION

【题目】《备考趣记》

【提示】从小学到大学，你经历了无数的考试。你有什么特别的法子在开夜车时保持头脑清醒？讲一个有趣的故事。

3. The Four Prohibitions 毋意毋必

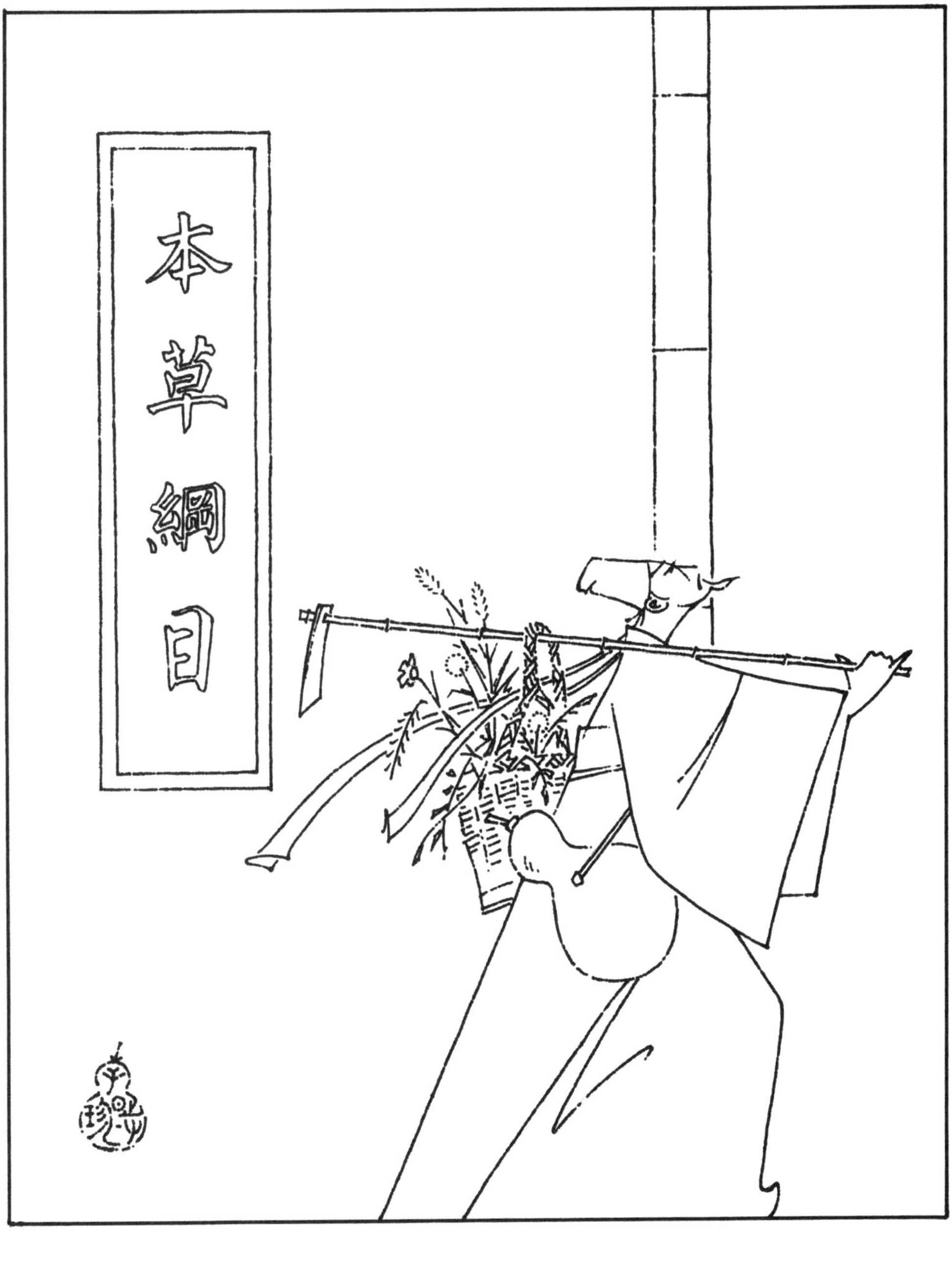

《论语》选段 *Analects* Passages

3-1. 子曰："由！诲女知之乎！知之为知之，不知为不知，是知也。"(2.17)

孔子说："子路，让我来教你什么叫知道吧。知道就是知道，不知道就是不知道，这就是知道啊！"

3-2. 子曰："盖有不知而作之者，我无是也。"(7.28)

孔子说："有人很无知却要创造理论，我没这样做过。"

3-3. 子绝四：毋意、毋必、毋固、毋我。(9.4)

孔子杜绝四种弊病：不猜测，不武断，不固执，不唯我。

3-4. 曾子曰："以能问于不能，以多问于寡，有若无，实若虚，犯而不校一昔者吾友尝从事于斯矣。"(8.5)

曾子说："自己有才能却向没有才能的人请教，自己知识多却向知识少的人请教，有学问却像没学问一样，充实却好像空虚，被人冒犯也不计较一从前我的朋友就是这样做的。"

词汇一 VOCABULARY I

1.	毋	wú	不要
2.	意	yì	to guess, to speculate
3.	诲	huì	教导
4.	女	rǔ	汝，你
5.	作	zuò	创造、建立（理论、学说）
6.	绝	jué	to cut off
7.	固	gù	stubborn
8.	杜绝	dùjué	to stop (a bad practice, etc.)
9.	弊病	bìbìng	malady, evil
10.	猜测	cāicè	to guess, to surmise
11.	武断	wǔduàn	arbitrary
12.	固执	gùzhí	stubborn
13.	唯	wéi	only, alone
14.	寡	guǎ	少
15.	实	shí	substantial
16.	虚	xū	空

17.	校	jiào	to be concerned, to dispute
18.	昔	xī	从前
19.	吾	wú	我，我的
20.	从事	cóngshì	to do, to be engaged in
21.	充实	chōngshí	substantial
22.	冒犯	màofàn	to offend
23.	计较	jìjiào	to mind, to care, to dispute, to haggle

虚词 FUNCTION WORDS

1.	之	zhī	(used to add emphasis)（诲女知之乎）
2.	盖	gài	大概（盖有不知而作之者，我无是也）
3.	无	wú	没有（同上）
4.	是	shì	这、这个（同上）
5.	毋	wú	不要（毋意、毋必、毋固、毋我）
6.	于	yú	向（以能问于不能，以多问于寡）
7.	若	ruò	像（有若无，实若虚）
8.	者	zhě	(used to pause, and for emphasis)（昔者吾友尝从事于斯矣）
9.	尝	cháng	曾经（同上）

专名 PROPER NAMES

1.	由	Yóu	仲由 (b. 542 BCE)，字子路，孔子的学生
2.	曾子	Zēngzǐ	名参 (505–436 BCE)，孔子的学生

解读 Exegeses

这一章讲的也是学习态度，就是要虚心学习。孔子的“四毋”是一种实事求是的精神，其基础就是承认自己的无知。

在日常生活中，人们常用“知之为知之，不知为不知”来教育孩子要老老实实地做人、求知，不要不懂装懂。进一步来说，这句格言中蕴藏着深刻的中国教育哲学的精神。人们应该学会在博大精深的“道”的面前表达自己的虔敬之心和谦恭之意。越学习，就越认识到自己的无知，就更要努力学习。

曾子在第四段中所说的话，完全秉承了孔子的思想。“有若无”、“实若虚”是一种谦虚的精神；“问于不能”，“问于寡”是一种谦逊的态度；“犯而不校”是一种谦和的胸怀。懂得不多的人以及跟自己持不同意见的人也能成为学习的对象。

词汇二 VOCABULARY II

1.	实事求是	shíshì qiúshì	to seek truth from facts, to be practical and realistic
2.	蕴藏	yùncáng	to contain, to store up
3.	虔敬	qiánjìng	reverent
4.	谦恭	qiāngōng	modest and respectful
5.	秉承	bǐngchéng	to act on orders
6.	谦逊	qiānxùn	modest, unassuming
7.	谦和	qiānhé	modest and amiable
8.	胸怀	xiōnghuái	mind, heart
9.	持	chí	to hold

事例 An Illustrative Story

A DOCTOR-TRAVELER 李时珍不耻下问

李时珍(1518–1593)是明代的名医。他费时二十七年编写的《本草纲目》，是明代以前药物学的总结性巨著。

中国有句话，叫“行万里路，读万卷书”。为了编《本草纲目》，李时珍读了八百余种、共万余卷的医书，也走遍了千山万水。李时珍穿着草鞋，背着药筐，远涉深山旷野，搜求民间验方，观察和收集药物标本。李时珍每到一地，就虚心地向各式各样的人物请教。其中有采药的、种田的、捕鱼的、砍柴的、打猎的，他们都热情地帮助他了解各种各样的药物。蕲州产的白花蛇是一种毒蛇，但可以用来制药。李时珍冒着生命危险，跟着捕蛇者上山观察，弄清了这种蛇的生长环境和习性。

《本草纲目》全书约有二百万字，记载药物一千八百九十二种，记载处方一万多个，附图一千多幅，成为我国药物学的空前巨著。这部书对世界医药学、植物学、动物学、矿物学、化学的发展也产生了深远的影响。该书出版后，很快就传到日本，以后又流传到欧美各国，先后被译成日、法、德、英、俄等十余种文字在国外出版。英国十九世纪生物学家达尔文称赞这部书是“中国古代医学的百科全书”。

词汇三 VOCABULARY III

1.	纲目	gāngmù	detailed outline (often used in a book title)
2.	药物学	yàowù xué	pharmacology
3.	总结性	zǒngjiéxìng	conclusive
4.	巨著	jùzhù	monumental work
5.	卷	juàn	a section of a book

6.	余	yú	more than, over
7.	草鞋	cǎoxié	straw sandals
8.	筐	kuāng	rectangular box woven from bamboo strips or wicker
9.	涉	shè	to wade
10.	旷野	kuàngyě	wilderness, prairie
11.	搜求	sōuqiú	to seek
12.	验方	yànfāng	effective medicine, proven formula
13.	标本	biāoběn	specimen, sample
14.	砍	kǎn	to cut, to chop
15.	柴	chái	firewood
16.	打猎	dǎliè	to go hunting
17.	蛇	shé	snake, serpent
18.	毒	dú	poison
19.	冒	mào	to risk, to brave
20.	习性	xíxìng	habits and characteristics
21.	约	yuē	approximately
22.	处方	chǔfāng	prescription
23.	附图	fùtú	attached map or drawing, figure
24.	幅	fú	measure word for paintings, etc.
25.	空前	kōngqián	unprecedented
26.	矿物	kuàngwù	mineral
27.	该	gāi	这
28.	百科全书	bǎikē quánshū	encyclopedia

专名 PROPER NAMES

1.	李时珍	Lǐ Shízhēn	one of the greatest physicians and pharmacologists in Chinese history (1518–1593)
2.	明	Míng	the Ming dynasty (1368–1644)
3.	本草纲目	*Běncǎo gāngmù*	*Compendium of Materia Medica*, a comprehensive medical book written by Li Shizhen
4.	蕲州	Qízhōu	town in present-day Hubei 湖北 Province
5.	达尔文	Dá'ěrwén	Charles Robert Darwin (1809–1882)

成语 Idioms

1. 毋意毋必
【课文】毋意、毋必、毋固、毋我。
2. 知之为知之，不知为不知
【课文】知之为知之，不知为不知，是知也。
3. 以多问寡
【课文】以能问于不能，以多问于寡。
4. 犯而不校
【课文】有若无，实若虚，犯而不校。
5. 实事求是
【课文】孔子的“四毋”是一种实事求是的精神。
6. 博大精深
【课文】人们应该学会在博大精深的“道”的面前表达自己的虔敬之心和谦恭之意。
7. 行万里路，读万卷书
【课文】中国有句话，叫“行万里路，读万卷书”。
8. 千山万水
【课文】李时珍读了万余卷的医书，也走遍了千山万水。
9. 深山旷野
【课文】李时珍远涉深山旷野，搜求民间验方。

词汇扩展 Vocabulary Expansion

1. 作
【课文】盖有不知而作之者，我无是也。
【例词】作家、作者、作品、作曲、作物、作为、作用、作风、创作、著作
2. 绝
【课文】子绝四：毋意、毋必、毋固、毋我。
【例词】绝妙、绝对、绝交、绝食、绝句、断绝、谢绝、隔绝、绝无仅有、绝代佳人
3. 固
【课文】同上。
【例词】固执、固定、固然、固有、固体、牢固、坚固、顽固、加固、巩固
4. 能
【课文】以能问于不能。

【例词】能力、能人、能手、能上能下、能文能武、能攻能收、能屈能伸、能说会道、能歌善舞、能者为师

5. 多

【课文】以多问于寡。

【例词】多情、多变、多疑、多功能、多才多艺、多愁善感、多谋善断、多此一举、多多益善、多管闲事

6. 实

【课文】有若无，实若虚。

【例词】实在、实际、实话、实力、实权、老实、结实、忠实、实事求是、实心实意

7. 虚

【课文】同上。

【例词】虚心、虚词、虚伪、空虚、谦虚、座无虚席、箭不虚发、虚情假意、虚张声势、虚虚实实

8. 犯

【课文】犯而不校。

【例词】犯病、犯法、犯愁、犯规、犯罪、犯人、冒犯、侵犯、犯错误、犯上作乱

练习 Exercises

一、选择题 MULTIPLE CHOICE

1. 越学习，就越认识到自己的 ________。
   a. 无能　　b. 无用
   c. 无知　　d. 无聊
2. 李时珍是 ________ 代的名医。
   a. 汉　　b. 唐
   c. 元　　d. 明
3. 《本草纲目》是我国明以前 ________ 的总结性巨著。
   a. 动物学　　b. 植物学
   c. 矿物学　　d. 药物学
4. 该书出版后，很快就传到日本，以后又 ________ 到欧美各国。
   a. 流行　　b. 流传
   c. 流动　　d. 流放

二、改错 CORRECTING MISTAKES

1. 人们应该学会在博大精深的“道”的面前表演自己的虔敬之心。
2. 曾子在第四段中所说的话，完全违背了孔子的思想。

3. 为了编《本草纲目》，李时珍读了八百余卷医书，
4. 李时珍穿着跑鞋，背着书包，走遍千山万水。
5. 《本草纲目》先后被译成日、法、德、英、俄等十余种语言在国外出版。

三、问答题 ANSWERING QUESTIONS

1. 孔子说他没做过什么事？
2. 孔子要杜绝哪四种弊病？
3. “有若无”、“实若虚”是一种什么精神？
4. “问于不能”、“问于寡”是一种什么态度？
5. “犯而不校”是一种什么胸怀？
6. 李时珍编写《本草纲目》费时多少年？
7. 李时珍虚心地向哪些人请教？
8. 李时珍冒着生命危险上山观察什么动物？他弄清了哪些问题？
9. 《本草纲目》全书有多少字？
10. 《本草纲目》记载了多少药物？多少处方？
11. 达尔文是怎么称赞《本草纲目》的？

四、讨论题 QUESTIONS FOR DISCUSSION

1. 曾子从哪三个方面来说明一个人应有的虚心学习的态度？
2. 李时珍为了编《本草纲目》学了很多理论知识和实践知识，请具体说明。

五、故事复述 RETELLING THE STORY

《李时珍不耻下问》

六、用本课的成语改写句子 REWRITING SENTENCES USING IDIOMS FROM THE CHAPTER

1. 这次口试，最主要的是不要不懂装懂，知道什么就说什么。
2. 我去中国开会时带了一大包书。本想在这长途旅行中读很多书的，结果一本都没看完。
3. 小李常年出差在外，走过很多地方，是一个见多识广的人。

七、选词 WORD CHOICE

1. 小云又会弹钢琴，又会拉小提琴，还喜欢唱歌、画画，真是（多才多艺、多谋善断、多多益善）啊！
2. 那位推销员（能文能武、能攻能守、能说会道），为公司拉来了很多客户。
3. 老赵是个极其（牢固、顽固、坚固）的人，从来听不进别人的意见。
4. 妈妈的胃不好，常常（犯病、犯规、犯愁）我们应该劝她去看医生。
5. 王经理在我们公司没有（实话、实力、实权），什么事都做不了主。

八、文译白 TRANSLATION FROM CLASSICAL CHINESE INTO MODERN CHINESE

文嘉①惜时《三日歌》

《昨日歌》："昨日兮昨日，昨日何其好！昨日过去了，今日徒烦恼。世人但知悔昨日，不觉今日又过了。水去汩汩流，花落日日少。万事立业在今日，莫待明朝悔今朝。"

《今日歌》："今日复今日，今日何其少！今日又不为，此事何时了？人生百年几今日，今日不为真可惜。若言姑待明朝至，明朝又有明朝事。为君聊赋今日诗，努力请从今日始。"

《明日歌》："明日复明日，明日何其多！我生待明日，万事成蹉跎。世人若被明日累，春去秋来老将至。朝看水东流，暮看日西坠。百年明日能几何？请君听我明日歌。"

【注释】①文嘉(1501–1583)：明朝书画家。

九、英译中 TRANSLATION FROM ENGLISH INTO CHINESE

GRINDING AN IRON ROD INTO A NEEDLE

The Tang dynasty poet Li Bai (李白) did not study very hard when he was a young boy. Once he saw an old lady grinding an iron rod on a stone and asked with curiosity, "Granny, what are you doing?" The lady said, "I am making a needle." Li Bai was quite puzzled: "How can you make a needle out of such a thick rod?" The lady answered, without even stopping her work, "As long as I grind it every day, the rod will become thinner and thinner, and it will one day turn into a needle." Li Bai was enlightened. He studied diligently ever since that moment and grew up to be one of the greatest poets in Chinese history. "As long as efforts are profound, an iron rod can be ground into a needle" (只要功夫深，铁棒磨成针) has become a popular proverb in China.

十、讲故事 STORYTELLING (根据下面的提示在网上找资料)

【题目】勤思好学的故事

【提示】毋意毋必、勤思好学是成功者的共同特质。比如，英国科学家牛顿（Isaac Newton）就有不少广泛流传的故事。讲一个这方面的故事，古今中外都可以。

4. Inferring by Analogy 举一反三

《论语》选段 *Analects* Passages

4-1. 子曰：“不愤不启，不悱不发。举一隅不以三隅反，则不复也。”(7.8)

孔子说：“不到学生急于弄通问题却又不能的时候，不去开导他；不到学生想表达思想却又苦于不能的时候，不去启发他。教给他一个方面，他却不能由此而推知其他三个方面，我就不重复了。”

4-2. 子谓子贡曰：“女与回也孰愈？”对曰：“赐也何敢望回？回也闻一以知十，赐也闻一以知二。”子曰：“弗如也。吾与女，弗如也。”(5.8)

孔子对子贡说：“你和颜回谁更好一些呢？”子贡回答说：“我怎么敢和颜回相比呢？颜回他听到一件事就可以推知十件事；我呢，听到一件事，只能推知两件事。”孔子说：“是不如他呀，我同意你说的，是不如他。”

4-3. 子贡曰：“贫而无谄，富而无骄，何如？”子曰：“可也。未若贫而乐道，富而好礼者也。”子贡曰：“《诗》云：‘如切如磋，如琢如磨’，其斯之谓与？”子曰：“赐也！始可与言《诗》已矣，告诸往而知来者。”(1.15)

子贡说：“贫穷而不谄媚，富有而不骄傲，怎么样？”孔子说：“不错。但还不如贫穷却乐于道，富裕却又好礼的人。”子贡说：“《诗经》上说的‘如切如磋，如琢如磨’，就是这个意思吧？”孔子说：“子贡啊，我可以同你谈论《诗经》了，你能从我已经讲过的话中领会到我还没有说到的意思。”

词汇一 VOCABULARY I

1.	愤	fèn	anger, resentment
2.	启	qǐ	to open, to inspire, to enlighten
3.	悱	fěi	inarticulate, unable to express one's emotion
4.	发	fā	to initiate, to enlighten
5.	举	jǔ	to cite (examples)
6.	隅	yú	corner, nook
7.	反	fǎn	to infer, to analogize
8.	复	fù	再
9.	弄通	nòngtōng	to get a good grasp
10.	开导	kāidǎo	to educate and enlighten, to help one straighten out wrong or muddled thinking

11.	苦于	kǔyú	to suffer (a disadvantage)
12.	推知	tuīzhī	to infer, to deduce
13.	谓	wèi	（对什么人）说
14.	愈	yù	better
15.	望	wàng	to view, to hope, to expect
16.	与	yǔ	同意
17.	谄	chǎn	to flatter, to fawn over
18.	可	kě	pretty good, not bad
19.	切	qiē	to cut, to slice
20.	磋	cuō	to grind and polish
21.	切磋	qiēcuō	to improve oneself through discussion with another
22.	琢	zhuó	to chisel, to carve
23.	磨	mó	to grind and polish
24.	琢磨	zhuómó	to carve and polish (jade), to refine and improve (literary works, moral status, etc.)
25.	往	wǎng	往日、过去
26.	谄媚	chǎnmèi	to flatter, to fawn over
27.	富裕	fùyù	rich, wealthy, prosperous
28.	领会	lǐnghuì	to understand, to comprehend, to grasp

虚词 FUNCTION WORDS

1.	与	yǔ	和（女与回也孰愈）
2.	孰	shú	谁（同上）
3.	何	hé	怎么（赐也何敢望回）
4.	以	yǐ	而（回也闻一以知十）
5.	弗	fú	不（弗如也。）
6.	何如	hérú	怎么样（贫而无谄，富而无骄何如）
7.	未若	wèiruò	不如（未若贫而乐道富，而好礼者也）
8.	其	qí	大概（其斯之谓与）
9.	与	yú	吧（同上）
10.	诸	zhū	之（告诸往而知来者）
11.	者	zhě	（的）事（同上）

专名 PROPER NAMES

1.	诗	Shī	*Classic of Poetry* (*Shijing* 诗经)
2.	子贡	Zǐgòng	姓端木，名赐 (b. 520 BCE), 孔子的学生

解读 Exegeses

我们现在用的很多词语和成语都是从《论语》中来的。比如从本章第一段中，至少能找到一个词语（“启发”）和一个成语（“举一反三”）的出处。

从这一章中，我们可以看到孔子对学生的要求是很高的。孔子的教学方法不是老师念讲稿、学生记笔记，死记硬背。学生要刻苦钻研、独立思考，还要能举一反三。在这个基础上，老师才能对他进行启发。

第三段中子贡与孔子讨论《诗经》提供了一个举一反三的好例子。子贡把《诗经》中说的“如切如磋，如琢如磨”用来比喻人的品格修养的不断提高。孔子听了很高兴，表扬他懂得了读诗的方法。后来“切磋琢磨”也成了一句成语，用来比喻在学习、研究上的互相商讨。

词汇二 VOCABULARY II

1.	出处	chūchù	source (of a quotation or allusion)
2.	死记硬背	sǐjì yìngbèi	mechanical memorization
3.	刻苦	kèkǔ	assiduous, hardworking, painstaking
4.	钻研	zuānyán	to study intensively, to dig into

事例 An Illustrative Story

TONES OF THE ZITHER 孔子学琴

孔子喜欢唱歌、作曲，还能弹琴。他曾跟鲁国一个叫师襄的有名的乐师学弹琴。

一次，师襄教了孔子一支乐曲。孔子埋头苦练了十天，师襄说：“你可以学新曲了。”孔子却说：“我只是刚刚把曲子弹熟，技法还没精呢！”又过了几天，师襄说：“你的技法熟练了，可以学新曲了。”孔子却说：“我还没有明白它的主题呢！”又过了几天，师襄又说：“现在你明白它的主题了，可以弹新曲了。”孔子仍然说：“我还没有体会到作曲家的为人呢！”

又过了好几天。孔子正弹琴时，忽然抬起头来，两眼闪烁着喜悦的光芒。他对师襄说：“我知道作曲家是怎样一个人了！这个人高高的个子，黝黑的脸，眼睛炯炯有神，像个统治四方的王者。莫非这曲子是周文王所作？我想除了他，别人是作不出这样好的曲子来的！”师襄听了，站起来说：“是呀，我的老师对我说过，这首曲子叫《文王操》，它的作者是周文王。”师襄对孔子佩服不已，躬身相拜。孔子急忙回礼，说：“我现在可以学弹新曲了！”

词汇三 VOCABULARY III

1.	琴	qín	a seven-stringed, plucked instrument, similar to the zither
2.	乐师	yuèshī	musician
3.	埋头	máitóu	to immerse oneself in, to be engrossed in
4.	技法	jìfǎ	skill, technique
5.	为人	wéirén	behavior, character
6.	闪烁	shǎnshuò	to twinkle, to glisten
7.	光芒	guāngmáng	rays of light, radiance
8.	黝黑	yǒuhēi	dark
9.	炯炯	jiǒngjiǒng	(of eyes) bright, shining
10.	莫非	mòfēi	难道
11.	操	cāo	a type of *qin* music
12.	佩服	pèifu	to admire
13.	躬身	gōngshēn	to bend at the waist, to bow
14.	拜	bài	to make obeisance

专名 PROPER NAMES

1.	师襄	Shī Xiāng	a Lu 鲁 musician
2.	周文王	Zhōu Wénwáng	King Wen of the Zhou, father of King Wu 武, founder of the Zhou dynasty (1046–256 BCE)

成语 Idioms

1. 举一反三
   【课文】举一隅不以三隅反，则不复也。
2. 不愤不启，不悱不发
   【课文】不愤不启，不悱不发。
3. 闻一知十
   【课文】回也闻一以知十。
4. 贫而无谄，富而无骄
   【课文】贫而无谄，富而无骄，何如？
5. 贫而乐道，富而好礼
   【课文】未若贫而乐道，富而好礼者也。
6. 切磋琢磨
   【课文】如切如磋，如琢如磨，其斯之谓与？
7. 告往知来
   【课文】赐也！始可与言《诗》已矣，告诸往而知来者。

8. 死记硬背
【课文】孔子的教学方法不是老师念讲稿、学生记笔记，死记硬背。
9. 炯炯有神
【课文】这个人高高的个子，黝黑的脸，眼睛炯炯有神，像个统治四方的王者。

词汇扩展 Vocabulary Expansion

1. 启
【课文】不愤不启，不悱不发。
【例词】启发、启程、启航、启示、启蒙、启事、启用、启动、启齿
2. 发
【课文】同上。
【例词】发生、发明、发动、发达、发扬、发现、发电、发火、发财、批发、抒发
3. 举
【课文】举一隅不以三隅反，则不复也。
【例词】举行、举动、举例、举一反三、举不胜举、举目无亲、举棋不定、举足轻重、举国欢腾、举世瞩目
4. 复
【课文】同上。
【例词】复信、复查、复试、复述、复赛、复交、复婚、复仇、复活节、复印机
5. 望
【课文】赐也何敢望回？
【例词】希望、盼望、远望、瞭望、失望、望尘莫及、望而生畏、望风而逃、望梅止渴、望眼欲穿
6. 贫
【课文】贫而无谄，富而无骄。
【例词】贫乏、贫苦、贫困、贫民、贫穷、贫弱、贫血、贫病交迫、贫而无谄、贫而乐道
7. 往
【课文】告诸往而知来者。
【例词】往来、往返、往常、往日、往往、交往、向往、往事如烟、古往今来、来来往往

练习 Exercises

一、选择题 MULTIPLE CHOICE

1. 很多成语都能从《论语》中找到 ________。
   a. 出处　　b. 出路
   c. 出口　　d. 出身
2. "切磋琢磨"这句成语是用来比喻在学习上的互相 ________。
   a. 商量　　b. 商谈
   c. 商讨　　d. 商洽
3. 孔子曾跟 ________ 国一个叫师襄的乐师学琴。
   a. 齐　　b. 鲁
   c. 秦　　d. 楚
4. 我还没有明白这支曲子的 ________ 呢！
   a. 旋律　　b. 题目
   c. 意义　　d. 主题
5. 孔子弹琴时，两眼闪烁着喜悦的 ________。
   a. 光明　　b. 光亮
   c. 光芒　　d. 光线

二、改错 CORRECTING MISTAKES

1. 学生要刻苦钻研、独立思想，还要能举一反三。
2. 孔子喜欢唱歌、作曲，还能弹钢琴。
3. 师襄教了孔子一支乐曲，孔子低头苦练了十天。
4. 我还没有体现到作曲家的为人呢！
5. 师襄对孔子喜欢不已，躬身相拜。

三、问答题 ANSWERING QUESTIONS

1. 从本章第一段中，你能找到哪个词语和哪个成语的出处？
2. 孔子说什么时候才需要开导、启发学生？
3. 子贡和颜回谁更好？为什么？
4. 子贡把诗经中说的"如切如磋，如琢如磨"用来比喻什么？
5. 现在"切磋琢磨"这句成语是用来比喻什么？
6. 孔子跟谁学琴？
7. 《文王操》的作者是谁？

四、讨论题 QUESTIONS FOR DISCUSSION

1. 根据本章的内容，介绍一下孔子的教学方法。
2. 师襄为什么对孔子佩服不已，躬身相拜？

五、故事复述 RETELLING THE STORY

《孔子学琴》

六、用本课的成语改写句子 REWRITING SENTENCES USING IDIOMS FROM THE CHAPTER

1. 这个电影明星高大英俊、眼睛明亮，怪不得那么多女孩子影迷喜欢他。
2. 你这样像老和尚念经似的读书是没用的，得用心去弄懂道理。
3. 这道题很难，我们得多花时间来商讨、研究。
4. 老赵从来不因为自己没钱而去讨好别人，他过得很开心，也很有尊严。

七、选词 WORD CHOICE

1. 小李中文说得这么好，真使我（望而生畏、望尘莫及、望眼欲穿）。
2. 孩子的（启示、启蒙、启动）教育非常重要，所以很多家长都要挑一个好的托儿所。
3. 这场比赛（举足轻重、举世瞩目、举棋不定），关系到我们校队能不能进入东部大学的决赛。
4. 包先生小时候家境（贫乏、贫困、贫弱），吃了很多苦，养成了他艰苦奋斗的精神。
5. （来来往往、往事如烟、古往今来），有多少名人勤奋好学的故事啊。

八、文译白 TRANSLATION FROM CLASSICAL CHINESE INTO MODERN CHINESE

朱熹①论读书

读书有三到，谓心到、口到、眼到。心不在此，则眼不看仔细。心眼既不专一，却只漫浪诵读，决不能记，记不能久也。三到之中，心到最急。心既到矣，眼口岂不到乎？

读书，始读，未知有疑；其次，则渐渐有疑；中则节节是疑。过了这一番，疑渐渐释，以至融会贯通，都无所疑，方始是学。

先须熟读，使其言皆若出自吾之口，继以精思，使其意皆若出自吾之心，然后可以有得也。

【注释】①朱熹(1130–1200)：南宋哲学家、教育家。

九、英译中 TRANSLATION FROM ENGLISH INTO CHINESE

1. The *Classic of Poetry* (诗经) is the earliest existing collection of Chinese poems. It comprises 305 poems, some written possibly as early as 1000 BCE.
2. The *Classic of Poetry* covers all aspects of the society of the Zhou dynasty, such as work and love, war and hunting, customs and marriage, sacrifices and feasts, and animals and plants.
3. The *Classic of Poetry* is not only a mirror reflecting the Zhou dynasty, but also valuable and important material in the study of the Chinese language from the eleventh century to the sixth century BCE.
4. The *Classic of Poetry* has spread widely in China and abroad. It has been translated into many foreign languages, including English, French, Japanese, and Russian.

十、辩论 DEBATING

【题目】《孔子的启发式教育》

【提示】（双方主要论点）：

正方—孔子的"不愤不启，不悱不发"的教育方法要求学生独立思考，调动了学生的积极性和创造性。

反方—孔子的启发式教育是一种精英教育，只有对少数最好的学生才能适用。

5. The Ultimate Joy 乐在其中

《论语》选段 *Analects* Passages

5-1. 子曰："知之者不如好之者，好之者不如乐之者。"(6.20)

孔子说："懂得它，不如爱好它；爱好它，又不如以它为乐。"

5-2. 子曰："默而识之，学而不厌，诲人不倦，何有于我哉？" (7.2)

孔子说："默默地记住所学的知识，学习不觉得厌烦，教人不知道疲倦，我还要什么呢？"

5-3. 子曰："饭疏食、饮水，曲肱而枕之，乐亦在其中矣。不义而富且贵，于我如浮云。"(7.16)

孔子说："吃粗粮，喝白水，弯着胳膊当枕头，乐趣也就在这中间了。用不正当的手段得来的富贵，对于我来说就像是浮云一样。"

5-4. 叶公问孔子于子路，子路不对。子曰："女奚不曰：'其为人也，发愤忘食，乐以忘忧，不知老之将至'云尔。"(7.18)

叶公问子路孔子是个什么样的人，子路不答。孔子说："你为什么不说'他这个人，发愤用功，连吃饭都忘了，快乐得把一切忧虑都忘了，连自己快要老了都不知道，等等'。"

5-5. 子曰："贤哉，回也！一箪食，一瓢饮，在陋巷，人不堪其忧，回也不改其乐。贤哉，回也！"(6.11)

孔子说："颜回多好啊！一箪饭，一瓢水，住在简陋的小巷里，别人都会受不了这种穷苦生活带来的烦恼，颜回却不改变他的好心情。颜回多好啊！"

词汇一 VOCABULARY I

1.	乐	yào	喜欢，爱好
2.	默	mò	silent
3.	识	zhì	志（誌）, to remember
4.	厌	yàn	to be weary of, to be fed up with
5.	倦	juàn	tired, slack
6.	厌烦	yànfán	to be sick of
7.	饭	fàn	吃
8.	疏食	shūshí	coarse food

9.	曲	qū	to bend
10.	肱	gōng	forearm
11.	枕	zhěn	to rest one's head on
12.	义	yì	righteous, just
13.	浮	fú	floating
14.	粗粮	cūliáng	coarse grains such as corn and millet (as distinct from wheat and rice)
15.	胳膊	gēbo	arm
16.	正当	zhèngdàng	proper, appropriate, legitimate
17.	忧虑	yōulǜ	worry, anxiety
18.	箪	dān	a bamboo vessel for holding cooked rice
19.	瓢	piáo	a ladle (often made of half of a dried gourd)
20.	陋	lòu	narrow and small, ugly, mean
21.	巷	xiàng	lane, alley
22.	堪	kān	to bear, to stand
23.	烦恼	fánnǎo	to be vexed, worried

虚词 FUNCTION WORDS

1.	何	hé	什么（何有于我哉）
2.	哉	zāi	呢（同上）
3.	且	qiě	而且（不义而富且贵）
4.	奚	xī	为什么（女奚不曰）
5.	云尔	yúněr	等等（同上）
6.	哉	zāi	affirmation（贤哉，回也）

专名 PROPER NAMES

1.	叶公	Shègōng	Duke of She (She was located in what is now Henan Province)

解读 Exegeses

虽然儒家提倡用学到的知识、本领为社会服务，但孔子也认为学习的主要目的是追求人格的自我完善。既然如此，学习的本身就应该是一个快乐的过程。

本章第一段中说了学习的三种境界：知之者是被动接受，好之者已是主动追求，乐之者则进入学习成为生活乐趣的境界。我们都知道，兴趣是最好的老师。只有发自内心的喜爱，才能学得又快又好。

第二至第四段是孔子的自画像。这是孔子以学为乐、好学不倦、安贫乐道、发愤忘食的生动写照。

第五段又是写颜回。颜回之所以是孔子最好的学生，是因为他好学（不迁怒、不贰过），能闻一知十，更因为他能在贫困中不改其乐。

孔子在《论语》中阐述了一系列关于学习和教育的理论，包括学以致道、有教无类、因材施教、敏而好学、学思结合、温故知新、博闻多见、择善而从、启发诱导和学无常师等等。这些思想代代相传，指导了中国二千五百年的教育事业。

词汇二 VOCABULARY II

1.	提倡	tíchàng	to advocate, to promote, to encourage
2.	人格	réngé	character, moral quality
3.	完善	wánshàn	perfection
4.	既然	jìrán	since, this being the case
5.	如此	rúcǐ	这样
6.	过程	guòchéng	course, process
7.	被动	bèidòng	passive
8.	主动	zhǔdòng	taking the initiative
9.	阐述	chánshù	to expound, to elaborate
10.	有教无类	yǒujiào wúlèi	to provide education for all people without discrimination
11.	类	lèi	kind, type, class
12.	因材施教	yīncái shījiào	to teach students according to their aptitudes
13.	因	yīn	on the basis of, in accordance with
14.	材	cái	material, talent, aptitude
15.	施	shī	to execute, to apply
16.	择	zé	to choose, to select
17.	诱导	yòudǎo	to guide, to lead, to induce

事例 An Illustrative Story

THE PLUM BLOSSOM PAINTER 王冕画梅

王冕是元代著名的画家、诗人。他年幼的时候，家里很穷。一天，父亲让他去放牛，王冕却偷偷溜进学堂听学生们读书。到了晚上回去的时候，才发现牛已跑得无影无踪了。

长大后，王冕不去追逐功名。他隐居在山中，白天耕耘，晚上作画。他盖了三间草屋，栽了上千树梅花，自称“梅花屋主”。当时向他求画的人很多，王冕便以他的画作交换粮米。他的朋友想推荐他当官，王冕却说："我有田可耕，有书可读，怎么肯给人当差呢？"他始终不为富贵所动，在清贫的生活中享受书画的乐趣。

王冕以画梅闻名。他的名作《墨梅图》枝叶繁茂，千花万蕊，洋溢着蓬勃的生气，又表现了孤傲倔强的性格。王冕的画梅是和其思想感情分不开的。他在一幅墨梅上题诗："凡桃俗李争芬芳，只有老梅心自常。"

词汇三 VOCABULARY III

1.	梅	méi	plum blossom
2.	放牛	fàngniú	to herd cattle
3.	偷偷	tōutōu	stealthily, secretly
4.	溜	liū	to go secretly and quietly
5.	学堂	xuétáng	学校 (old term)
6.	无影无踪	wúyǐng wúzōng	(to vanish or disappear) without a trace
7.	踪	zōng	footprint, trace
8.	追逐	zhuīzhú	to chase, to pursue, to seek
9.	功名	gōngmíng	official rank and academic degree (determined by performance in the imperial examinations)
10.	隐居	yǐnjū	to retire from public life, to live in seclusion
11.	耕耘	gēngyún	to till and weed
12.	盖	gài	to build (a house)
13.	栽	zāi	to plant, to grow
14.	当差	dāngchāi	to do a duty (as a clerk or servant)
15.	繁茂	fánmào	lush, luxuriant
16.	蕊	ruǐ	flower bud
17.	洋溢	yángyì	to be permeated with, to brim with
18.	蓬勃	péngbó	vigorous, flourishing, full of vitality
19.	生气	shēngqì	life, vitality
20.	孤傲	gū'ào	proud and aloof
21.	孤	gū	solitary, isolated, alone
22.	傲	ào	proud, haughty
23.	倔强	juéjiàng	unyielding, stubborn
24.	题	tí	to inscribe (a poem, etc.)
25.	凡	fán	ordinary
26.	桃	táo	peach (blossoms)
27.	俗	sú	vulgar, in poor taste
28.	李	lǐ	plum (blossoms)
29.	争	zhēng	to contend, to vie, to strive
30.	芬芳	fēnfāng	fragrance

专名 PROPER NAMES

1. 王冕 Wáng Miǎn a painter and poet (1287–1359)
2. 元 Yuán the Yuan dynasty (1271–1368)

成语 Idioms

1. 乐在其中
   【课文】饭疏食、饮水，曲肱而枕之，乐亦在其中矣。
2. 默而识之
   【课文】默而识之，学而不厌，诲人不倦，何有于我哉？
3. 学而不厌
   【课文】同上。
4. 诲人不倦
   【课文】同上。
5. 发愤忘食
   【课文】发愤忘食，乐以忘忧，不知老之将至。
6. 乐以忘忧
   【课文】同上。
7. 箪食瓢饮
   【课文】一箪食，一瓢饮，在陋巷。
8. 不堪其忧
   【课文】人不堪其忧，回也不改其乐。
9. 不改其乐
   【课文】同上。
10. 安贫乐道
   【课文】这是孔子以学为乐、好学不倦、安贫乐道、发愤忘食的生动写照。
11. 有教无类
   【课文】孔子在《论语》中阐述了一系列关于学习和教育的理论，包括学以致道、有教无类、因材施教、敏而好学、学思结合、温故知新、博闻多见、择善而从、启发诱导和学无常师等等。
12. 因材施教
   【课文】同上。
13. 博闻多见
   【课文】同上。
14. 择善而从
   【课文】同上。
15. 学无常师
   【课文】同上。

16. 代代相传
【课文】这些思想代代相传，指导了中国二千五百年的教育事业。
17. 无影无踪
【课文】到了晚上回去的时候，才发现牛已跑得无影无踪了。

词汇扩展 Vocabulary Expansion

1. 默
【课文】默而识之，学而不厌，诲人不倦，何有于我哉？
【例词】默写、默读、默认、默许、沉默、幽默、默不作声、默默无闻、默默无语、潜移默化
2. 厌
【课文】同上。
【例词】厌烦、厌倦、厌恶、厌弃、厌战、厌世、讨厌、百看不厌、贪得无厌、喜新厌旧
3. 食
【课文】饭疏食、饮水，曲肱而枕之，乐亦在其中矣。
【例词】食宿、食言、食指、饮食、主食、素食、甜食、绝食、食无求饱、衣食无忧
4. 义
【课文】不义而富且贵，于我如浮云。
【例词】义务、义气、义父、正义、意义、定义、起义、义正词严、义不容辞、义无反顾
5. 贵
【课文】同上。
【例词】贵宾、贵客、贵族、贵重、宝贵、富贵、高贵、权贵、贵客盈门、高抬贵手
6. 忘
【课文】发愤忘食，乐以忘忧，不知老之将至。
【例词】忘本、忘我、健忘、难忘、遗忘、忘年之交、发愤忘食、废寝忘食、得意忘形、忘恩负义
7. 乐
【课文】同上。
【例词】乐观、乐趣、乐意、欢乐、安乐、乐在其中、乐天知命、乐极生悲、安贫乐道、安居乐业

练习 Exercises

一、选择题 MULTIPLE CHOICE

1. 学习的本身就应该是一个 ________ 的过程。
   a. 紧张　　b. 快乐
   c. 痛苦　　d. 烦恼
2. 本章第一段中说了学习的三种 ________。
   a. 情况　　b. 方法
   c. 境界　　c. 过程
3. 王冕盖了三间草屋，栽了上千树 ________。
   a. 桃花　　b. 李花
   c. 樱花　　d. 梅花
4. 他在清贫的生活中享受书画的 ________。
   a. 快乐　　b. 乐趣
   c. 趣味　　d. 味道

二、改错 CORRECTING MISTAKES

1. 王冕是清代著名的画家、诗人。
2. 王冕年幼的时候，家里很富。
3. 父亲让他去放牛，王冕却偷偷溜进教堂。
4. 他隐居在山中，白天写诗，晚上作画。
5. 王冕以他的画作交换钱财。
6. 王冕以画竹闻名。

三、问答题 ANSWERING QUESTIONS

1. 孔子认为学习的主要目的是什么？
2. 为什么说颜回是孔子最好的学生？
3. 孔子在《论语》中阐述了哪些关于学习和教育的理论？
4. 王冕长大后做什么？
5. 王冕自称什么？
6. 王冕为什么不想当官？
7. 王冕在一幅墨梅上题写了什么诗句？

四、讨论题 QUESTIONS FOR DISCUSSION

1. 本章第一段说了学习的三种境界。请结合自己的体会讨论。
2. 根据第二至第四段，说说孔子的生活态度。

五、故事复述 RETELLING THE STORY

《王冕画梅》

六、用本课的成语改写句子 REWRITING SENTENCES USING IDIOMS FROM THE CHAPTER

1. 方先生去过三十多个国家旅行，知识非常丰富，是一本活辞典。
2. 我的钱包刚刚还在，怎么一下子就不见了？一定是让人给偷了。
3. 戴教授真是一个好老师，他不但上课很生动，而且在指导学生的时候极其耐心。
4. 刘先生根据他的两个孩子的特点进行培养：儿子好动，就叫他打网球；女儿安静，就教她弹钢琴。

七、选词 WORD CHOICE

1. 吴大中是一个很讲（义气、义务、正义）的人，他把朋友的事看得比自己的还重。
2. 小夏已经把《红楼梦》读了好多遍了，这个暑假她说还要再读一遍，真是（贪得无厌、喜新厌旧、百看不厌）。
3. 汪太太是个（乐在其中、乐天知命、乐极生悲）的人，从来不发愁，整天开开心心。
4. 这个花瓶是清朝的，非常（高贵、贵重、富贵），请你不要摸它。
5. 张玲平时上课总是举手发言，可是今天她（默默无闻、默不作声、潜移默化），不知发生了什么事？

八、文译白 TRANSLATION FROM CLASSICAL CHINESE INTO MODERN CHINESE

1. 王冕《墨梅》："我家洗砚池边树，个个花开淡墨痕。不要人夸好颜色，只留清气满乾坤①。"
2. 王冕《白梅》："冰雪林中著此身，不同桃李混芳尘。忽然一夜清香发，散作乾坤万里春。"
3. 齐已②《早梅》："万木冻欲折，孤根暖独回。村前深雪里，昨夜一枝开。"
4. 李公明③《早梅》："东风才有又西风，群木山中叶叶空。只有梅花吹不尽，依然新白抱新红。"

【注释】①乾坤qiánkūn：天地、世界。②齐已(ca. 860–ca. 937)：唐朝诗僧。③李公明：宋朝诗人。

九、英译中 TRANSLATION FROM ENGLISH INTO CHINESE

1. Plum blossoms are seen in China as the heralds of spring. Their beauty, fragrance, and symbolic meaning have been popular themes for numerous poets and painters.
2. Plum blossoms, pine trees, and bamboo have been called the "Three Friends in the Cold Season" (岁寒三友) because all can withstand chilly weather.
3. Plum blossoms, orchids, bamboo, and chrysanthemums are the "Four Gentlemen" (四君子), so named for their shared spirit of purity and nobility. They are often seen on traditional four-panel Chinese screens.

十、专题研究 TOPICAL RESEARCH

范仲淹在《睢阳学舍书怀》诗中写道："瓢思颜子心还乐"。结合第一章中范仲淹的故事和本章第五段《论语》语录，解释这句诗。

PART II

Morality 修身篇

6. Filial Piety 孝弟为本

《论语》选段 *Analects* Passages

6-1. 有子曰："其为人也孝弟，而好犯上者，鲜矣；不好犯上，而好作乱者，未之有也。君子务本，本立而道生。孝弟也者，其为仁之本与！"(1.2)

有子说："孝顺父母，敬爱兄长，却喜好反对上级的人是很少见的。不喜好反对上级却喜好造反的人是没有的。君子致力于根本，根本建立了，道也就有了。孝顺父母、敬爱兄长，这就是仁的根本啊！"

6-2. 子曰："弟子入则孝，出则弟，谨而信，汎爱众，而亲仁，行有余力，则以学文。"(1.6)

孔子说："年轻人在家要孝顺父母，出外要敬爱兄长。谨慎而诚信，广泛地爱众人，亲近那些有仁德的人。这样做了还有余力的话，就再去学习文化知识。"

6-3. 子夏问孝。子曰："色难。有事，弟子服其劳；有酒食，先生馔。曾是以为孝乎？"(2.8)

子夏问什么是孝，孔子说："脸色最难。有了事情，小辈去做；有了酒饭，让长辈吃。难道这就算是孝了吗？"

词汇一 VOCABULARY I

1.	孝	xiào	filial piety
2.	弟	tì	same as 悌, love and respect for one's elder brother
3.	犯上	fànshàng	to go against one's superior
4.	鲜	xiǎn	少
5.	作乱	zuòluàn	to rebel
6.	乱	luàn	disorder, chaos, upheaval, riot
7.	务	wù	to attend to, to devote one's efforts to
8.	本	běn	stem, root, origin, basis, foundation
9.	孝顺	xiàoshùn	filial piety
10.	造反	zàofǎn	to rebel, to revolt
11.	致力	zhìlì	to devote oneself to
12.	谨	jǐn	谨慎, prudent, circumspect
13.	汎	fàn	广泛, broadly, extensively
14.	亲	qīn	亲近, to be close to
15.	余力	yúlì	strength and energy to spare
16.	色	sè	脸色, facial expression

17. 弟子 dìzǐ 年轻人
18. 服 fú to serve
19. 先生 xiānsheng 父兄
20. 馔 zhuàn food, to eat and drink
21. 小辈 xiǎobèi the younger generation
22. 长辈 zhǎngbèi the older generation

虚词 FUNCTION WORDS

1. 其 qí 如果（其为人也孝弟，而好犯上者，鲜矣）
2. 者 zhě to pause for emphasis （同上）
3. 其 qí 真是（孝弟也者，其为仁之本与）
4. 与 yú 啊 （同上）
5. 则 zé 就
6. 其 qí 那个（有事，弟子服其劳）
7. 曾是 zēngshì 竟然（曾是以为孝乎）
8. 以为 yǐwéi 作为（同上）

专名 PROPER NAMES

1. 有子 Yǒuzǐ 姓有名若 (b. 518 BCE)，孔子的学生

解读 Exegeses

古人说“百善孝为先”。说明孝敬父母是人类发展过程中形成的一种最基本的美德，是其他一切伦理道德的基础。一个人首先应该爱自己的父母，其次才能谈到爱他人、爱集体、爱社会、爱祖国……试想，一个人如果连自己的父母都不爱，连孝敬父母、报答养育之恩都做不到，谁还相信他是个有爱心、有责任感的人呢？谁又相信他能够无私奉献、报效国家呢？所以古人有云：“忠臣必出于孝子之门”。

家庭乃社会细胞，家庭的稳固和睦有着不可忽视的社会意义。当然，万事都是相互的。“父慈子孝”，父亲对儿子慈爱，儿子就对父亲孝顺。“兄友弟恭”，哥哥对弟弟友好，弟弟自然对哥哥恭敬。做人由最基本的孝悌做起，自然能逐渐推广到“老吾老以及人之老，幼吾幼以及人之幼”的境界。

在《论语》中，有关“孝悌”的章节达十六处之多，足以见得孝悌观念在儒家学说中的地位。“孝悌”的本质要求是“敬”。随着物质文明的进步，子女对待父母最大的问题已不再是能否在物质上供养的问题，而是敬与不敬的问题了。所以“孝敬”、“孝顺”成了常用词汇。

孔子在《孝经》中说：“夫孝，德之本也，教之所由生也。”孔子在本章

第二段又说，实行孝道以后，“行有余力，则以学文”。“教”这个字的左边是个“孝”字，右边是个“文”字，是不是意味着教育就是在孝的基础上学习文化呢？

词汇二 VOCABULARY II

1.	集体	jítǐ	group, team
2.	报答	bàodá	to repay another's kindness
3.	养育	yǎngyù	to bring up, to raise and educate
4.	恩	ēn	kindness, favor, grace
5.	责任	zérèn	responsibility
6.	感	gǎn	sense, feeling
7.	无私	wúsī	selfless, unselfish
8.	奉献	fèngxiàn	to devote, to dedicate
9.	报效	bàoxiào	to render a service to, to repay somebody's kindness by working hard for him
10.	臣	chén	official under a sovereign, subject
11.	乃	nǎi	是
12.	细胞	xìbāo	cell
13.	稳固	wěngù	firm, stable
14.	和睦	hémù	harmony, concord
15.	忽视	hūshì	to disregard, to neglect
16.	慈	cí	kind, benevolent, loving
17.	推广	tuīguǎng	to spread, to popularize, to make known
18.	观念	guānniàn	sense, concept, mentality
19.	供养	gòngyǎng	to offer provisions (especially to one's parents)
20.	意味	yìweì	to signify, to mean, to imply

事例 An Illustrative Story

GRANDMA AND THE OFFICE 李密陈情

李密是西晋文学家。他出生六个月丧父，四岁时母亲改嫁，他是由祖母抚养成人的。祖母对他关怀备至，他对祖母也十分孝敬。祖母生病时，他日夜在旁服侍。

因为祖母年迈，李密不出去做官，在家乡教书。后来，晋武帝下诏书叫他进京做官。当时李密的祖母已九十六岁，年老多病。于是他向晋武帝上表陈述家里情况，说明自己无法遵命赴京的原因。这就是千古名篇《陈情表》。

李密在表中说得委婉动人。许多词语，为后人经常引用。如他以“急如星火”来形容情势急迫，以“狼狈”形容进退两难，以“茕茕孑立，形影相吊”形容孤苦伶仃、无依无靠，以“日薄西山、气息奄奄、人命危浅、朝不虑夕”形容情况危险。晋武帝看了表，为李密对祖母的孝心所感动，不仅同意他暂不赴京，还嘉奖他孝敬长辈的诚心。

李密在祖母去世、服丧期满后出仕，官至太守。

词汇三 VOCABULARY III

1.	陈	chén	to state
2.	改嫁	gǎijià	(of a woman) to remarry
3.	抚养	fúyǎng	to provide subsistence, to bring up
4.	备	bèi	fully, in every possible way
5.	服侍	fúshi	to wait upon, to attend
6.	年迈	niánmài	年老
7.	诏书	zhàoshū	imperial edict
8.	表	biǎo	a memorial to the emperor
9.	陈述	chénshù	to state
10.	遵命	zūnmìng	to obey orders
11.	赴	fù	去、到
12.	委婉	wěiwǎn	mild and tactful
13.	情势	qíngshì	situation
14.	急迫	jípò	urgent, pressing, imperative
15.	狼狈	lángbèi	in a difficult position, in a dilemma
16.	狼	láng	wolf
17.	狈	bèi	a kind of wolf with short forelegs
18.	茕茕孑立	qióngqióng jiélì	standing all alone
19.	形影相吊	xíngyǐng xiāngdiào	“body and shadow comforting each other”—extremely lonely
20.	孤苦伶仃	gūkǔ língdīng	lonely and helpless
21.	日薄西山	rìbó xīshān	“the sun approaching the western hills”—old age
22.	气息奄奄	qìxī yǎnyǎn	at one’s last gasp, at the point of death
23.	朝不虑夕	zhāobù lǜxī	“not knowing in the morning what may happen in the evening”—to be in a precarious state
24.	嘉奖	jiājiǎng	to commend, to cite
25.	服丧	fúsāng	to be in mourning (for the death of a kinsman, etc.)

26.	出仕	chūshì	to take a government office
27.	太守	tàishǒu	prefect

专名 PROPER NAMES

1.	李密	Lǐ Mì	a literary man (224–287)
2.	西晋	Xī Jìn	the Western Jin dynasty (265–316)
3.	晋武帝	Jìn Wǔdì	Emperor Wu of the Jin (r. 265–290)

成语 Idioms

1. 孝弟为本
【课文】孝弟也者，其为仁之本与！
2. 犯上作乱
【课文】不好犯上，而好作乱者，未之有也。
3. 君子务本
【课文】君子务本，本立而道生。
4. 本立道生
【课文】同上。
5. 行有余力
【课文】行有余力，则以学文。
6. 养育之恩
【课文】一个人如果连孝敬父母、报答养育之恩都做不到，谁还相信他是个有爱心、有责任感的人呢？
7. 父慈子孝
【课文】“父慈子孝”，父亲对儿子慈爱，儿子就对父亲孝顺。
8. 兄友弟恭
【课文】“兄友弟恭”，哥哥对弟弟友好，弟弟自然对哥哥恭敬。
9. 关怀备至
【课文】祖母对他关怀备至，他对祖母也十分孝敬。
10. 委婉动人
【课文】李密在表中说得委婉动人。
11. 急如星火
【课文】他用“急如星火”来形容情势急迫。
12. 进退两难
【课文】他以“狼狈”形容进退两难。
13. 茕茕孑立
【课文】他以“茕茕孑立，形影相吊”形容孤苦伶仃、无依无靠。

14. 形影相吊
【课文】同上。
15. 孤苦伶仃
【课文】同上。
16. 无依无靠
【课文】同上。
17. 日薄西山
【课文】他以“日薄西山、气息奄奄、人命危浅、朝不虑夕”形容情况危险。
18. 气息奄奄
【课文】同上。
19. 人命危浅
【课文】同上。
20. 朝不虑夕
【课文】同上。

词汇扩展 Vocabulary Expansion

1. 本
【课文】君子务本，本立而道生。
【例词】本科、本行、本质、本钱、剧本、资本、本来面目、本末倒置、舍本逐末、一本万利
2. 立
【课文】同上。
【例词】独立、对立、孤立、私立、立交桥、立等可取、立足之地、立竿见影、建功立业、成家立业
3. 道
【课文】同上。
【例词】道德、道理、公道、地道、道听途说、歪门邪道、志同道合、任重道远、处世之道、养生之道
4. 生
【课文】同上。
【例词】生平、生动、生老病死、生离死别、生龙活虎、生气勃勃、生花妙笔、生意兴隆、生财有道、贪生怕死
5. 余
【课文】行有余力，则以学文。
【例词】余地、余生、余党、多余、其余、课余、业余、余味无穷、余音绕梁、余波荡漾

6. 众

【课文】谨而信，汎爱众，而亲仁。

【例词】大众、群众、观众、众志成城、众怒难犯、众口一词、众星捧月、众叛亲离、众所周知、万众一心

7. 难

【课文】色难。

【例词】难看、难听、难道、难得、难怪、难过、难为情、难能可贵、难兄难弟、面有难色

练习 Exercises

一、选择题 MULTIPLE CHOICE

1. 做人由最基本的孝悌做起，自然能逐渐推广到“老吾老以及人之老，幼吾幼以及人之幼”的 ________。

   a. 境界　　b. 情况

   c. 场面　　d. 形势

2. 在《论语》中，有关“孝悌”的章节达十六处之多，足以见得孝悌观念在儒家学说中的 ________。

   a. 地点　　b. 地形

   c. 地方　　d. 地位

3. 因为祖母年迈，李密不出去做官，在家乡 ________。

   a. 种田　　b. 教书

   c. 经商　　d. 做官

4. 于是他向晋武帝上表 ________ 家里情况，说明自己无法遵命赴京的原因。

   a. 讲述　　b. 叙述

   c. 表述　　d. 陈述

二、改错 CORRECTING MISTAKES

1. 哥哥对弟弟友好，弟弟自然对哥哥孝顺。
2. 在《论语》中，有关“孝悌”的语录达十六处之多。
3. 孝悌”的本质要求是“养”。
4. 成语“日薄西山”是形容黄昏的景色。

三、问答题 ANSWERING QUESTIONS

1. 李密怎么会是在祖母抚养下长大成人的？
2. 李密和他祖母的关系怎么样？
3. 李密为什么不出去做官，在家乡教书？

4. 李密无法遵命赴京的原因是什么？
5. 李密的《陈情表》写得怎么样？
6. 李密在《陈情表》中是怎么形容孤苦伶仃、无依无靠的？
7. 李密在《陈情表》中是怎么形容情况危险的？
8. 李密在什么时候出仕做官？

四、讨论题 QUESTIONS FOR DISCUSSION

1. 为什么说“百善孝为先”？
2. 古人说“忠臣必出于孝子之门”，但有时候忠孝却难以两全。李密当时就处于这样困境。他在《陈情表》中是怎么诚恳又巧妙地处理这个难题的？

五、故事复述 RETELLING THE STORY

《李密陈情》

六、用本课的成语改写句子 REWRITING SENTENCES USING IDIOMS FROM THE CHAPTER

1. 王先生刚来美国时谁都不认识，硬是靠着他自己的努力，成为一个有名的电气工程师。
2. 我大学毕业了，还找到了一个很理想的工作，但我永远不会忘记我妈妈为了抚养我而辛苦工作的情景。
3. 你听过《弯弯的月亮》那首歌吗？那么抒情，那么好听，我一下子就被吸引住了。
4. 周明很喜欢他最近认识的女朋友，可是他的父母却觉得他还年轻，应该专心学习，他现在真不知道怎么办才好。

七、选词 WORD CHOICE

1. 我家隔壁的高先生真是（生气勃勃、生意兴隆、生财有道），几年前还看他骑自行车，现在居然开起了奔驰轿车。
2. 陆先生昨天被公司解雇了，他伤心地说：“这么大的公司为什么没有我的（立竿见影、立足之地、立等可取）呢？
3. 那位二胡演奏家拉的《二泉映月》多美啊！到现在还是（余音绕梁、余波荡漾、余味无穷），那旋律老在我的脑子里转悠。
4. 我们学校的辩论队真令人（佩服、征服、信服），从两年前的全国三十五名，一下子跳到了今年的第一名。
5. 那位经理做了很多不得人心的事，现在是（众所周知、众叛亲离、众怒难犯），谁都不听他的。

八、文译白 TRANSLATION FROM CLASSICAL CHINESE INTO MODERN CHINESE

《陈情表》选段

1. 臣少多疾病。九岁不行。零丁孤苦，至于成立。既无叔伯，终鲜兄弟。
2. 臣无祖母，无以至今日。祖母无臣，无以终余年。母孙二人，更相为命。
3. 臣密今年四十有四，祖母刘今年九十有六；是以臣尽节于陛下之日长，报刘之日短也。

九、英译中 TRANSLATION FROM ENGLISH INTO CHINESE (每句要用一句成语)

1. The emperor summoned Li Mi to serve at court but Li Mi's grandmother needed his care, so he had a real dilemma.
2. Li Mi's grandmother was ninety-six years old and sick; she was like the setting sun.
3. He was as lonely as if he were accompanied only by his shadow.

十、讲故事 STORYTELLING (根据下面的提示在网上找资料)

【题目】古代孝子的故事

【提示】以下故事供选择时参考：王祥卧冰、孟宗哭竹、董永葬父、鲍出负母、汉文尝药、杨香打虎。

7. Righteousness and Profit 君子喻义

《论语》选段 *Analects* Passages

7-1. 子曰："君子喻于义，小人喻于利。"(4.16)

孔子说："君子明白大义，小人知道谋取利益。"

7-2. 子曰："君子周而不比，小人比而不周。"(2.14)

孔子说："君子团结而不与人勾结，小人与人勾结而不团结。

7-3. 子曰："君子和而不同，小人同而不和。"(13.23)

孔子说："君子讲求和谐而非一致，小人讲求一致而非和谐。"

7-4. 子曰："君子成人之美，不成人之恶；小人反是。"(12.16)

孔子说："君子成全别人的好事，而不助长别人的恶处。小人则与此相反。"

7-5. 子曰："君子坦荡荡，小人长戚戚。"(7.36)

孔子说："君子心胸宽广，小人经常发愁。"

7-6. 子曰："君子道者三，我无能焉：仁者不忧，知者不惑，勇者不惧。"子贡曰："夫子自道也！"(14.28)

孔子说："君子之道有三个方面，我都未能做到：仁德的人不忧愁，聪明的人不迷惑，勇敢的人不畏惧。"子贡说："这正是老师的自我表述啊！"

词汇一 VOCABULARY I

1. 喻 yù to understand, to know
2. 谋取 móuqǔ to try to gain, to seek
3. 周 zhōu circumference, unity, harmony
4. 比 bǐ collusion
5. 团结 tuánjié to unite
6. 勾结 gōujié to collude, to gang up on
7. 和 hé harmony, to mingle
8. 同 tóng same, to agree without giving serious thought to the matter, to readily subscribe to (somebody's viewpoint)

9.	讲求	jiǎngqiú	to stress, to strive for
10.	和谐	héxié	harmony
11.	成	chéng	to help somebody to accomplish his goals
12.	是	shì	这
13.	成全	chéngquán	to help somebody to accomplish his goals
14.	助长	zhùzhǎng	to encourage (a bad habit, etc.), to foment
15.	坦荡	tǎndàng	bighearted, contented and composed
16.	坦	tǎn	(of a road, etc.) level and broad
17.	荡	dàng	level
18.	长	cháng	常
19.	戚戚	qīqī	woeful and worried
20.	知	zhì	智
21.	惑	huò	to be puzzled, bewildered
22.	迷惑	míhuò	to be puzzled, bewildered
23.	畏惧	wèijù	to fear
24.	表述	biǎoshù	表达和陈述

解读 Exegeses

在中国的古籍中，作者很少给专门名词下定义。比如在《论语》中，"君子"和"小人"用得很多，但孔子也没在某一段里给这两个词下过全面、准确的定义。本章所收的语录每段说了一个方面，综合起来，我们可以对这两个词有比较清楚的理解。

君子和小人的根本区别就在义、利二字。君子重义轻利，小人见利忘义。

君子与众人融洽相处，小人结党营私。

君子独立思考，讲求原则；小人盲目附和，人云亦云。

君子心胸开阔，无所畏惧；小人患得患失，愁眉苦脸。

作为君子，孔子认为其必需的品格有许多，他强调指出了其中的三个方面：仁、智、勇。

读了这一章的语录，同学们能不能给"君子"和"小人"下个定义呢？

词汇二 VOCABULARY II

1.	定义	dìngyì	definition
2.	某	mǒu	certain (used to refer to a person or a thing)
3.	融洽	róngqià	harmonious, on friendly terms
4.	结党营私	jiédǎng yíngsī	to form a clique to pursue selfish interests

5. 盲目 mángmù blind
6. 附和 fùhè to echo, to chime in with, to parrot another's opinions
7. 人云亦云 rényún yìyún to parrot what another says
8. 患 huàn 担心, to worry

事例 An Illustrative Story

THE PROMISSORY NOTES 冯谖焚券

战国时期，齐国有个宰相叫孟尝君。有一次，他叫他的门客冯谖到他的封地薛邑去讨债。

冯谖到了薛邑，了解到由于年成不好，很多百姓都还不出钱。于是，他置办了酒席，请借债的人都来赴宴。冯谖叫大家拿出债券来核对，有能力偿还的给他定下归还期限。对没能力偿还的，冯谖把他们的债券集中起来，当众烧掉了。

孟尝君看见冯谖回来了，就问他："债都收完了吗？"。冯谖回答道："收完了。"孟尝君又问冯谖买了什么回来。冯谖回答道："买了个'义'字回来。我看您的府上，金银绸缎，不计其数，所以我替你买了稀有的东西回来了。"

后来孟尝君政治上失势了，被免去了宰相的职务，他的门客都离开了他。只有冯谖不走，还为孟尝君驾车前往薛邑。

薛邑的百姓，一听说孟尝君罢相回来了，扶老携幼，在路旁迎接。孟尝君一到，他们争献酒食，问候起居。孟尝君感慨地对冯谖说："这就是先生以前替我买的'义'，我今天终于看到了！"

词汇三 VOCABULARY III

1. 焚 fén to burn
2. 券 quàn certificate, ticket
3. 门客 ménkè a hanger-on of an aristocrat
4. 封地 fēngdì fief
5. 讨 tǎo to demand, to ask for
6. 债 zhài debt
7. 年成 niánchéng the year's harvest
8. 置办 zhìbàn to purchase, to procure, to prepare
9. 酒席 jiǔxí banquet, feast
10. 赴宴 fùyàn to attend a banquet
11. 核对 héduì to check (the facts), to verify

12.	偿还	chánghuán	to repay
13.	期限	qīxiàn	time limit, deadline
14.	当众	dāngzhòng	in the presence of all, in public
15.	绸缎	chóuduàn	silks and satins
16.	不计其数	bùjì qíshù	countless, innumerable
17.	稀有	xīyǒu	rare, unusual
18.	失势	shīshì	to lose power and influence, to fall into disgrace
19.	免（职）	miǎn	to be removed from office
20.	职务	zhíwù	post, duties
21.	驾	jià	to drive (a vehicle)
22.	罢（官）	bà	to be removed from office
23.	相	xiàng	宰相
24.	扶	fú	to support with the hand
25.	携	xié	to take somebody by the hand
26.	起居	qǐjū	daily life
27.	感慨	gǎnkǎi	deep feeling, thoughts

专名 PROPER NAMES

1.	冯谖	Féng Xuān	a personal name
2.	齐	Qí	State of Qi, annexed by Qin in 221 BCE
3.	孟尝君	Mèngcháng jūn	Lord Mengchang (fl. 294 BCE), a prince and prime minister of Qi
4.	薛邑	Xuēyì	Xue City, in present-day Pixian 邳县, Jiangsu 江苏 Province

---

成语 Idioms

1. 君子喻于义，小人喻于利
   【课文】君子喻于义，小人喻于利。
2. 周而不比
   【课文】君子周而不比，小人比而不周。
3. 和而不同
   【课文】君子和而不同，小人同而不和。
4. 君子成人之美
   【课文】君子成人之美，不成人之恶。
5. 君子坦荡荡，小人长戚戚
   【课文】君子坦荡荡，小人长戚戚。

6. 仁者不忧
   【课文】仁者不忧，知者不惑，勇者不惧。
7. 知者不惑
   【课文】同上。
8. 勇者不惧
   【课文】同上。
9. 夫子自道
   【课文】子贡曰：“夫子自道也！”
10. 重义轻利
    【课文】君子重义轻利，小人见利忘义。
11. 见利忘义
    【课文】同上。
12. 结党营私
    【课文】君子与众人融洽相处，小人结党营私。
13. 人云亦云
    【课文】小人盲目附和，人云亦云。
14. 心胸开阔
    【课文】君子心胸开阔，无所畏惧。
15. 患得患失
    【课文】小人患得患失，愁眉苦脸。
16. 愁眉苦脸
    【课文】同上。
17. 不计其数
    【课文】您的府上，金银绸缎，不计其数。
18. 扶老携幼
    【课文】薛邑的百姓扶老携幼，在路旁迎接。

词汇扩展 Vocabulary Expansion

1. 利
   【课文】君子喻于义，小人喻于利。
   【例词】利益、利息、利润、利用、利害、利己、胜利、顺利、利令智昏、损人利己
2. 周
   【课文】君子周而不比，小人比而不周。
   【例词】周围、周到、周密、周全、周详、周转、周年、周而复始、周游世界、众所周知

3. 和
【课文】君子和而不同，小人同而不和。
【例词】和谐、和睦、和谈、和解、和约、和棋、和声、和平共处、和风细雨、和颜悦色

4. 同
【课文】同上。
【例词】同胞、同党、合同、同义词、同心同德、同甘共苦、同舟共济、同床异梦、同病相怜、求同存异

5. 美
【课文】君子成人之美，不成人之恶；小人反是。
【例词】美术、美满、优美、壮美、秀美、健美、甜美、美不胜收、美中不足、美名远扬

6. 恶
【课文】同上。
【例词】恶果、恶习、恶意、恶梦、恶化、恶劣、丑恶、邪恶、万恶之源、恶有恶报

7. 反
【课文】同上。
【例词】反动、反悔、反击、反省、反问句、反义词、反客为主、反守为攻、反败为胜、反复无常

8. 忧
【课文】仁者不忧，知者不惑，勇者不惧。
【例词】忧愁、忧虑、忧伤、忧郁、忧患、担忧、分忧、忧国忧民、忧心如焚、无忧无虑

练习 Exercises

一、选择题 MULTIPLE CHOICE

1. 在中国的古籍中，作者很少给专门名词下 ________。
   a. 定理　　b. 定论
   c. 定律　　d. 定义
2. 本章所收的语录每段说了一个方面， ________ 起来，我们可以对这两个词有比较清楚的理解。
   a. 结合　　b. 综合
   c. 联合　　d. 组合
3. 君子心胸 ________，无所畏惧。
   a. 开朗　　b. 开放
   c. 开阔　　d. 开展

4. 孟尝君叫冯谖到他的封地薛邑去 ________。
   a. 讨饭　b. 讨钱
   c. 讨债　d. 讨价
5. 冯谖叫大家拿出 ________ 来核对。
   a. 债权　b. 债券
   c. 债款　d. 债务
6. 孟尝君一到，薛邑的百姓扶老携幼，争献 ________。
   a. 金银　b. 绸缎
   c. 钱财　d. 酒食

二、改错 CORRECTING MISTAKES

1. 战国时期，秦国有个宰相叫孟尝君。
2. 冯谖到了薛邑，了解到很多百姓都不肯还钱。
3. 冯谖置办了酒席，请放债的人都来赴宴。
4. 对没能力偿还的，冯谖把他们的债券集中起来，定下归还期限。
5. 孟尝君政治上失势后，冯谖离开了他。

三、问答题 ANSWERING QUESTIONS

1. 君子和小人的根本区别在哪里？
2. 孔子认为君子应具有哪三种必需的品格？
3. 冯谖到薛邑去，给孟尝君买回来什么？
4. 为什么薛邑的很多百姓都还不出钱？
5. 孟尝君政治上失势后被免去了什么职务？

四、讨论题 QUESTIONS FOR DISCUSSION

1. 请给君子和小人下个定义，并具体说明两者的区别。
2. 用《冯谖焚券》的故事来说明君子重义轻利的道理。

五、故事复述 RETELLING THE STORY

《冯谖焚券》

六、用本课的成语改写句子 REWRITING SENTENCES USING IDIOMS FROM THE CHAPTER

1. 看着你不开心的样子，我都觉得难受。有什么天大的事，快告诉我吧。
2. 小芳，你怎么每做一件事情都东想西想，怕这怕那的？这样怎么办得了大事啊？
3. 我们现在讨论的问题很重要，你不要人家说什么就跟着说什么，能不能拿出一些你自己的观点来？

4. 每年除夕，纽约时报广场上人山人海，大家都想亲眼看到水晶球掉下来这一激动人心、令人难忘的场面。

七、选词 WORD CHOICE

1. 站在长城上放眼望去，辽阔的原野、起伏的山岗、茂密的树林，风景真是（美名远扬、美不胜收、美中不足）。
2. 今天是我请你吃饭，你怎么倒动手做起菜来，这不是（反守为攻、反复无常、反客为主）了吗？
3. 孙老师跟学生说话时总是（和风细雨、和平共处、和颜悦色）的，怪不得学生都那么喜欢她。
4. 小琴真是个（无忧无虑、忧国忧民、忧心如焚）的姑娘。昨天她的男朋友刚和她分手了，今天还是高高兴兴的。
5. 今年的经济形势很糟糕，很多公司的（利益、利润、利息）都大大低于去年同时期。

八、文译白 TRANSLATION FROM CLASSICAL CHINESE INTO MODERN CHINESE

孟子论舍生取义①

鱼我所欲也，熊掌亦我所欲也。二者不可得兼，舍鱼而取熊掌者也。生我所欲也，义亦我所欲也。二者不可得兼，舍生而取义者也。生亦我所欲，所欲有甚于生者，故不为苟得也。死亦我所恶，所恶有甚于死者，故患有所不辟也。

【注释】①本段选自《孟子·告子上》。

九、英译中 TRANSLATION FROM ENGLISH INTO CHINESE (每句要用一句成语)

1. Professor Wang is a famous scholar; he has published numerous books and articles.
2. He never parrots the words of others, but expresses his own opinions.
3. She is mindful of personal gains and losses, so she knits her brows in anxiety all the time.

十、讲故事 STORYTELLING (根据下面的提示在网上找资料)

【题目】《冯谖客孟尝君》
【关键词】长铗归来乎、食无鱼、出无车、无以为家

8. Three Introspections Daily 三省吾身

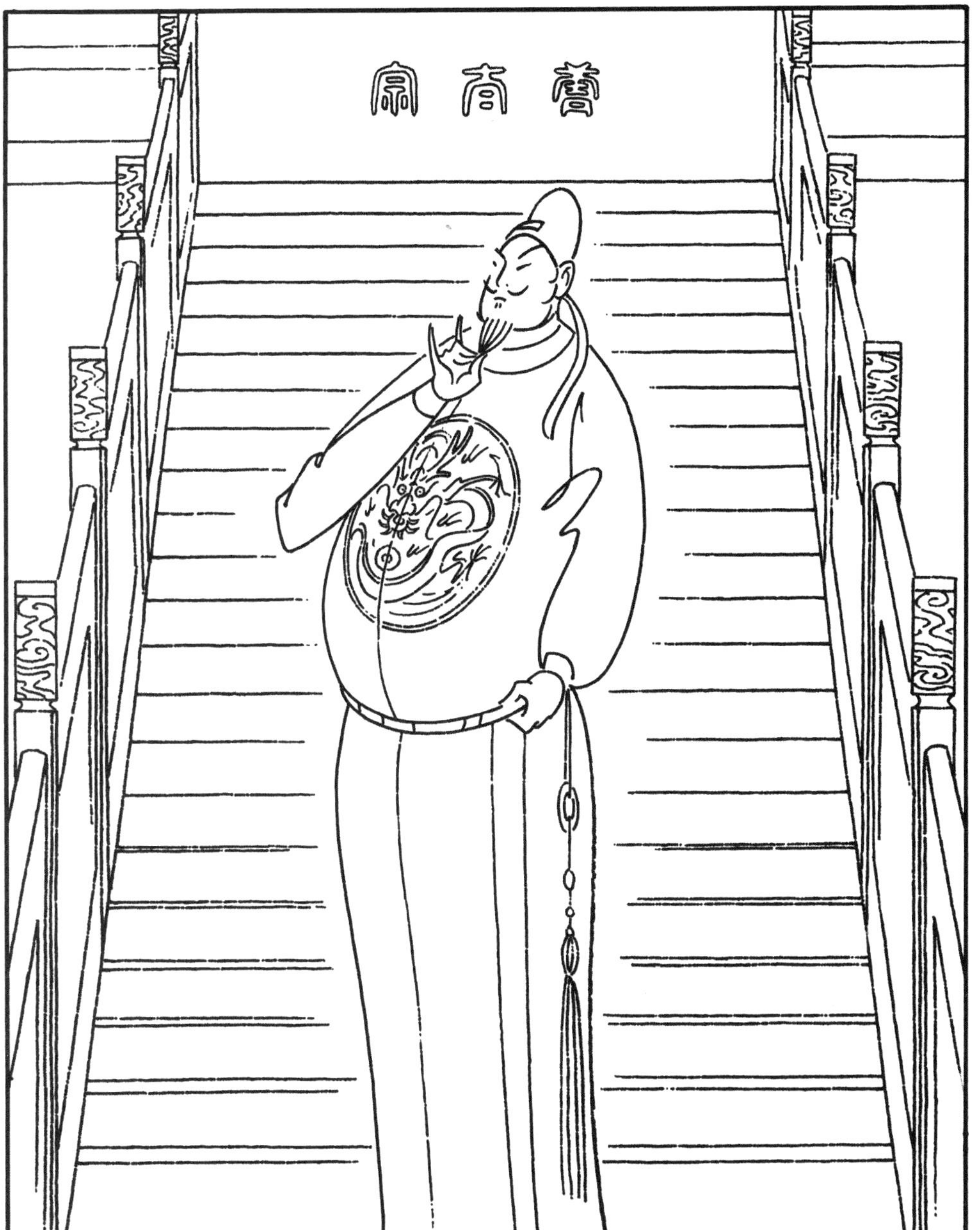

《论语》选段 *Analects* Passages

8-1. 曾子曰："吾日三省吾身：为人谋而不忠乎？与朋友交而不信乎？传不习乎？" (1.4)

曾子说："我每天三次反省自己：为别人办事没有不忠诚吧？同朋友交往没有不诚实吧？老师传授给我的学业没有不复习吧？"

8-2. 子曰："三人行，必有我师焉：择其善者而从之，其不善者而改之。" (7.21)

孔子说："三个人一起走路，其中必定有人可以作我的老师。我选择他好的地方向他学习，看到他不好的地方，就改掉自己的缺点。"

8-3. 子曰："见贤思齐焉，见不贤而内自省也。" (4.17)

孔子说："见到贤人，就向他看齐。见到不好的人，就自我反省。"

8-4. 子曰："过而不改，是谓过矣。" (15.30)

孔子说："有了过错而不改正，这才真叫错了。"

8-5. 子贡曰："君子之过也，如日月之食焉。过也，人皆见之；更也，人皆仰之。" (19.21)

子贡说："君子的过错好比日食月食。他犯过错，人们都看得见；他改正过错，人们都仰望着他。"

8-6. 子夏曰："小人之过也必文。" (19.8)

子夏说："小人犯了过错一定会掩饰。"

词汇一 VOCABULARY I

1. 省 xǐng to examine (oneself), to reflect, to be introspective
2. 日 rì 每天
3. 身 shēn 自身，自己
4. 谋 móu to work for, to plot, to seek, to consult
5. 交 jiāo to associate with, to have friendly contact with
6. 传 chuán to teach, to pass on (knowledge, skills, etc.)
7. 行 xíng 走
8. 从 cóng 跟从, to follow
9. 齐 qí to keep up with, to emulate

10. 食 shí eclipse
11. 更 gēng 改
12. 仰 yǎng to face upward, to look up to, to admire
13. 日食 rìshí solar eclipse
14. 月食 yuèshí lunar eclipse
15. 文 wén to cover up, to paint over
16. 掩饰 yǎnshì to cover up, to gloss over

虚词 FUNCTION WORDS

1. 皆 jiē 都（过也，人皆见之）
2. 必 bì 一定（小人之过也必文）

解读 Exegeses

“人非圣贤，孰能无过？”但关键不在于有没有过失，而在于能否改正过失，今后不再重犯同样的错误。儒家十分重视个人的道德修养，以求塑造成理想人格。而本章所讲的反省，则是自我修养的基本方法。

反省，好像镜子，可以看到自己的本来面目；反省，好像清水，可以洗净内心的污垢。我们每天检讨自己做过的事，都会发现有对与不对的地方。比如今天发了试卷，如果你的成绩不太理想，你就得找找原因：是否上课不够专心，或是平时学习上不求甚解，又或是考试时粗心大意、答非所问？只要找出不足之处，努力改正，成绩一定会有所进步。如果我们把做得正确的保持下去，做得不够的加以改进，我们的学问和道德就会日益提高。

词汇二 VOCABULARY II

1. 非 fēi 不是
2. 关键 guānjiàn key, crux
3. 能否 néngfǒu 能不能
4. 塑造 sùzào to model, to mold, to portray
5. 反省 fǎnxǐng introspection, self-examination
6. 本来面目 běnlái miànmù one’s true colors
7. 本来 běnlái original
8. 面目 miànmù face, appearance
9. 污垢 wūgòu dirt, filth
10. 检讨 jiǎntǎo to examine oneself, to do some soul searching
11. 不求甚解 bùqiú shènjiě not to seek to understand things thoroughly

12.	甚	shèn	很
13.	解	jiě	理解、了解
14.	粗心大意	cūxīn dàyì	careless, negligent
15.	不足	bùzú	deficiency, inadequacy
16.	日益	rìyì	(to advance) each day

事例 An Illustrative Story

CRITICS OF THE EMPEROR 唐太宗闻过则喜

唐太宗李世民是历史上少有的圣君明主，他以广开言路、虚心纳谏而著称。

太宗刚即位时，屡次出游打猎。一个名叫孙伏伽的官员进谏，认为这给后代树立了不好的榜样。太宗高兴地说："你能指出我的过失，我能改正过失，天下就能治理好了！"

太宗痛恨贪官污吏，要对他们严加惩处。一次，他暗中派人给高官们送礼。有一名官员接受了礼物，太宗要下诏处死他。一个名叫裴矩的官员就进谏说："官吏受贿固然应该受罚，然而陛下用计谋欺骗他，又将他绳之以法，这不是用道德引导人的办法。"太宗听后对群臣说："裴矩能在朝堂之上跟我争论，如果人人如此，天下能治不好吗？"

杜正伦、韦挺、虞世南和姚思廉都能不顾个人安危、经常犯颜直谏。有一次太宗特地宴请他们四人，并对他们说："我听说神龙的颔下长有逆鳞，触犯逆鳞者死。人君也有这种情况。你们不怕触犯我的'逆鳞'，补救我的过失，我还会担心危亡吗？想到你们的诚意，所以设宴来同乐。"

唐太宗时最有名的直臣叫魏征。关于他的故事，下面还要讲到。

词汇三 VOCABULARY III

1.	纳谏	nàjiàn	(of an emperor) to accept an admonition
2.	纳	nà	to receive, to accept, to admit
3.	谏	jiàn	admonition
4.	著称	zhùchēng	famous, celebrated
5.	即位	jíwèi	to ascend to the throne
6.	屡次	lǚcì	多次
7.	进谏	jìnjiàn	to present an admonition to the emperor
8.	贪官污吏	tānguān wūlì	corrupt officials
9.	贪污	tānwū	corruption, graft
10.	严	yán	strict, severe
11.	惩处	chéngchǔ	to penalize, to punish

12.	诏	zhào	imperial edict
13.	处死	chǔsǐ	to execute, to put to death
14.	贿	huì	bribe
15.	固然	gùrán	虽然
16.	罚	fá	punishment
17.	陛下	bìxià	Your Majesty
18.	计谋	jìmóu	scheme, stratagem
19.	绳之以法	shéngzhī yǐfǎ	to prosecute someone in accordance with the law
20.	朝堂	cháotáng	imperial court
21.	犯颜	fànyán	to incur the displeasure of an elder or superior by one's words
22.	颔	hàn	chin
23.	逆	nì	contrary, counter
24.	鳞	lín	scale (of a fish, etc.)
25.	触犯	chùfàn	to offend, to violate, to go against

专名 PROPER NAMES

1.	唐太宗	Táng Tàizōng	Emperor Taizong of the Tang (r. 626–649)
2.	孙伏伽	Sūn Fújiā	Tang dynasty courtier
3.	裴矩	Péi Jù	Tang dynasty minister (547–627)
4.	杜正伦	Dù Zhènglún	Tang dynasty courtier (d. 658)
5.	韦挺	Wéi Tǐng	Tang dynasty courtier
6.	虞世南	Yú Shìnán	Tang dynasty courtier and calligrapher (558–638)
7.	姚思廉	Yáo Sīlián	Tang dynasty courtier and historian (557–637)
8.	魏征	Wèi Zhēng	Tang dynasty courtier (580–643)

成语 Idioms

1. 三省吾身
   【课文】吾日三省吾身。
2. 见贤思齐
   【课文】见贤思齐焉，见不贤而内自省也。
3. 过而不改
   【课文】过而不改，是谓过矣。
4. 人非圣贤，孰能无过
   【课文】人非圣贤，孰能无过？

5. 不求甚解
【课文】是否上课不够专心，或是平时学习上不求甚解？
6. 粗心大意
【课文】又或是考试时粗心大意、答非所问？
7. 答非所问
【课文】同上。
8. 闻过则喜
【课文】唐太宗闻过则喜。
9. 广开言路
【课文】唐太宗以广开言路、虚心纳谏而著称。
10. 贪官污吏
【课文】太宗痛恨贪官污吏，要对他们严加惩处。
11. 绳之以法
【课文】陛下用计谋欺骗他，又将他绳之以法。
12. 犯颜直谏
【课文】杜正伦等人都能不顾个人安危、经常犯颜直谏。

词汇扩展 Vocabulary Expansion

1. 交
【课文】与朋友交而不信乎？
【例词】交际、交流、交情、交谈、交通、交易所、交响乐、交头接耳、交浅言深、交游广阔
2. 传
【课文】传不习乎？
【例词】传播、传媒、传说、传授、传奇、传神、传真、传家宝、传教士、传宗接代
3. 善
【课文】择其善者而从之，其不善者而改之。
【例词】善良、善意、善变、完善、改善、和善、善罢甘休、善始善终、善有善报、慈善事业
4. 改
【课文】同上。
【例词】改革、改善、改行、改嫁、改期、改朝换代、改头换面、改恶从善、改邪归正、改过自新
5. 思
【课文】见贤思齐焉。

【例词】思考、思念、思路、思维、思乡、心思、意思、思想库、思潮起伏、思绪万千

6. 齐

【课文】同上。

【例词】齐唱、齐奏、齐全、齐备、齐集、齐名、齐声、齐心合力、齐头并进，并驾齐驱

7. 仰

【课文】更也，人皆仰之。

【例词】仰望、仰慕、仰卧、仰泳、信仰、敬仰、久仰、瞻仰、仰天大笑、仰天长叹

练习 Exercises

一、选择题 MULTIPLE CHOICE

1. ________ 十分重视个人的道德修养。
   a. 道家　　b. 儒家
   c. 法家　　d. 兵家
2. 反省，好像镜子，可以看到自己的本来 ________。
   a. 面孔　　b. 面貌
   c. 面目　　d. 面庞
3. 如果我们把做得正确的 ________ 下去，我们的学问和道德就会日益提高。
   a. 保持　　b. 保证
   c. 保护　　d. 保卫
4. 你能指出我的过失，我能改正过失，天下就能 ________ 好了！
   a. 管理　　b. 整理
   c. 清理　　d. 治理
5. 想到你们的 ________，所以设宴来同乐。
   a. 诚心　　b. 诚意
   c. 诚实　　d. 诚恳

二、改错 CORRECTING MISTAKES

1. 孙伏伽认为唐太宗出游打猎给后代树立了好榜样。
2. 孙伏伽指出了唐太宗的过失，唐太宗很不高兴。
3. 唐太宗派人给高官们送礼是为了表扬他们。
4. 裴矩说唐太宗用计谋欺骗一个官吏，又将他绳之以法，是一个聪明的办法。

三、问答题 ANSWERING QUESTIONS

1. 曾子每天从哪三个方面反省自己?
2. 唐太宗叫什么名字?他以什么而著称?
3. 裴矩为什么要在朝堂上跟唐太宗争论?
4. 唐太宗为什么要宴请杜正伦等四人?
5. 唐太宗时最有名的直臣叫什么名字?

四、讨论题 QUESTIONS FOR DISCUSSION

1. 你觉得"三省吾身"是必要的吗?为什么?
2. 你能做到"闻过则喜"吗?请举例说明。

五、故事复述 RETELLING THE STORY

《唐太宗闻过则喜》

六、用本课的成语改写句子 REWRITING SENTENCES USING IDIOMS FROM THE CHAPTER

1. 我真是糊涂,昨天去买衣服,结果把钱包留在试衣间里了。
2. 小王不太下功夫去理解老师讲课的内容,所以到了做功课的时候就老打电话来问我。
3. 我特别喜欢念伟人的故事,因为我可以向他们学习呀。
4. 那个在台上作报告的人没回答听众的问题,他是没听懂问题还是不愿意回答问题?

七、选词 WORD CHOICE

1. 我们班的小花特别喜欢(交流、交谈、交际),全校的人她几乎都认识。
2. 上个周末我去看了龙舟赛。看他们那么(并驾齐驱、齐心合力、齐头并进)划船的样子,我想我们做其他事情又何尝不是如此呢?
3. 王董事长,(久仰、信仰、敬仰)大名,今天很荣幸能见到您。
4. 小云,你怎么房间整理到一半就去看电视了呢?做事要(善罢甘休、善始善终、善有善报),懂吗?
5. 那个国家的经济糟透了,人民怨声载道,看来是到了(改头换面,改朝换代,改过自新)的时候了。

八、中译英 TRANSLATION FROM CHINESE INTO ENGLISH

回天之力①

一次,唐太宗下令重修乾元殿②。这本来不是一件大事,可是,有一个叫张玄素的却上了一道奏折,批评此举。他说,修了阿房宫③,秦朝倒了;修了章华台,楚国败了;修了乾元殿,隋朝垮了。这都是历史的教训。现在，我们唐朝百废待兴，陛下却要大兴土木。陛下的过失超过了隋炀帝。张玄素竟敢把英明的君主唐太宗比作暴君隋炀帝，满朝文武都为他捏一把汗。但是，唐太宗不仅没有发怒，反而被深深地感动了。他想，张玄素敢于冒死直谏，还不是为了唐朝的江山？因此，唐太宗收回了他的命令，停止重修乾元殿，并且嘉奖了张玄素。魏征听到了这个结局，感叹道："张公论事，有回天之力！"

【注释】①选自《新唐书 · 张玄素传》。②乾元殿：读 Qiányuándiàn。③阿房宫：读 Ēpáng gōng。

九、英译中 TRANSLATION FROM ENGLISH INTO CHINESE

1. Taizong was the second emperor of the Tang dynasty. He ruled for twenty-three years and brought about one of the most prominent eras of peace and prosperity in China's history. People lived and worked in such harmony and contentment that no one would take any articles left by the wayside and doors were not bolted at night.
2. Wei Zheng once told Emperor Taizong of the Tang, "Water can carry a boat, but it can also capsize it [水能载舟，亦能覆舟]. The common people are like water, and the monarch is like the boat. If the monarch treats the common people with kindness and virtue, the common people will love the monarch. If the monarch is tyrannical and is not attentive to the common people's needs, the people will consider him an enemy and betray him."

十、辩论 DEBATING

【题目】《反省的必要性》

【提示】正方—反省能使人发现自己的错误和缺点，从而能扬长避短，不断前进。

反方—反省是朝后看，是消极的态度；我们应该向前看，勇往直前。

9. Strength in Adversity 君子固穷

《论语》选段 *Analects* Passages

9-1. 在陈绝粮。从者病，莫能兴。子路愠见曰："君子亦有穷乎？"子曰："君子固穷；小人穷斯滥矣。"(15.2)

孔子一行在陈国断了粮食。随从的人病得起不来。子路很不高兴地来见孔子，说道："君子也有穷困的时候吗？"孔子说："君子在穷困中仍然坚定，小人穷困了就无所不为了。"

9-2. 子曰："岁寒然后知松柏之后凋也。"(9.28)

孔子说："到了寒冷的季节，才知道松柏是最后凋谢的。"

9-3. 子曰："士志于道，而耻恶衣恶食者，未足与议也。"(4.9)

孔子说："一个士有志于道，但又以穿得不好、吃得不好为耻辱，那就不值得跟他谈论了。"

9-4. 子曰："衣敝缊袍，与衣狐貉者立，而不耻者，其由也与？"(9.27)

孔子说："穿着破旧的棉袍，与穿着狐貉皮袍的人站在一起而不觉得难为情的，大概只有仲由吧。"

9-5. 子欲居九夷。或曰："陋，如之何？"子曰："君子居之，何陋之有！"(9.14)

孔子想到九夷去居住。有人说："那里非常落后，怎么能去呢？"孔子说："有君子住那儿，还落后什么呢？"

词汇一 VOCABULARY I

1.	固	gù	firm
2.	穷	qióng	predicament
3.	莫	mò	不
4.	兴	xīng	起来
5.	滥	làn	reckless, unrestrained
6.	岁	suì	年
7.	松	sōng	pine tree
8.	柏	bǎi	cypress
9.	凋	diāo	to wither
10.	凋谢	diāoxiè	to wither and fall
11.	士	shì	scholar-official

12.	耻	chǐ	to feel ashamed of
13.	恶	è	坏
14.	足	zú	to deserve
15.	议	yì	to discuss
16.	耻辱	chǐrǔ	shame, disgrace, humiliation
17.	值得	zhíde	to merit, to deserve
18.	衣	yī	穿
19.	敝	bì	破旧
20.	缊	yùn	old or reused cotton or silk wadding
21.	袍	páo	robe, gown
22.	狐	hú	fox
23.	貉	hé	raccoon dog

虚词 FUNCTION WORDS

1.	莫	mò	不（从者病，莫能兴）
2.	斯	sī	则，就（小人穷斯滥矣）
3.	未足	wèizú	不值得（士志于道，而耻恶衣恶食者，未足与议也）
4.	也	yě	吧（衣敝缊袍，与衣狐貉者立，而不耻者，其由也与）
5.	或	huò	有人（或曰："陋，如之何？"）
6.	如之何	rúzhīhé	怎么办（同上）

专名 PROPER NAMES

1.	陈	Chén	State of Chen, in present-day Henan Province
2.	九夷	Jiǔyí	a general term for the various minorities in the east

---

解读 Exegeses

本章第一段又说到君子的一个特征，那就是在艰难困苦中仍能坚定不移，保持高尚的情操。孔子这段话是"在陈绝粮"，最困难的时候说的，所以也是"夫子自道"。

孔子又说："岁寒然后知松柏之后凋也。"中国人很喜欢用形象的语言、用比喻来说明一种思想，常常能做到言简意赅，寓意深刻。松柏四季常青，傲霜立雪，姿态挺拔，象征坚强不屈。自从孔子说了这段话以后，中国人都喜欢松树的品格。因为相近的道理，中国人还喜欢梅花和竹子。常有人把松、竹、梅画在一幅画中，叫"岁寒三友"。

词汇二 VOCABULARY II

1.	情操	qíngcāo	sentiment, value
2.	言简意赅	yánjiǎn yìgāi	terse but comprehensive
3.	寓意	yùyì	implied meaning, moral
4.	姿态	zītài	posture, pose
5.	挺拔	tǐngbá	tall and straight
6.	象征	xiàngzhēng	to symbolize, to signify
7.	不屈	bùqū	unbending, unyielding

事例 An Illustrative Story

A DETERMINED HISTORIAN 司马迁发愤著书

司马迁是西汉时期的史学家、文学家。他在汉武帝的朝廷里做史官，当时叫太史令。他立志要编写一部从远古到汉武帝、上下三千年的史书。公元前一百零四年，司马迁开始编写《史记》。

公元前九十九年，一个叫李陵的将军率兵出击匈奴，兵败投降。汉武帝问司马迁对李陵的看法。司马迁说，李陵投降，是因为寡不敌众，又没有救兵，责任不全在他身上。汉武帝听了很不高兴，就把司马迁投进监狱，并处以宫刑。司马迁悲痛欲绝，甚至想到了自杀。可是他又想到，人总有一死，但死的意义是不同的，“或重于泰山，或轻于鸿毛”。他想到了孔子、屈原、左丘明和孙膑等人，想到了他们忍辱负重所取得的成果。他决心效法孔子编撰《春秋》，写出一部同样能永垂不朽的史书。

三年后他被赦出狱，更加发愤写作《史记》。公元前九十一年，基本上完成了这部五十二万多字的不朽名著。《史记》是中国第一部纪传体的史书，对后世史学影响深远。《史记》语言生动，塑造了很多历史人物的形象，也是一部优秀的文学作品。

词汇三 VOCABULARY III

1.	史学家	shǐxuéjiā	historian
2.	太史令	tàishǐlìng	title of the historian in the Han court
3.	远古	yuǎngǔ	remote antiquity
4.	击	jī	to attack
5.	投降	tóuxiáng	to surrender
6.	投	tóu	to throw, to put in
7.	监狱	jiānyù	prison
8.	宫刑	gōngxíng	punishment by castration
9.	鸿	hóng	wild goose

10.	效法	xiàofǎ	to follow the model of, to learn from
11.	编撰	biānzhuàn	to compile and write
12.	永垂不朽	yǒngchuí bùxiǔ	to be immortal (due to fame, accomplishment, etc.)
13.	垂	chuí	to hang down, to hand down
14.	朽	xiǔ	rotten, decayed
15.	赦	shè	to pardon, to give amnesty
16.	纪传体	jìzhuàntǐ	history presented in a series of biographies
17.	纪	jì	biographies of emperors
18.	传	zhuàn	biography
19.	体	tǐ	style, form
20.	部	bù	measure word for books, films, etc.

专名 PROPER NAMES

1.	司马迁	Sīmǎ Qiān	a Han historian (b. ca. 145 BCE)
2.	西汉	Xī Hàn	Western Han dynasty (202 BCE–8 CE)
3.	史记	Shǐjì	*Records of the Grand Historian*
4.	李陵	Lǐ Líng	a Han general (d. 74 BCE)
5.	匈奴	Xiōngnú	the Huns, a race of Asian nomads
6.	泰山	Tàishān	Mount Tai in Shandong 山东 Province
7.	屈原	Qū Yuán	China's earliest great poet (ca. 340–ca. 278 BCE), who wrote his masterpieces in exile
8.	左丘明	Zuǒ Qiūmíng	a historian of the Spring and Autumn period (770–476 BCE) who wrote the history *Zuozhuan* 左传 while blind
9.	孙膑	Sūn Bìn	a military strategist of the Warring States period; he was punished by having his kneecaps removed but ultimately defeated his rival

成语 Idioms

1. 君子固穷

   【课文】君子固穷；小人穷斯滥矣。

2. 松柏后凋

   【课文】岁寒然后知松柏之后凋也。

3. 恶衣恶食

   【课文】士志于道，而耻恶衣恶食者，未足与议也。

4. 艰难困苦
【课文】君子的一个特征是在艰难困苦中仍能坚定不移，保持高尚的情操。
5. 坚定不移
【课文】同上。
6. 言简意赅
【课文】用比喻来说明一种思想，常常能做到言简意赅，寓意深刻。
7. 寓意深刻
【课文】同上。
8. 四季常青
【课文】松柏四季常青，傲霜立雪，姿态挺拔，象征坚强不屈。
9. 傲霜立雪
【课文】同上。
10. 坚强不屈
【课文】同上。
11. 岁寒三友
【课文】常有人把松、竹、梅画在一幅画中，叫“岁寒三友”。
12. 寡不敌众
【课文】李陵投降，是因为寡不敌众。
13. 悲痛欲绝
【课文】司马迁悲痛欲绝，甚至想到了自杀。
14. 重于泰山
【课文】人总有一死，但死的意义是不同的，“或重于泰山，或轻于鸿毛”。
15. 轻于鸿毛
【课文】同上。
16. 忍辱负重
【课文】他想到了他们忍辱负重所取得的成果。
17. 永垂不朽
【课文】他决心效法孔子编撰《春秋》，写出一部同样能永垂不朽的史书。

词汇扩展 Vocabulary Expansion

1. 从
【课文】从者病，莫能兴。
【例词】从前、从此、从简、从速、从古到今、从上到下、从头到尾、从无到有、从小到大、从早到晚
2. 病
【课文】同上。

【例词】病房、病假、病情、病危、病句、急性病、慢性病、职业病、流行病、卧病在床

3. 兴

【课文】同上。

【例词】兴奋、兴办、兴起、兴建、兴旺发达、兴师动众、兴利除弊、兴风作浪、兴修水利、生意兴隆

4. 见

【课文】子路愠见曰："君子亦有穷乎？"

【例词】见贤思齐、见义勇为、见多识广、见机行事、见仁见智、见缝插针、见好就收、见风是雨、见利忘义、见钱眼开

5. 穷

【课文】同上。

【例词】穷苦、穷困、贫穷、无穷、穷于应付、穷山恶水、穷途末路、穷则思变、智穷力竭、穷凶极恶

6. 寒

【课文】岁寒然后知松柏之后凋也。

【例词】寒假、寒风、寒冷、寒热、寒心、严寒、寒暑表、寒来暑往、寒风刺骨、饥寒交迫

7. 后

【课文】同上。

【例词】后代、后方、后果、后悔、后门、后路、后继有人、后来居上、后起之秀、幕后英雄

8. 衣

【课文】士志于道，而耻恶衣恶食者，未足与议也。

【例词】衣柜、衣架、雨衣、毛衣、睡衣、衣食住行、衣冠楚楚、衣着入时、衣锦还乡、丰衣足食

练习 Exercises

一、选择题 MULTIPLE CHOICE

1. 君子在艰难困苦中仍能坚定不移，保持高尚的 ________。
   a. 情绪　　b. 情感
   c. 情操　　d. 情况
2. 中国人很喜欢用 ________ 的语言来说明一种思想。
   a. 形容　　b. 形象
   c. 形式　　d. 形势

3. 自从孔子说了这段话以后，中国人都喜欢松树的 ________。
   a. 品德　　b. 品质
   c. 品行　　d. 品格
4. 司马迁在 ________ 的朝廷里做史官。
   a. 汉文帝　　b. 汉武帝
   c. 汉高祖　　d. 汉景帝
5. 人总有一死，但死的 ________ 是不同的。
   a. 意思　　b. 意义
   c. 意见　　d. 意志
6. 司马迁想到了孔子、屈原、左丘明和孙膑等人 ________ 所取得的成果。
   a. 坚定不移　　b. 坚强不屈
   c. 艰难困苦　　d. 忍辱负重
7. 《史记》是中国第一部纪传体的史书，对后世史学影响 ________。
   a. 深远　　b. 深长
   c. 深厚　　d. 深入

二、改错 CORRECTING MISTAKES

1. 中国人喜欢梅花，主要是因为梅花很好看。
2. 司马迁立志要编写一部从远古到汉武帝、上下五千年的史书。
3. 司马迁决心效法屈原编撰《春秋》，写出一部同样能永垂不朽的史书。
4. 常有人把松树、竹子和菊花画在在一幅画中，叫“岁寒三友”。

三、问答题 ANSWERING QUESTIONS

1. 为什么说孔子关于“君子固穷”的那段话是“夫子自道”？
2. 为什么中国人喜欢松树？
3. “岁寒三友”指的是什么？
4. 李陵率兵去攻打什么人？
5. 司马迁说李陵兵败的原因是什么？
6. 汉武帝为什么把司马迁投进监狱？

四、讨论题 QUESTIONS FOR DISCUSSION

1. 《史记》是一部什么样的书？
2. 为什么松、竹、梅被称为“岁寒三友”？它们各有什么特色？又有什么共同点？

五、故事复述 RETELLING THE STORY

《司马迁发愤著书》

六、用本课的成语改写句子 REWRITING SENTENCES USING IDIOMS FROM THE CHAPTER

1. 《红楼梦》这本小说含意很深，我每读一遍都有新的发现、新的体会。
2. 冬天到了，所有的花都凋谢了，只有梅花不怕严寒，开得那么鲜艳美丽。
3. 李平明知当兵很危险，但没人能动摇他的志向，他要当一名优秀的军人，
4. 我家的后院有很多树，但只有一棵树一年到头不掉叶子，你猜这是什么树？

七、选词 WORD CHOICE

1. "老公，我们昨天买的"谷歌"股票今天涨了二十多块呢！""老婆，我看你还是（见机行事、见钱眼开、见好就收），快把它卖掉吧。"
2. 期末到了，我要准备大考、完成论文，还要开钢琴独奏会……真是 （穷于应付、穷途末路、智穷力竭），只好不睡觉了！
3. 就搬一张床，我一个人帮你就行了，何必（兴风作浪、兴旺发达、兴师动众），叫那么多人来帮忙呢？
4. 彭先生喜欢跑步，多少年了，（寒风刺骨、饥寒交迫、寒来暑往）他每天晨跑，从不间断。
5. 李强初中的时候糊里糊涂，学习成绩不怎么样。可是进入高中后，他（后来居上、后起之秀、后继有人），一下子成了全班第一。

八、文译白 TRANSLATION FROM CLASSICAL CHINESE INTO MODERN CHINESE

刘禹锡①《陋室铭》②

山不在高，有仙则名。水不在深，有龙则灵。斯是陋室，惟吾德馨。苔痕上阶绿，草色入帘青。谈笑有鸿儒，往来无白丁③。可以调素琴，阅金经④。无丝竹之乱耳，无案牍之劳形。南阳诸葛⑤庐，西蜀子云⑥亭。孔子云："何陋之有？"

【注释】①刘禹锡(772–842)，唐代诗人。②铭：一种押韵的文体。③白丁：没有官职的人，这里指没有学问的人。④金经：指佛经。⑤诸葛：诸葛亮(181–234)，三国时蜀国丞相。⑥子云：杨雄(53–18 BCE)，西汉文学家。

九、英译中 TRANSLATION FROM ENGLISH INTO CHINESE

1. In 99 BCE, a general named Li Ling led his troops to attack the Huns but he was defeated and he surrendered.
2. Everyone will die but the weights of deaths vary. One person's death might be heavier than Mount Tai, whereas someone else's death might be lighter than a feather.

3. Sima Qian's *Shiji* is respected as a model of biographical literature with high literary value, and it still serves as a textbook for the study of classical Chinese worldwide.
4. The great use of characterization and plot in the *Shiji* also influenced fictional writing, including the classical short stories of the Tang dynasty as well as the vernacular novels of the late imperial period.

十、讲故事 STORYTELLING (根据下面的提示在网上找资料)

【题目】《史记》人物故事

【提示】司马迁在《史记》中写了很多生动的历史人物，如项羽、荆轲、蔺相如、韩信、李广等。请你讲一个人物故事。

10. The Long Journey 任重道远

《论语》选段 *Analects* Passages

10-1. 曾子曰："士，不可以不弘毅，任重而道远。仁以为己任，不亦重乎？死而后已，不亦远乎？"(8.7)

曾子说："士不可以不弘大而刚毅，因为他责任重大而道路遥远。把实现仁作为自己的责任，难道还不重大吗？死而后已，难道路程还不遥远吗？"

10-2. 子曰："志士仁人，无求生以害仁，有杀身以成仁。"(15.9)

孔子说："志士仁人，没有贪生怕死而损害仁的，只有勇于牺牲来成全仁的。"

10-3. 子曰："三军可夺帅也，匹夫不可夺志也。"(9.26)

孔子说："一国军队的主帅可以被夺去，但一个男子汉的志向是夺不走的。"

10-4. 曾子曰："可以托六尺之孤，可以寄百里之命，临大节而不可夺也。君子人与？君子人也。"(8.6)

曾子说："可以把年幼的君主托付给他，可以把国家的政权委托给他，面临重要关头而不动摇屈服。这样的人是君子吗？是君子啊！"

词汇一 VOCABULARY I

1.	任	rèn	mission, task
2.	弘	hóng	great, magnificent
3.	毅	yì	firm, resolute
4.	已	yǐ	to stop, to cease, to end
5.	刚毅	gāngyì	resolute and steadfast
6.	求	qiú	to seek, to strive for
7.	害	hài	to do harm to, to impair
8.	贪	tān	greedy
9.	损害	sǔnhài	to harm, to damage
10.	牺牲	xīshēng	to sacrifice one's life, to die a martyr's death
11.	三军	sānjūn	the army (of a large state)
12.	夺	duó	to take by force
13.	帅	shuài	commander-in-chief

14.	匹夫	pǐfū	ordinary man
15.	托	tuō	to entrust
16.	尺	chǐ	unit of length measuring one-third of a meter today, but a shorter length in ancient times
17.	孤	gū	orphan
18.	寄	jì	to consign
19.	里	lǐ	unit of length equal to half of a kilometer
20.	命	mìng	fate, destiny
21.	临	lín	to face, to encounter
22.	大节	dàjié	political integrity
23.	托付	tuōfù	to entrust, to commit something to somebody's care
24.	动摇	dòngyáo	to vacillate, to waver
25.	屈服	qūfú	to surrender, to yield

虚词 FUNCTION WORDS

1.	可以	kěyǐ	应当（士，不可以不弘毅）
2.	而后	érhòu	然后（死而后已，不亦远乎）
3.	有	yǒu	to initiate a sentence（有杀身以成仁）
4.	可	kě	能（三军可夺帅也）

解读 Exegeses

死亡是一般人不太愿意谈论的话题，可是在这一章的语录中，“任重道远”和“杀身成仁”这两句常用的成语都谈到了死亡，并且都讨论了死亡和“仁”的关系。

“任重道远”我们在日常生活中用得很多，可读了原文才知道孔子讲的是一个人一生中的大事。为什么任重？是因为肩负着“仁”。为什么道远？是因为要“死而后已”。“仁”是儒家终身追求的目标。

“杀身成仁”说明了儒家的生死观是以“仁”为最高原则的。生命对每个人来讲都是十分宝贵的，但还有比生命更重要的，那就是“仁”。孔子所培养的就是这样有道德、有知识、有才干的人，他可以受命辅佐幼君，可以执掌国家政权，在生死关头会视死如归、舍生取义。这就是具有君子品格的人。自古以来，孔子的这些话激励着多少志士仁人为国家和民族英勇献身，留下了很多感人的故事。

词汇二 VOCABULARY II

1.	话题	huàtí	topic (of a conversation or talk)
2.	肩负	jiānfù	to undertake, to shoulder
3.	终身	zhōngshēn	lifelong
4.	观	guān	outlook, view
5.	培养	péiyǎng	to foster, to train
6.	才干	cáigàn	ability, competence
7.	辅佐	fǔzuǒ	to assist a ruler in governing a country
8.	执掌	zhízhǎng	to wield, to be in control of
9.	关头	guāntóu	juncture, moment
10.	激励	jīlì	to encourage, to inspire

事例 An Illustrative Story

DEATH OF A PREMIER 文天祥杀身成仁

文天祥生在南宋末年。他年轻时刻苦读书，二十岁就考取了状元。

在元军从北方对南宋大举进攻时，文天祥在危急关头被任命为丞相，组织军队进行抵抗。他在一二七八年兵败被俘，被押送到元朝的首都大都。元朝政府不断派各种人来劝降，都被文天祥严词拒绝了。在狱中，他写下了名篇《正气歌》。

一二八二年十二月八日，元朝的皇帝元世祖忽必烈亲自召见文天祥，劝他投降，并要封他做丞相。文天祥回答道："我是大宋的宰相。国家灭亡了，我只求速死！"忽必烈毫无办法，下令处死文天祥。

次日，文天祥被押解到刑场。文天祥向南方跪拜后，端坐在椅子上，从容就义，年仅四十七岁。死后在他的衣带上发现一首诗："孔曰成仁，孟曰取义，唯其义尽，所以仁至。读圣贤书，所学何事？而今而后，庶几无愧。"

文天祥是中国的民族英雄。他的诗篇《过零丁洋》中的最后一联"人生自古谁无死，留取丹心照汗青"成为千古传诵的名句。

词汇三 VOCABULARY III

1.	末年	mònián	last years of a dynasty or reign
2.	状元	zhuàngyuán	title conferred on the top scorer in the highest-level imperial examination
3.	大举进攻	dàjǔ jìngōng	to mount a large-scale offensive
4.	丞相	chéngxiàng	prime minister
5.	俘	fú	to capture, to take prisoner

6.	押送	yāsòng	to send under escort, to escort
7.	严词	yáncí	in strong terms, in stern words
8.	拒绝	jùjué	to refuse, to reject
9.	正气	zhèngqì	righteousness, the spiritual strength of the right and just
10.	召见	zhàojiàn	to call in (a subordinate), to summon (an envoy)
11.	速	sù	快
12.	次日	cìrì	第二天
13.	刑场	xíngchǎng	execution ground
14.	跪	guì	to kneel
15.	端	duān	upright, proper
16.	从容	cōngróng	calm, unhurried
17.	就义	jiùyì	to be executed for championing a just cause, to die a martyr's death
18.	仅	jǐn	only, 差不多
19.	唯	wéi	因为
20.	庶几	shùjǐ	almost, nearly
21.	愧	kuì	to be ashamed, conscience-stricken
22.	联	lián	a poetic couplet
23.	丹	dān	红色
24.	汗青	hànqīng	(history) book

专名 PROPER NAMES

1.	文天祥	Wén Tiānxiáng	Southern Song prime minister (1236–1283)
2.	大都	Dàdū	元朝的首都，现在的北京
3.	元世祖	Yuán Shìzǔ	Emperor Shizu of the Yuan (r. 1260–1294), founder of the Yuan dynasty
4.	忽必烈	Hūbìliè	Kublai Khan, Emperor Shizu of the Yuan
5.	零丁洋	Língdīngyáng	an area of the sea just outside the mouth of the Pearl River 珠江

成语 Idioms

1. 任重道远
   【课文】士，不可以不弘毅，任重而道远。
2. 死而后已
   【课文】死而后已，不亦远乎。

3. 志士仁人
【课文】志士仁人，无求生以害仁，有杀身以成仁。
4. 求生害仁
【课文】同上。
5. 杀身成仁
【课文】同上。
6. 贪生怕死
【课文】志士仁人，没有贪生怕死而损害仁的。
7. 托孤寄命
【课文】可以托六尺之孤，可以寄百里之命。
8. 大节不夺
【课文】临大节而不可夺也。
9. 生死关头
【课文】在生死关头会视死如归、舍生取义。
10. 视死如归
【课文】同上。
11. 舍生取义
【课文】同上。
12. 大举进攻
【课文】元军从北方对南宋大举进攻。
13. 严词拒绝
【课文】元朝政府不断派各种人来劝降，都被文天祥严词拒绝了。
14. 从容就义
【课文】文天祥向南方跪拜后，端坐在椅子上，从容就义。

词汇扩展 Vocabulary Expansion

1. 任
【课文】任重而道远。
【例词】担任、兼任、连任、离任、聘任、任重道远、任人唯亲、任人唯贤、任劳任怨、胜任愉快
2. 重
【课文】同上。
【例词】重点、重音、重视、重用、保重、贵重、尊重、重男轻女、重金聘请、重兵压境
3. 求
【课文】志士仁人，无求生以害仁，有杀身以成仁。

【例词】求爱、求婚、求和、求降、求之不得、求贤若渴、求胜心切、求同存异、求全责备、求神拜佛

4. 害

【课文】同上。

【例词】害怕、害病、害虫、谋害、迫害、损害、危害、害群之马、利害关系、为民除害

5. 托

【课文】可以托六尺之孤，可以寄百里之命，临大节而不可夺也。

【例词】托付、托福、托盘、托运、托病、拜托、寄托、委托、托儿所、所托非人

6. 寄

【课文】同上。

【例词】寄放、寄存、寄宿、寄养、寄费、邮寄、寄予希望、寄托哀思、寄居他乡、寄人篱下

7. 临

【课文】同上。

【例词】临时、临行、临别赠言、临门一脚、临渴掘井、临危不惧、临阵脱逃、大难临头、欢迎光临、双喜临门

练习 Exercises

一、选择题 MULTIPLE CHOICE

1. “仁”是儒家终身追求的 ________。

   a. 目标　　b. 目的

   c. 目录　　d. 目光

2. 儒家的生死观是以“仁”为最高 ________ 的。

   a. 原因　　b. 原则

   c. 原理　　d. 原由

3. 元朝的首都叫大都，在现在的 ________。

   a. 西安　　b. 洛阳

   c. 北京　　d. 南京

4. 次日，文天祥被押解到 ________。

   a. 战场　　b. 刑场

   c. 操场　　d. 广场

二、改错 CORRECTING MISTAKES

1. 死亡是一般人经常谈论的题目。
2. 孔子关于“任重道远”和“杀身成仁”的两段话都讨论了死亡和“仁”的联系。
3. 生命对每个人来讲都是十分宝贝的。
4. 文天祥生在北宋末年。
5. 文天祥年轻时刻苦读书，二十岁就考取了博士。
6. 元朝政府不断派各种人来求降，都被文天祥严词拒绝了。
7. 元世祖忽必烈亲自会见文天祥，劝他投降。

三、问答题 ANSWERING QUESTIONS

1. 孔子提出“任重道远”；为什么任重？为什么道远？
2. 儒家的生死观是以什么为最高原则的？
3. 孔子说的君子应是什么样的人？
4. 文天祥在危急关头被任命为什么？
5. 元世祖忽必烈为什么要召见文天祥？
6. 文天祥临刑前为什么要向南方跪拜？
7. 文天祥死后在哪里发现了一首诗？
8. 文天祥的诗篇《过零丁洋》中的最后一联是怎么写的？

四、讨论题 QUESTIONS FOR DISCUSSION

1. “仁”是儒家学说的一个重要概念，请说明一下。
2. 文天祥死后在他的衣带上发现的一首诗中说道：“孔曰成仁”。结合本章中孔子关于仁的论述，讨论文天祥对仁的实践。

五、故事复述 RETELLING THE STORY

《文天祥杀身成仁》

六、用本课的成语改写句子 REWRITING SENTENCES USING IDIOMS FROM THE CHAPTER

1. 我家隔壁的吴先生真是个胆小鬼。一天小偷进了他的家，他竟然扔下妻子孩子不管，自己一个人逃了出来。
2. 四川地震的时候，很多人在极其危险的时刻，不顾自己的安危而抢救别人。
3. 章局长为官正派，一次他的一个下级官员给他送礼，他不但没收，还把送礼的人教育了一番。
4. 屈原坚持正义、投江自杀的故事感动世人，所以人们每到端午节就吃粽子来纪念他。

七、选词 WORD CHOICE

1. 老田，我要去中国工作几个月，我家的房子和花园就（拜托、委托、寄托）你照顾一下了。
2. 李明因父母离婚，从小寄养在叔叔家，所以他常有(寄托哀思、寄居他乡、寄人篱下）的感觉。
3. 老马在公司里做什么事都（任人唯亲、任劳任怨、胜任愉快），人缘关系非常好。
4. 你平时不念书，明天要考试了才开夜车，这不是（临门一脚、临渴掘井、临阵脱逃）吗！
5. 小云昨天网球比赛输了，全是因为她（求全责备、求神拜佛、求胜心切），打得太猛，球出界太多了。

八、中译英 TRANSLATION FROM CHINESE INTO ENGLISH

1. 汉武帝在病危时，把年仅八岁的太子托付给大臣霍光。太子即位后就是汉昭帝。可是汉昭帝在二十一岁时就去世了。霍光又拥立了年轻的汉宣帝。霍光忠心耿耿地辅佐两个小皇帝，没有辜负汉武帝托孤的重任。
2. 三国时期蜀汉的君主刘备去世前把国家的政事托付给大臣诸葛亮。诸葛亮竭尽全力辅佐刘备的儿子，一直到自己病逝，真是“可以寄百里之命”的忠臣。
3. 明朝末年，清朝的军队打到了长江边上。史可法带兵坚守扬州。扬州城被清军打破后，史可法坚决不投降，壮烈牺牲。他是个大节不夺的民族英雄。

九、英译中 TRANSLATION FROM ENGLISH INTO CHINESE

1. Wen Tianxiang is one of the most famous symbols of loyalty and patriotism in China. His patriotic poems are still widely taught in schools today.
2. Kublai Khan wanted to employ Wen Tianxiang as his chief minister but Wen refused to accept the Mongol emperor's offer.
3. One day Kublai Khan visited Wen Tianxiang in person and asked what would satisfy him. Wen replied that he wished for a swift death. Accordingly, Kublai Khan ordered his execution to take place the following day.
4. During his house arrest in the west of Beijing, Wen Tianxiang wrote his famous "Song of Righteousness" (正气歌). The house still stands in its original place and has been turned into a temple bearing his name.

十、讲故事 STORYTELLING (根据下面的提示在网上找资料)

【题目】《正气歌》人物故事

【提示】文天祥在他的《正气歌》中列举了很多有浩然正气的历史人物：

在齐太史简，在晋董狐笔。

在秦张良椎，在汉苏武节。

为严将军头，为嵇侍中血。
为张睢阳齿，为颜常山舌。
或为辽东帽，清操厉冰雪。
或为出师表，鬼神泣壮烈。
或为渡江楫，慷慨吞胡羯。
或为击贼笏，逆竖头破裂。

这些人物依次是：齐太史兄弟、董狐、张良、苏武、严颜、嵇绍、张巡、颜杲卿、管宁、诸葛亮、祖逖、段秀实。请选其中一人讲故事。

PART III

Wisdom 处世篇

11. Self-Reliance 君子求己

《论语》选段 *Analects* Passages

11-1. 子曰："君子求诸己，小人求诸人。" (15.20)

孔子说："君子求之于自己，小人求之于别人。"

11-2. 子曰："不患人之不己知，患不知人也。" (1.16)

孔子说："不怕别人不了解自己，只怕自己不了解别人。"

11-3. 子曰："君子病无能焉，不病人之不己知也。" (15.18)

孔子说："君子只怕自己没有才能，不怕别人不了解自己。"

11-4. 子曰："躬自厚，而薄责于人，则远怨矣。" (15.14)

孔子说："多责备自己而少责备别人，那就可以避免别人的怨恨了。"

11-5. 司马牛忧曰："人皆有兄弟，我独亡！"子夏曰："商闻之矣：'死生有命，富贵在天'。君子敬而无失，与人恭而有礼；四海之内皆兄弟也。君子何患乎无兄弟也？" (12.5)

司马牛忧愁地说："别人都有兄弟，就我没有！"子夏说："我听说过：'死生有命，富贵在天。'君子只要敬业而不出差错，对人恭敬而合乎礼节，天下人就都是自己的兄弟了。君子为什么要担心没有兄弟呢？"

词汇一 VOCABULARY I

1.	处世	chǔshì	to conduct one's life, philosophy of life
2.	病	bìng	to worry
3.	躬	gōng	身体、亲自
4.	厚	hòu	深、重、thick, deep
5.	薄	bó	light, slight
6.	责	zé	to reproach, to blame
7.	怨	yuàn	resentment, enmity
8.	责备	zébèi	to reproach, to blame
9.	避免	bìmiǎn	to avoid, to refrain from
10.	忧	yōu	worry, sorrow
11.	独	dú	lonely, alone

12. 敬 jìng respectful
13. 失 shī 过失
14. 恭 gōng respectful
15. 敬业 jìngyè respectful of work, conscientious at work
16. 差错 chācuò mistake, error
17. 礼节 lǐjié courtesy, etiquette, protocol
18. 担心 dānxīn to worry

虚词 FUNCTION WORDS

1. 诸 zhū 之于（君子求诸己，小人求诸人）
2. 何 hé 何必（君子何患乎无兄弟也）
3. 乎 hū (to pause)（同上）

专名 PROPER NAMES

1. 司马牛 Sīmǎ Niú 孔子的学生

解读 Exegeses

本章讲了一个处世的根本原则：求人不如求己。人生在世，不可能不求人。但是如果你处处先求己，事事严于求己，那么求人的事就可以减到最低限度。

如果你想在一门课拿到好成绩，到期末的时候去跟老师谈，解释各种原因，希望老师"高抬贵手"，就是求人了。如果你从学期初就努力学习，每个作业都认真完成，每个考试都取得高分，每堂课都积极参加讨论，期终的成绩就不用担心了。

大学毕业找工作时，如果你求人帮忙，"开后门"，常常费时费力，也不一定有好的结果。如果你以优秀成绩毕业，课外又积累了很多工作经验，各家公司都争着要你，哪里还用得着求人呢？

如果你能处处求己，再加上"敬而无失"、"恭而有礼"，那么，不但事业上会很成功，你也会有很多朋友，"四海之内皆兄弟也"。

词汇二 VOCABULARY II

1. 限度 xiàndù limit
2. 开后门 kāi hòumén to handle business underhandedly, to "let in through the back door"
3. 积累 jīlěi to accumulate

事例 An Illustrative Story

THE TASTE OF GALL 勾践卧薪尝胆

春秋时期，吴国和越国是邻国。公元前496年，吴王阖闾发兵攻打越国，没想到被越王勾践打得大败，中箭受了重伤，回到吴国就死了。

吴王阖闾死后，儿子夫差即位。他念念不忘报仇，每次经过宫门，手下的人就会喊："夫差！你忘了越王杀你父亲的仇吗？"夫差流着眼泪说："不，不敢忘。"过了两年，吴王夫差率领大军打败了越国。越王勾践带了五千个残兵败将逃到会稽，最后只能求和投降。

勾践到了吴国，夫差叫勾践给他喂马、牵马。过了三年，夫差认为勾践真心归顺了他，就放勾践回国。

勾践回到越国后，立志报仇雪耻。他在房间里挂上一个苦胆，每逢吃饭的时候，先尝一尝苦味，门外的士兵就问："你忘了会稽的耻辱吗？"晚上他就睡在柴草上，唯恐眼前的安逸消磨了志气。他亲自到田里与农夫一起干活，妻子也纺线织布。经过十年的艰苦奋斗，越国终于兵精粮足，转弱为强。

公元前473年，勾践带兵出征，灭了吴国。夫差求和不成，羞愧地拔剑自杀了。

词汇三 VOCABULARY III

1.	薪	xīn	firewood
2.	胆	dǎn	gallbladder, gall
3.	发兵	fābīng	to dispatch troops
4.	箭	jiàn	arrow
5.	重伤	zhòngshāng	severe injury
6.	念念不忘	niànniàn bùwàng	to bear in mind constantly
7.	报仇	bàochóu	to avenge
8.	仇	chóu	hatred, enmity
9.	手下	shǒuxià	subordinates
10.	残兵败将	cánbīng bàijiàng	remnants of a routed army
11.	残	cán	deficient, remaining
12.	求和	qiúhé	to sue for peace
13.	归顺	guīshùn	to submit, surrender
14.	雪耻	xuěchǐ	to avenge an insult, to wipe out a disgrace
15.	逢	féng	to meet, to come across, to happen upon
16.	柴草	cháicǎo	firewood

17. 唯恐 wéikǒng to worry
18. 安逸 ānyì easy and comfortable
19. 消磨 xiāomó to wear down, to sap
20. 纺线 fǎngxiàn to spin cotton into yarn
21. 织布 zhībù to weave cotton cloth
22. 羞愧 xiūkuì ashamed, abashed

专名 PROPER NAMES

1. 勾践 Gōujiàn king of Yue (r. 497–465 BCE)
2. 春秋 Chūnqiū the Spring and Autumn period (770–476 BCE)
3. 吴 Wú State of Wu
4. 越 Yuè State of Yue
5. 阖闾 Hélǘ king of Wu (r. 514–496 BCE)
6. 夫差 Fūchāi king of Wu (r. 495–473)
7. 会稽 Kuàijī a prefecture, in what is now Shaoxing 绍兴, Zhejiang 浙江 Province

---

成语 Idioms

1. 君子求己
   【课文】君子求诸己，小人求诸人。
2. 薄责于人
   【课文】躬自厚，而薄责于人，则远怨矣。
3. 死生有命
   【课文】商闻之矣："死生有命，富贵在天"。
4. 富贵在天
   【课文】同上。
5. 敬而无失
   【课文】君子敬而无失，与人恭而有礼；四海之内皆兄弟也。
6. 恭而有礼
   【课文】同上。
7. 四海之内皆兄弟也
   【课文】同上。
8. 高抬贵手
   【课文】如果你想在一门课拿到好成绩，希望老师"高抬贵手"，就是求人了。
9. 卧薪尝胆
   【课文】勾践卧薪尝胆

10. 念念不忘
【课文】他念念不忘报仇，每次经过宫门，手下的人就会喊："夫差！你忘了越王杀你父亲的仇吗？"
11. 残兵败将
【课文】越王勾践带了五千个残兵败将逃到会稽。
12. 报仇雪耻
【课文】勾践回到越国后，立志报仇雪耻。
13. 兵精粮足
【课文】经过十年的艰苦奋斗，越国终于兵精粮足，转弱为强。
14. 转弱为强
【课文】同上。

词汇扩展 Vocabulary Expansion

1. 厚
【课文】躬自厚，而薄责于人，则远怨矣。
【例词】厚意、厚礼、厚利、浓厚、深厚、雄厚、厚此薄彼、厚古薄今、厚颜无耻、高官厚禄
2. 薄
【课文】同上。
【例词】薄弱、薄情、薄命、薄暮、单薄、淡薄、轻薄、刻薄、浅薄、薄利多销
3. 责
【课文】同上。
【例词】责任、责备、责令、责问、责打、责罚、责怪、责骂、负责、职责
4. 怨
【课文】同上。
【例词】怨恨、怨言、抱怨、埋怨、怨气冲天、怨声载道、怨天怨地、怨天尤人、恩恩怨怨、任劳任怨
5. 独
【课文】人皆有兄弟，我独亡！
【例词】独立自主、独立思考、独立王国、独善其身、独挡一面、独来独往、独一无二、独家经营、独家新闻、独木难支
6. 死
【课文】死生有命，富贵在天。
【例词】死而后已、死而无怨、死里逃生、死路一条、死生有命、死不改悔、死无对证、死记硬背、死灰复燃、生死存亡

7. 敬
【课文】君子敬而无失，与人恭而有礼。
【例词】敬爱、敬祝、敬酒、敬礼、敬意、敬重、崇敬、恭敬、孝敬、敬而远之

8. 恭
【课文】同上。
【例词】恭顺、恭维、恭谨、谦恭、恭贺新禧、恭喜发财、恭候光临、洗耳恭听、恭敬不如从命

练习 Exercises

一、选择题 MULTIPLE CHOICE

1. 本章讲了一个处世的根本 ________：求人不如求己。
   a. 原因　b. 原理
   c. 原则　d. 原由
2. 如果你处处先求己，事事严于求己，那么求人的事就可以减到最低 ________。
   a. 限制　b. 限度
   c. 限量　d. 限期
3. 如果你从学期初就努力学习，期终的成绩就不用 ________ 了。
   a. 放心　b. 称心
   c. 省心　d. 担心
4. 勾践吃饭的时候，门外的士兵就问：“你忘了会稽的 ________ 吗？”
   a. 失败　b. 投降
   c. 归顺　d. 耻辱
5. 晚上勾践就睡在柴草上，唯恐眼前的安逸消磨了 ________。
   a. 志气　b. 志向
   c. 志愿　d. 志趣
6. 夫差求和不成，________ 地拔剑自杀了。
   a. 羞辱　b. 羞愧
   c. 害羞　d. 怕羞

二、改错 CORRECTING MISTAKES

1. 孔子说：“不怕自己不了解别人，只怕别人不了解自己。”
2. 孔子说：“多责备别人而少责备自己，那就可以避免别人的怨恨了。”
3. 大学毕业找工作时，如果你求人帮忙，“开后门”，就会有好的结果。
4. 吴王阖闾发兵攻打越国，把越王勾践打得大败。
5. 越王勾践带了五千个残兵败将逃到绍兴。

6. 勾践到了吴国，夫差叫勾践给他放牛。
7. 经过三年的艰苦奋斗，越国终于兵精粮足，转弱为强。

三、问答题 ANSWERING QUESTIONS

1. 本章讲了一个什么样的处世的根本原则？
2. 吴王阖闾是怎么死的？
3. 吴王夫差是怎么死的？
4. 夫差为什么会放勾践回国？
5. 勾践为什么要卧薪尝胆？
6. 勾践是怎么艰苦奋斗的？

四、讨论题 QUESTIONS FOR DISCUSSION

1. 大学生想拿到好成绩，应该怎样求己不求人？
2. 大学毕业要找到好工作，应该怎样求己不求人？

五、故事复述 RETELLING THE STORY

《勾践卧薪尝胆》

六、用本课的成语改写句子 REWRITING SENTENCES USING IDIOMS FROM THE CHAPTER

1. 我跟哥哥下象棋，被他杀得只剩几个棋子了，我爸爸在一旁说："你这么几个小兵和一个将，看来只能投降了。"
2. 你看，那个拳击手刚刚还被打倒在地下，现在反而连连出击，好像比他的对手更厉害了。
3. 小江今天因为上学晚了，把车开得飞快，被警察抓住，他只好一个劲儿地解释，要求警察放了他这一次。
4. 白立胜的女朋友离开他已经一年多了，可是他还老想着她呢。

七、选词 WORD CHOICE

1. 今天天气这么冷，你穿得这么（淡薄、轻薄、单薄），会生病的！
2. 林秘书工作中出了差错，她的老板不但不（责令、责怪、责骂）她，反而给了她很多安慰。
3. 小孟对他的父母非常（崇敬、恭敬、孝敬），每次回家总是给父母买来很多好吃的东西，还问长问短，关心备至。
4. 胡老板，（恭贺新禧，恭喜发财，恭候光临）啊，你的新饭店真是又漂亮，又气派！
5. 小花大学毕业了，并找到了一份很好的工作，终于能在经济上（独立自主、独立思考、独来独往）了。

八、文译白 TRANSLATION FROM CLASSICAL CHINESE INTO MODERN CHINESE

汪洙①《神童诗》

天子重英豪，文章教尔曹；
万般皆下品，惟有读书高。

少小须勤学，文章可立身；
满朝朱紫贵，尽是读书人。

学问勤中得，萤窗万卷书；
三冬今足用，谁笑腹空虚。

自小多才学，平生志气高；
别人怀宝剑，我有笔如刀。

朝为田舍郎，暮登天子堂；
将相本无种，男儿当自强。

【注释】①汪洙：北宋学者，著有《神童诗》一组，今选五首。

九、英译中 TRANSLATION FROM ENGLISH INTO CHINESE

BEAUTIFUL XI SHI

Xi Shi 西施 was one of the renowned Four Beauties of ancient China. She was said to have lived at the end of the Spring and Autumn period in the State of Yue.

King Goujian of Yue was once imprisoned after being defeated in a war against King Fuchai of Wu. The State of Yue later became a tributary state to Wu. Secretly planning his revenge, Goujian trained beautiful women and offered them to Fuchai as tribute. His minister, Fan Li 范蠡, found Xi Shi and presented her to Fuchai in 490 BCE.

Bewitched by the beauty of Xi Shi, Fuchai forgot all about his state affairs, and, at her instigation, killed his best advisor, the great general Wu Zixu 伍子胥. The strength of Wu dwindled, and in 473 BCE Goujian launched a strike and routed the Wu army. King Fuchai lamented that he should have listened to Wu Zixu and then committed suicide.

After the fall of Wu, Fan Li retired from his ministerial post and lived with Xi Shi on a fishing boat; they roamed like fairies in the misty wilderness of Lake Tai 太湖, and no one has seen them since.

十、作文 COMPOSITION

【题目】《卧薪尝胆的启示》

【提示】越王勾践先打败了吴王阖闾，后来被阖闾的儿子吴王夫差打败了。最后，勾践又打败了夫差。从这段历史中，你得到了什么启示？

12. Three Beneficial Friends 益者三友

《论语》选段 *Analects* Passages

12-1. 孔子曰："益者三友，损者三友。友直，友谅，友多闻，益矣。友便辟，友善柔，友便佞，损矣。"(16.4)

孔子说："有益的交友有三种，有害的交友有三种。同正直的人交友，同诚信的人交友，同见闻广博的人交友，是有益的。同歪门邪道的人交朋友，同阿谀奉承的人交朋友，同花言巧语的人交朋友，是有害的。"

12-2. 孔子曰："益者三乐，损者三乐。乐节礼乐，乐道人之善，乐多贤友，益矣。乐骄乐，乐佚游，乐宴乐，损矣。"(16.5)

孔子说："有益的爱好有三种，有害的爱好有三种。爱好得到礼乐的节制，爱好称道别人的好处，爱好交很多有贤德的朋友，这是有益的。爱好放纵的快乐，爱好尽情的游玩，爱好吃喝的乐趣，这是有害的。"

12-3. 子曰："群居终日，言不及义，好行小慧，难矣！"(15.17)

孔子说："一群人整天在一起，话说不到道义上，只喜欢卖弄小聪明，这种人是很难有成就的。"

12-4. 子贡问曰："有一言而可以终身行之者乎？"子曰："其恕乎！己所不欲，勿施于人。"(15.23)

子贡问："有没有一个字可以终身奉行的呢？"孔子说："大概是恕吧！自己不要的，也不要给别人。"

词汇一 VOCABULARY I

1.	益	yì	benefit, profit
2.	损	sŭn	harm, damage
3.	谅	liàng	honest, sincere
4.	便辟	piánpì	dishonest, evil
5.	善柔	shànróu	flattery
6.	便佞	piánnìng	fawning, servile
7.	歪门邪道	wāimén xiédào	crooked ways, dishonest practices
8.	歪	wāi	askew, crooked
9.	邪	xié	evil, heretical, irregular
10.	阿谀	ēyú	to fawn over

11. 奉承 fèngchéng to flatter
12. 节 jié to control, to be moderate in
13. 善 shàn 好
14. 骄 jiāo undisciplined, willful, arrogant
15. 佚游 yìyóu unrestrained gaiety
16. 节制 jiézhì to practice temperance in, to exercise moderation in
17. 称道 chēngdào to speak approvingly of, to commend
18. 放纵 fàngzòng self-indulgent, undisciplined, unmannered
19. 尽情 jìnqíng to one's heart's content, as much as one likes
20. 行 xíng to do, to practice, to carry out
21. 慧 huì intelligence, wisdom
22. 卖弄 màinòng to show off, to parade
23. 恕 shù forgiveness, magnanimity
24. 欲 yù 想要
25. 施 shī to give, to grant
26. 奉行 fèngxíng to pursue, to practice

虚词 FUNCTION WORDS

1. 者 zhě 吗（有一言而可以终身行之者乎）
2. 乎 hū 吧（其恕乎）
3. 勿 wù 不要（己所不欲，勿施于人）
4. 于 yú 给（同上）

解读 Exegeses

人生有“三情”，即亲情、友情和爱情。这三情中，亲情最长，爱情最深，友情最广。一个人一生要交很多朋友，因此处世之道也就是交友之道。

俗语说“在家靠父母，出门靠朋友”，说明朋友之重要。又说：“近朱者赤，近墨者黑”，说明朋友对一个人的影响之大。那么，交什么样的朋友呢？孔子提出要交三种益友，不交三种损友。良朋益友可以给你带来很多好处，帮你做一个品德高尚的人，在事业上取得成功。反之，损友的坏处也是很大的。“乐宴乐”的就是平时说的酒肉朋友，整天在一起大吃大喝。那些“便辟”、“便佞”的人更是狐群狗党，他们谄媚奉承、见风使舵、花言巧语，把你带上邪路。那么，怎么识别朋友呢？如果你和一些朋友在一起，“群居终日，言不及义”，你就要警惕了。

词汇二 VOCABULARY II

1.	朱	zhū	vermilion, bright red
2.	赤	chì	红
3.	见风使舵	jiànfēng shǐduò	to act as the occasion dictates
4.	使	shǐ	to use, to operate
5.	舵	duò	rudder, helm
6.	识别	shíbié	to distinguish, to discern, to judge
7.	警惕	jǐngtì	to be on guard against, vigilant

事例 An Illustrative Story

THE SLASHED MAT 管宁割席

东汉末年，管宁与华歆一起读书。两人每天坐在一张席子上学习。

一天，他们在园中锄土种菜，忽然看见土中有一块黄金。管宁毫不动心，视若无睹。华歆捡起黄金看了好一会儿，才忍痛丢下。

又有一次，管宁和华歆正在读书时，外面传来一阵锣声。这准是哪个大官从这儿路过。管宁头也没抬，继续念书。华歆坐不住了，跑出去看。只见前面有人鸣锣开道，大官坐着一顶八人抬的大轿子，好不威风！

华歆回到房间后，却大吃一惊：管宁竟用刀子把席子割为两截！他正坐在自己的那头专心地读书呢。华歆问管宁为什么要这样做，管宁答道："你不配再做我的朋友了！"

从此以后，两人分手了。管宁潜心读书，成为德高望重的学者。华歆先跟孙权，后投曹操。虽然他做了高官，但道德、学问却不如管宁。

词汇三 VOCABULARY III

1.	割	gē	to cut, to slash
2.	席	xí	straw mat
3.	锄	chú	hoe, to hoe
4.	毫不	háobù	not at all
5.	睹	dǔ	to see
6.	捡	jiǎn	to pick up (from the ground)
7.	忍	rěn	to bear, to endure
8.	阵	zhèn	measure word for anything that occurs for an unusually brief duration—such as rain, wind, business, etc.
9.	锣	luó	gong
10.	准	zhǔn	definitely, certainly
11.	鸣锣	míngluó	to beat gongs

12. 鸣 míng to ring, to sound
13. 顶 dǐng measure word for things that serve as (or might have) a top cover, such as hats, etc.
14. 轿子 jiàozi sedan chair
15. 好不 hǎobù 非常、十分
16. 威风 wēifēng imposing, awe-inspiring
17. 却 què but, yet, however
18. 截 jié section
19. 配 pèi to deserve, to be worthy of, qualified
20. 分手 fēnshǒu to separate, to part company with
21. 潜心 qiánxīn to concentrate, to devote oneself to something

专名 PROPER NAMES

1. 管宁 Guǎn Níng scholar (158–241)
2. 华歆 Huà Xīn Three Kingdoms period official from the State of Wei 魏 (157–231)
3. 孙权 Sūn Quán king of Wu 吴 (r. 229–252)
4. 曹操 Cáo Cāo king of Wei 魏 (155–220)

成语 Idioms

1. 歪门邪道
   【课文】同歪门邪道的人交朋友，同阿谀奉承的人交朋友，同花言巧语的人交朋友，是有害的。
2. 花言巧语
   【课文】同上。
3. 言不及义
   【课文】群居终日，言不及义，好行小慧，难矣！
4. 好行小慧
   【课文】同上。
5. 己所不欲，勿施于人
   【课文】其恕乎！己所不欲，勿施于人。
6. 近朱者赤，近墨者黑
   【课文】俗语说："近朱者赤，近墨者黑"，说明朋友对一个人的影响之大。
7. 良朋益友
   【课文】良朋益友可以给你带来很多好处。

8. 狐群狗党
【课文】那些“便辟”、“便佞”的人更是狐群狗党，他们谄媚奉承、见风使舵、花言巧语，把你带上邪路。
9. 谄媚奉承
【课文】同上。
10. 见风使舵
【课文】同上。
11. 视若无睹
【课文】管宁毫不动心，视若无睹。
12. 鸣锣开道
【课文】只见前面有人鸣锣开道，大官坐着一顶八人抬的大轿子，好不威风！
13. 德高望重
【课文】管宁潜心读书，成为德高望重的学者。

词汇扩展 Vocabulary Expansion

1. 益
【课文】益者三友，损者三友。
【例词】益处、益友、益鸟、益虫，有益、得益、公益、收益、损益、延年益寿
2. 损
【课文】同上。
【例词】损害、损坏、损伤、损失、损毁、亏损、磨损、损人利己、损公肥私、损兵折将
3. 节
【课文】乐节礼乐，乐道人之善，乐多贤友，益矣。
【例词】节省、节制、节目、节译、节选、章节、细节、节衣缩食、开源节流、节节胜利
4. 游
【课文】乐骄乐，乐佚游，乐宴乐，损矣。
【例词】游览、游行、游戏、旅游、春游、导游、郊游、游乐场、游山玩水、游牧民族
5. 群
【课文】群居终日，言不及义，好行小慧，难矣！
【例词】群众、群岛、群居、群英会、群星灿烂、群策群力、群龙无首、群情激愤、鹤立鸡群、超群绝伦

6. 终
   【课文】同上。
   【例词】终日、终年、终点、终结、终止、终身伴侣、终身大事、始终如一、善始善终
7. 日
   【课文】同上。
   【例词】日新月异、日积月累、日理万机、日日夜夜、日思夜想、日薄西山、日暮途穷、旭日东升、风和日暖、夜以继日

练习 Exercises

一、选择题 MULTIPLE CHOICE

1. 有没有一个字可以终身 ________ 的呢？
   a. 奉承　　b. 奉行
   c. 奉陪　　d. 奉送
2. “乐宴乐” 的就是整天在一起 ________ 的酒肉朋友。
   a. 歪门邪道　　b. 阿谀奉承
   c. 花言巧语　　d. 大吃大喝
3. 如果你和一些朋友在一起，“群居终日，言不及义”，你就要 ________ 了。
   a. 警惕　　b. 警告
   c. 警戒　　d. 警卫

二、改错 CORRECTING MISTAKES

1. 在亲情、友情和爱情中，友情最长。
2. 华歆捡起黄金看了好一会儿，才放进自己的口袋里。
3. 大官坐着一顶四人抬的大轿子，好不威风！
4. 华歆先跟孙权，后投曹操，成为德高望重的学者。

三、问答题 ANSWERING QUESTIONS

1. 孔子提出要交哪三种益友，不交哪三种损友？
2. 人生有哪“三情”？
3. 哪两句俗语说明朋友之重要？
4. 管宁与华歆坐在什么上面一起读书？
5. 看到黄金以后，管宁怎么样？
6. 听到窗外的锣声以后，管宁怎么样？
7. 管宁为什么要割席？

四、讨论题 QUESTIONS FOR DISCUSSION

1. 本章第二段中的“乐”字有三个读音。请说明这个字在这不同的读音时的词义及用法。
2. 用锄土时发现黄金和读书时窗外有大官经过的两个事例来说明管宁和华歆为什么会走上不同的道路。

五、故事复述 RETELLING THE STORY

《管宁割席》

六、用本课的成语改写句子 REWRITING SENTENCES USING IDIOMS FROM THE CHAPTER

1. 小云要上大学了，爸妈一再叮嘱她在学校里要努力学习，还要多交好朋友。
2. 小文为了买一个电脑游戏跟妈妈说了半天好话，可他妈妈还是没答应。
3. 许大爷深受大家的尊重，村里有什么问题都要征求他的意见。
4. 小钱为人没有原则，经常做些不正派的事，你离他远一点。

七、选词 WORD CHOICE

1. 中国的经济发展真是（旭日东升，夜以继日，日新月异），变化之大令人惊叹。
2. 我最喜欢看奥斯卡颁奖大会了。那时候电影明星齐聚一堂，真是（群情激愤，群星灿烂，超群绝伦）！
3. 小李从小没了爸爸，他的妈妈多少年来一直（节衣缩食，开源节流，节节上升）才培养他上了大学。
4. 喂，你可不能把公司的东西往家里拿呀，你知道这是一种什么行为吗？这叫（损人利己，损公肥私，损兵折将）！
5. 小芬说找男朋友是找一个 （终身伴侣、终身大事、始终如一），可是小芳说没那么严重，不好了可以再换一个。

八、中译英 TRANSLATION FROM CHINESE INTO ENGLISH (几种关于朋友的称呼)

1. 刎颈之交指即使掉脑袋也不变心的朋友。
2. 忘年之交指不计年岁长幼，以才能德行为主的交往。
3. 君子之交指重在道义、但看上去很平淡的朋友。
4. 金石之交指交谊深厚，如金石之坚固。
5. 肺腑之交指无话不谈、推心置腹的朋友。
6. 贫贱之交指在贫困时结交的朋友。

九、英译中 TRANSLATION FROM ENGLISH INTO CHINESE (美国关于友谊的名言)

1. Friendship is a plant of slow growth and must undergo and withstand the shocks of adversity before it is entitled to the appellation. (George Washington)
2. In the end we will remember not the words of our enemies but the silence of our friends. (Martin Luther King Jr.)
3. The ornaments of a house are the friends who frequent it. (Ralph Waldo Emerson)
4. Friendship is a sheltering tree. (Samuel Coleridge)
5. All love that has not friendship for its base is like a mansion built upon the sand. (Ella Wheeler Wilcox)
6. The holy passion of friendship is of so sweet and steady and loyal and enduring a nature that it will last through a whole lifetime, if not asked to lend money. (Mark Twain)

十、讲故事 STORYTELLING (根据下面的提示在网上找资料)

【题目】《高山流水》

【关键词】俞伯牙、钟子期、知音

13. Words and Deeds 听言观行

《论语》选段 *Analects* Passages

13-1. 宰予昼寝。子曰："朽木不可雕也，粪土之墙不可圬也，于予与何诛？"子曰："始吾于人也，听其言而信其行；今吾于人也，听其言而观其行。于予与改是。"(5.10)

宰予白天睡觉。孔子说："腐朽的木头无法雕刻，肮脏的土墙无法粉刷。对于宰予这个人，我还能有什么责备呢？"孔子说："起初我对于人，听了他话便相信他的行为；现在我对于人，听了他的话还要观察他的行为。宰予使我有了这个改变。"

13-2. 子曰："众恶之，必察焉。众好之，必察焉。"(15.28)

孔子说："如果大家都厌恶他，就必须考察一下；如果大家都喜欢他，也必须考察一下。"

13-3. 子贡问曰："乡人皆好之，何如？"子曰："未可也。""乡人皆恶之，何如？"子曰："未可也。不如乡人之善者好之，其不善者恶之。"(13.24)

子贡问道："一乡的人都喜欢他，怎么样？"孔子说："还不行。""一乡的人都厌恶他，怎么样？"孔子说："还不行。不如乡里的好人喜欢他，乡里的坏人厌恶他。"

13-4. 子曰："君子不以言举人，不以人废言。"(15.23)

孔子说："君子不凭一个人说的话来举荐他，也不因为对一个人的看法而废弃他的话。"

13-5. 子路曰："子行三军，则谁与？"子曰："暴虎冯河，死而不悔者，吾不与也。必也临事而惧，好谋而成者也。"(7.11)

子路说："如果您统率三军，找谁共事？"孔子说："赤手空拳和老虎搏斗，徒步涉水过河，至死都不会后悔的人，我是不会和他共事的。我要共事的，一定要是遇事小心谨慎，善于谋划而能完成任务的人。"

词汇一 VOCABULARY I

1. 寝 qǐn 睡觉
2. 雕 diāo to carve
3. 粪 fèn manure, dirty

4.	圬	wū	trowel
5.	诛	zhū	to reproach
6.	腐朽	fǔxiǔ	rotten
7.	粉刷	fěnshuā	to whitewash, to plaster
8.	察	chá	to examine, to scrutinize
9.	厌恶	yànwù	to detest
10.	考察	kǎochá	to inspect, to examine
11.	乡	xiāng	village, township
12.	举	jǔ	to recommend, to promote
13.	废	fèi	to abandon
14.	凭	píng	to rely on
15.	废弃	fèiqì	to discard, to abandon
16.	行	xíng	to run, to administer
17.	暴虎	bàohǔ	to fight a tiger barehanded
18.	冯河	pínghé	to wade across a river
19.	悔	huǐ	to regret
20.	惧	jù	to be afraid
21.	统率	tǒngshuài	to command
22.	赤手空拳	chìshǒu kōngquán	barehanded, unarmed
23.	拳	quán	fist
24.	搏斗	bódòu	to wrestle, to fight
25.	徒步	túbù	on foot
26.	后悔	hòuhuǐ	to regret
27.	谋划	móuhuà	to plan, to scheme

虚词 FUNCTION WORDS

1. 未 wèi 不（未可也）
2. 可 kě 可以、行（同上）
3. 以 yǐ 根据（君子不以言举人，不以人废言）

专名 PROPER NAMES

1. 宰予 Zǎiyú 孔子的学生 (522–458 BCE)

解读 Exegeses

《论语》中都是语录，很少写到情景和故事。本章的第一段很简练地叙述了一个有趣的小故事，使我们对孔子和他的学生增加了一点了解。

"宰予昼寝"，我们不知道他是睡午觉还是上课时打瞌睡，但孔子因此而非常生气，严厉地批评了他。可见他对学生的要求是很严格的。

孔子提出的"听其言而观其行"是识别一个人的基本方法。本章的第二、第三段也说明，孔子不会人云亦云，随波逐流。即使别人的意见都一致，他也要根据事实，经过思考，做出自己的判断。

孔子在第五段中说明了他喜欢哪种类型的人。"暴虎冯河"是有勇无谋，鲁莽冒险。中国古典名著《水浒传》中有"武松打虎"的故事。武松赤手空拳打死了一只大老虎，但是像武松那样武艺高强的人是绝无仅有的。另外一部古典名著《三国演义》中有个诸葛亮。他是最好的军事家，打了很多胜仗，可是他一生都很谨慎，要求自己做到"临事而惧"。如果孔子听到诸葛亮这样说，一定会很高兴的。

词汇二 VOCABULARY II

1.	简练	jiǎnliàn	succinct
2.	严厉	yánlì	stern, severe
3.	云	yún	说
4.	随波逐流	suíbō zhúliú	to go with the flow, to follow other people's views and actions
5.	逐	zhú	追
6.	判断	pànduàn	to judge, to decide
7.	类型	lèixíng	type
8.	鲁莽	lǔmǎng	crude and rash
9.	武艺	wǔyì	martial arts

事例 An Illustrative Story

TALKING A GOOD GAME 赵括纸上谈兵

公元前二百六十二年，秦国的军队进攻赵国的长平。赵王派老将廉颇带二十万军队守住长平。廉颇知道秦军远道而来，不能持久，所以尽管秦军几次三番挑战，廉颇始终坚守阵地，不跟秦军交战。

于是，秦国就在赵国散布谣言说："廉颇老了，不敢出战。秦国就是怕赵国让年轻力壮的赵括带兵！"他们所说的赵括，是赵国名将赵奢的儿子。赵括从小熟读兵书，高谈阔论，自以为天下无敌。

赵王听信了谣言，就拜赵括为大将。可是赵括的母亲坚决反对，因为赵奢临终前叮嘱过：赵括只会纸上谈兵，不要让他当大将。但是赵王却不肯更改他的决定。

公元前二百六十年，赵括领兵二十万到了长平，取代廉颇。他下命令说："秦军再来挑战，必须迎头痛击。敌人逃跑了，就得穷追猛打，非杀得他们片甲不留不可！"

秦国的大将白起，故意打了几个败仗。赵括不知是计，拼命追赶。白起把赵军引进了包围圈。赵括带兵想冲出重围，秦军万箭齐发，把赵括射死了。赵军听到主将被杀，纷纷投降。白起把这四十万降卒全杀了，赵国从此走向衰亡。

词汇三 VOCABULARY III

1.	持久	chíjiǔ	lasting, enduring, protracted
2.	尽管	jǐnguǎn	even though, despite
3.	番	fān	次
4.	挑战	tiǎozhàn	to challenge to a battle
5.	始终	shǐzhōng	from beginning to end, throughout
6.	阵地	zhèndì	military position
7.	交战	jiāozhàn	to wage war, to be at war against each other
8.	谣言	yáoyán	rumor
9.	兵书	bīngshū	books on military strategy
10.	敌	dí	敌手、对手、 rivals of equal strength
11.	拜	bài	to appoint (a government official)
12.	临终	línzhōng	on one's deathbed
13.	叮嘱	dīngzhǔ	to enjoin and urge repeatedly
14.	取代	qǔdài	to replace
15.	穷追	qióngzhuī	to pursue relentlessly
16.	猛	měng	fierce, vigorous
17.	甲	jiǎ	armor
18.	计	jì	stratagem, scheme, plot
19.	拼命	pīnmìng	to risk one's life
20.	包围	bāowéi	to surround, to encircle
21.	纷纷	fēnfēn	numerous and disorderly
22.	卒	zú	soldier
23.	衰亡	shuāiwáng	to decline and fall (as a nation)

专名 PROPER NAMES

1.	赵括	Zhào Kuò	a Zhao general (d. 260 BCE)
2.	水浒传	Shuǐhǔ zhuàn	*The Water Margin*, one of the Four Great Classical Novels
3.	武松	Wǔ Sōng	a hero in *The Water Margin*
4.	三国演义	Sānguó yǎnyì	*Romance of the Three Kingdoms*, one of the Four Great Classical Novels

5.	诸葛亮	Zhūgě Liàng	a strategist (181–234) of the Three Kingdoms period
6.	秦	Qín	State of Qin
7.	赵	Zhào	State of Zhao
8.	长平	Chángpíng	An ancient city in present-day Shanxi 山西 Province
9.	廉颇	Lián Pō	a Zhao general (fl. 251 BCE)
10.	赵奢	Zhào Shē	a Zhao general
11.	白起	Bái Qǐ	a Qin general (d. 257 BCE)

成语 Idioms

1. 听言观行
【课文】今吾于人也，听其言而观其行。
2. 朽木不可雕也
【课文】朽木不可雕也，粪土之墙不可圬也，于予与何诛？
3. 以言举人
【课文】君子不以言举人，不以人废言。
4. 以人废言
【课文】同上。
5. 暴虎冯河
【课文】暴虎冯河，死而不悔者，吾不与也。
6. 死而不悔
【课文】同上。
7. 临事而惧
【课文】必也临事而惧，好谋而成者也。
8. 好谋而成
【课文】同上。
9. 赤手空拳
【课文】赤手空拳和老虎搏斗的人，我是不会和他共事的。
10. 随波逐流
【课文】孔子不会人云亦云，随波逐流。
11. 有勇无谋
【课文】“暴虎冯河”是有勇无谋，鲁莽冒险。
12. 武艺高强
【课文】像武松那样武艺高强的人是绝无仅有的。
13. 绝无仅有
【课文】同上。
14. 纸上谈兵
【课文】赵括纸上谈兵。

15. 远道而来
【课文】廉颇知道秦军远道而来，不能持久。
16. 几次三番
【课文】尽管秦军几次三番挑战，廉颇始终坚守阵地。
17. 年轻力壮
【课文】秦国就是怕赵国让年轻力壮的赵括带兵！
18. 高谈阔论
【课文】赵括从小熟读兵书，高谈阔论，自以为天下无敌。
19. 天下无敌
【课文】同上。
20. 迎头痛击
【课文】秦军再来挑战，必须迎头痛击。
21. 穷追猛打
【课文】敌人逃跑了，就得穷追猛打，非杀得他们片甲不留不可！
22. 片甲不留
【课文】同上。

词汇扩展 Vocabulary Expansion

1. 听
【课文】始吾于人也，听其言而信其行。
【例词】听从、听觉、听课、听说、听众、旁听、收听、动听、听而不闻、听天由命
2. 观
【课文】今吾于人也，听其言而观其行。
【例词】观察、观看、观望、观点、观感、观念、主观、客观、乐观、悲观
3. 察
【课文】众恶之，必察焉。
【例词】察看、察觉、观察、考察、视察、洞察、警察、侦察、察颜观色、明察秋毫
4. 乡
【课文】乡人皆好之，何如？
【例词】乡村、乡亲、乡音、乡情、乡思、乡愁、故乡、水乡、同乡、他乡
5. 何
【课文】乡人皆好之，何如？
【例词】何必、何苦、何不、何尝、何妨、何乐不为、何去何从、何以见得、何足挂齿、居心何在

6. 废
   【课文】君子不以言举人，不以人废言。
   【例词】废除、废物、废品、废墟、残废、荒废、废话连篇、废寝忘食、半途而废、过期作废
7. 悔
   【课文】暴虎冯河，死而不悔者，吾不与也。
   【例词】悔过、悔改、悔悟、后悔，反悔、忏悔、悔之莫及、悔不当初、悔过自新、悔恨交加

练习 Exercises

一、选择题 MULTIPLE CHOICE

1. 对于宰予这个人，听了他的话还要 ________ 他的行为。
   a. 相信　　b. 观察
   c. 责备　　d. 改变
2. 孔子主张根据事实，经过思考，做出自己的判断，不要 ________。
   a. 以人废言　　b. 以言举人
   c. 人云亦云　　d. 高谈阔论
3. 孔子对学生的要求是很 ________ 的。
   a. 严肃　　b. 严厉
   c. 严重　　d. 严格
4. “武松打虎”是 ________ 中的一个故事。
   a. 《水浒传》　　b. 《西游记》
   c. 《红楼梦》　　d. 《三国演义》
5. 诸葛亮一生都很 ________。
   a. 勇敢　　b. 鲁莽
   c. 积极　　d. 谨慎
6. 纸上谈兵讲的是 ________ 的故事。
   a. 赵奢　　b. 赵括
   c. 白起　　d. 廉颇
7. 赵括是战国时期 ________ 国的将军。
   a. 吴　　b. 越
   c. 赵　　d. 秦
8. 这位常胜将军每次打仗都把敌人打得 ________。
   a. 迎头痛击　　b. 穷追猛打
   c. 片甲不留　　d. 天下无敌

二、改错 CORRECTING MISTAKES

1. 孔子说，对于宰予，责备是很有用的。
2. 如果一个村子的人都喜欢一个人，这个人一定是最好的人。
3. 君子要凭一个人说的话来推荐他。
4. “临事而惧”的人都是胆小鬼。
5. 廉颇老了，不敢跟秦军交战了。
6. 赵括从小熟读兵法，高谈阔论，天下无敌。
7. 赵王听了赵奢的话，就拜赵括为大将。
8. 赵括的二十万兵都被白起杀死了。

三、问答题 ANSWERING QUESTIONS

1. 《论语》中有没有很多情景和故事？
2. 孔子对学生的要求严不严？你怎么知道？
3. 长平大战是哪两国之间的战争？
4. 长平大战发生在哪一年？
5. 廉颇为什么不跟秦军交战？
6. 秦国为什么要在赵国散布谣言？
7. 赵括的母亲为什么反对自己的儿子当大将？
8. 赵括到了长平后下了什么命令？
9. 白起为什么故意打了几个败仗？
10. 赵括是怎么死的？

四、讨论题 QUESTIONS FOR DISCUSSION

1. 宰予白天睡觉这件事，对孔子有什么影响？
2. 宰予只不过在白天睡了个觉，孔子为什么生这么大的气？
3. 根据这章的语录，讲一讲孔子识别人的方法。
4. 《三国演义》中的诸葛亮是个什么样的人？
5. 赵括在长平大战中犯了什么错误？

五、故事复述 RETELLING THE STORY

《赵括纸上谈兵》

六、用本课的成语改写句子 REWRITING SENTENCES USING IDIOMS FROM THE CHAPTER

1. 妈妈一次又一次地跟小峰说，每天起床以后就把自己的房间整理干净，可他还是做不到。
2. 你说你很会做菜，还给我说了那么多菜谱，可你这几个菜实在是做得不怎么样，看来你是只会说不会做的了。

3. 明天我家有客人从很远的地方来，我们怎么招待他们呢？
4. 高先生喜欢谈论时事政治。一到聚会的时候，大家都只听他一个人大谈特谈他的见解了。

七、选词 WORD CHOICE

1. 我只不过是帮了你一点儿小忙，你（何苦、何必、何妨）送我这么好的礼物呢？
2. 在生物实验室里工作很不容易，除了必须非常仔细和耐心以外，还得有敏锐的（观看、观察、观望）能力。
3. 我离开自己的家乡很久了，每到中秋节，天上的一轮明月常常会引起我的（乡情、乡音、乡愁）。
4. 小刘中学的时候很贪玩，不用功，结果没考上好大学，他现在非常（后悔、反悔、忏悔）。
5. 做一件事要成功，最主要的是要持之以恒，不能（废话连篇、半途而废、过期作废）。

八、中译英 TRANSLATION FROM CHINESE INTO ENGLISH

1. 孔子对学生要求很严格，但在其他章节中，我们也看到孔子跟他的学生亲切交谈的场面。
2. 以前，中国的老师常常会在课堂上批评一个学生，或者表扬一个学生。现在这样的时做法已经比较少了。
3. 战国时期中国分成秦、楚、齐、燕、韩、赵、魏七个国家，最后秦国统一了中国。
4. 公元前二百三十年，秦始皇灭掉韩国，到公元前二百二十一年灭齐，他用了十年时间消灭了六国。
5. 秦始皇虽然是个暴君，但他能识别人才，用了一批有本领的文臣武将，所以能打败六国。
6. 赵奢很了解自己的儿子，知道他只会纸上谈兵，正像一句成语所说的："知子莫若父"。
7. 白起把赵国的四十万降卒引进一个山谷，堵住两头，从山上扔下树木和石头，把他们全部活埋了。
8. 廉颇和白起是战国时期的"四大名将"中的两个。如果赵王不用赵括取代廉颇，长平大战还不知是什么结局呢。
9. 《三国演义》中有许多战争的故事和战术运用的事例，所以有人把这本小说当成一本兵书来读。
10. 中国有句话叫"少不读水浒，老不读三国"。这是说年轻人读《水浒》会学小说中的好汉打打杀杀，老年人读《三国》就会学一肚子的阴谋诡计。

九、英译中 TRANSLATION FROM ENGLISH INTO CHINESE (每句中至少要用一句成语)

1. Confucius was very upset by Zai Yu's sleeping during the day and sighed, "Rotten wood cannot be carved!"
2. We should not recommend a person on account of his words; nor do we dismiss words on account of their speaker.
3. Wu Song killed a tiger with his bare hands, but how many people possess martial arts at as high a level as he?
4. Qin spread rumors: "Lian Po is old and does not dare fight. Qin is the most afraid of Zhao Kuo, who is young and strong!"
5. Zhao Kuo read many books on battle strategy and thought of himself as having no rival in the world.
6. Zhao Kuo ordered, "If the Qin army comes to attack, we must face them head on; if they flee, we must pursue them relentlessly!"

十、讲故事 STORYTELLING (根据下面的提示在网上找资料)

1. 【题目】《武松打虎》
   【提示】武松喝醉酒以后，在景阳岗上打死了一只大老虎。
2. 【题目】《空城计》
   【提示】诸葛亮用了一个将军叫马谡，他也只会纸上谈兵。
3. 【题目】《将相和》
   【提示】这是发生在赵国的将军廉颇和丞相蔺相如之间的一个故事。

14. Advancing and Retreating 用行舍藏

《论语》选段 *Analects* Passages

14-1. 子谓颜渊曰："用之则行，舍之则藏，惟我与尔有是夫。"(7.11)

孔子对颜渊说："用我呢，我就去干；不用我，我就隐居起来，只有我和你才能做到这样吧！"

14-2. 子曰："邦有道，危言危行；邦无道，危行言孙。"(14.3)

孔子说："国家有道，说话和行为都要正直；国家无道，行为要正直，但说话要谦逊。"

14-3. 子曰："宁武子，邦有道则知，邦无道则愚。其知可及也，其愚不可及也。"(5.21)

孔子说："宁武子在国家有道时便显露才智，在国家无道时就像很愚昧。他的才智别人还赶得上，他的愚昧却没人赶得上。"

14-4. 子曰："天下有道则见，无道则隐。邦有道，贫且贱焉，耻也，邦无道，富且贵焉，耻也。"(8.13)

孔子说："天下有道，就出来工作；天下无道，就隐居起来。国家有道，贫穷而地位低下是一种耻辱；国家无道，有钱并居高位也是一种耻辱。"

词汇一 VOCABULARY I

1.	舍	shě	to abandon, to give up
2.	藏	cáng	to hide, to conceal
3.	尔	ěr	你
4.	邦	bāng	feudal state
5.	危	wēi	high, upright, honest
6.	孙	xùn	逊, respectful and compliant
7.	愚	yú	foolish, stupid
8.	显露	xiǎnlù	to become visible
9.	愚昧	yúmèi	ignorant, dull
10.	见	xiàn	现, to emerge, to appear
11.	隐	yǐn	to hide, to retire, to live like a hermit
12.	贱	jiàn	lowly, humble

虚词 FUNCTION WORDS

1. 惟 wéi 只有（惟我与尔有是夫）
2. 夫 fú 啊（同上）
3. 焉 yān (used to pause, and for emphasis) (邦有道，贫且贱焉，耻也)

专名 PROPER NAMES

1. 宁武子 Níng Wǔzǐ a courtier of the State of Wei 卫

解读 Exegeses

儒家提倡学以致用，就是要做官，为社会贡献知识才能。但如果没人要用你呢？孔子说："用之则行，舍之则藏"，"有道则见，无道则隐"。这是孔子为官处世的一条重要原则，也是孔子一生实践的总结。他在鲁国从政，做到代理宰相。以后又周游列国十四年，希望能有施展抱负的机会。四处碰壁后，他就"隐"、"藏"起来，专注于教育和编订古籍。

孔子的传人孟子进一步发挥了孔子的思想，他说："达则兼济天下，穷则独善其身"。因为君子当官的目的主要是为国家建功立业，并非自己升官发财，所以没有官当，也能看淡名利，致力于提升自己的道德品格。孔子在这儿称赞颜回能做到用行舍藏。在别处他还说颜回能身居陋巷而不改其乐。这种能进能退、积极乐观的思想，对几千年来中国的知识分子影响深远。

词汇二 VOCABULARY II

1. 施展 shīzhǎn to put (a plan) into practice
2. 抱负 bàofù aspiration, ambition
3. 碰壁 pèngbì to run up against a stone wall, to be rebuffed
4. 传人 chuánrén disciple, exponent
5. 发挥 fāhuī to fully utilize (one's abilities)
6. 达 dá successful, prominent
7. 兼 jiān concurrently, simultaneously
8. 济 jì to aid, to relieve

事例 An Illustrative Story

WORLD AND ISLAND 苏东坡仰俯皆宽

苏轼，号东坡居士，在诗、文、书、画等方面，都取得了登峰造极的成就。然而，他的人生道路却是坎坷不平的。

他二十一岁中进士，但不久就卷入北宋朝廷的政治斗争的旋涡中。他受到诬陷，被捕入狱。出狱以后，苏轼被降职到黄州。他公余带领家人开荒种田，帮补生计。“东坡居士”的别号便是他在那时为自己起的。

新皇帝即位后，苏轼被调回朝廷，当上皇帝的秘书。在两年中，他为皇帝起草诏令达八百多件，也提了很多建议。但后来他又被排挤出朝廷，调到杭州当太守。苏轼在杭州兴修水利，疏浚西湖，用挖出的泥筑了一道堤坝，就是著名的“苏堤”，现在还是西湖上的一道风景线。

他再次回朝廷后，当上兵部尚书和礼部尚书等高官。但不久又被贬到被称为天涯海角的海南岛。虽然那里生活很艰苦，但他泰然处之，写了很多诗文。

苏轼一生，在政治上经历了三起三落。为官时，忧国忧民，勤于政务；失意时，也胸襟坦荡，为善一方。在顺境与逆境的变更中，完成人格的修养。苏轼在一首词中写道：“用舍由时，行藏在我”，引自孔子的“用之则行，舍之则藏”。苏轼的仰俯皆宽的人生态度，赢得了后世广泛的崇敬。

词汇三 VOCABULARY III

1.	俯	fǔ	to bow (one's head)
2.	号	hào	alias, byname, cognomen
3.	居士	jūshì	a scholar without an office, a lay Buddhist
4.	登峰造极	dēngfēng zàojí	to reach the summit, to reach the height of perfection
5.	坎坷	kǎnkě	bumpy, rough
6.	旋涡	xuánwō	whirlpool, vortex
7.	诬陷	wūxiàn	to frame someone
8.	捕	bǔ	to catch, to arrest
9.	狱	yù	prison, jail
10.	公余	gōngyú	spare time after work
11.	开荒	kāihuāng	to cultivate virgin soil
12.	帮补	bāngbǔ	to help, to supply
13.	生计	shēngjì	livelihood, means of livelihood
14.	别号	biéhào	alias, byname, cognomen

15.	起草	qǐcǎo	to draft
16.	诏令	zhàolìng	imperial edict
17.	排挤	páijǐ	to push aside, to push out
18.	兴修	xīngxiū	to start construction (on a large project), to build
19.	疏浚	shūjùn	to dredge
20.	堤坝	dībà	dikes and dams
21.	兵部	bīngbù	the Ministry of War
22.	尚书	shàngshū	minister
23.	礼部	lǐbù	the Ministry of Rites
24.	天涯海角	tiānyá hǎijiǎo	the ends of the earth, the remotest corners of the world
25.	涯	yá	margin, limit
26.	泰然	tàirán	calm, composed
27.	顺境	shùnjìng	favorable circumstances
28.	逆境	nìjìng	unfavorable circumstances
29.	变更	biàngēng	change, alteration
30.	词	cí	a poetic genre

专名 PROPER NAMES

1.	苏轼	Sū Shì	a poet, prose writer, and calligrapher (1037–1101)
2.	黄州	Huángzhōu	a city in present-day Hubei 湖北 Province
3.	杭州	Hángzhōu	a city in present-day Zhejiang Province
4.	西湖	Xīhú	West Lake, a famous tourist spot in Hangzhou
5.	海南岛	Hǎinán dǎo	Hainan Island

成语 Idioms

1. 用之则行，舍之则藏
   【课文】用之则行，舍之则藏，惟我与尔有是夫。
2. 危言危行
   【课文】邦有道，危言危行。
3. 危行言逊
   【课文】邦无道，危行言孙。
4. 愚不可及
   【课文】其知可及也，其愚不可及也。
5. 有道则见，无道则隐
   【课文】天下有道则见，无道则隐。

6. 学以致用
【课文】儒家提倡学以致用。
7. 周游列国
【课文】他在鲁国从政，以后又周游列国十四年。
8. 四处碰壁
【课文】四处碰壁后，他就专注于教育和编订古籍。
9. 兼济天下
【课文】孟子说："达则兼济天下，穷则独善其身"。
10. 独善其身
【课文】同上。
11. 建功立业
【课文】君子当官的目的主要是为国家建功立业，并非自己升官发财。
12. 升官发财
【课文】同上。
13. 仰俯皆宽
【课文】苏东坡仰俯皆宽。
14. 登峰造极
【课文】苏轼在诗、文、书、画等方面，都取得了登峰造极的成就。
15. 坎坷不平
【课文】然而，他的人生道路却是坎坷不平的。
16. 天涯海角
【课文】不久他又被贬到被称为天涯海角的海南岛。
17. 泰然处之
【课文】虽然那里生活很艰苦，但他泰然处之，写了很多诗文。
18. 胸襟坦荡
【课文】失意时，也胸襟坦荡，为善一方。
19. 为善一方
【课文】同上。

词汇扩展 Vocabulary Expansion

1. 用
【课文】用之则行，舍之则藏，惟我与尔有是夫。
【例词】使用、适用、实用、食用、试用、用行舍藏、用之不竭、用武之地、用兵如神、古为今用
2. 行
【课文】同上。

【例词】行为、行动、行政、行军、行善、行之有效、行成于思、及时行乐、日行千里、言行一致

3. 舍
【课文】同上。
【例词】舍得、取舍、施舍、舍己为人、舍身救人、舍生取义、舍生忘死、舍近就远、舍本逐末、难分难舍

4. 藏
【课文】同上。
【例词】藏书、暗藏、收藏、隐藏、珍藏、储藏、矿藏、藏龙卧虎、东躲西藏、包藏祸心

5. 危
【课文】邦有道，危言危行。
【例词】危害、危机、危急、危难、安危、危言危行、危急存亡、危机四伏、危在旦夕、临危不惧

6. 智（知）
【课文】邦有道则知，邦无道则愚。
【例词】智慧、智力、智谋、智商、才智、机智、理智、明智、智勇双全、智穷力竭

7. 隐
【课文】天下有道则见，无道则隐。
【例词】隐藏、隐瞒、隐私、隐患、隐忧、隐居、隐士、隐姓埋名、隐隐约约、隐隐作痛

练习 Exercises

一、选择题 MULTIPLE CHOICE

1. 国家有道，说话和行为都要 ________。
   a. 正直　　b. 谦虚
   c. 谨慎　　d. 泰然
2. 宁武子的才智别人还赶得上，他的 ________ 却没人赶得上。
   a. 聪明　　b. 愚昧
   c. 勤奋　　d. 正直
3. 国家无道，有钱并居高位也是一种 ________。
   a. 光荣　　b. 危险
   c. 耻辱　　d. 幸福
4. 这种能进能退的思想，对几千年来中国的知识分子影响 ________。
   a. 深刻　　b. 深长
   c. 深厚　　d. 深远

5. “东坡居士”的别号是苏轼在 ________ 时为自己起的。
   a. 杭州　　b. 苏州
   c. 青州　　d. 黄州
6. 兵部尚书相当于现在的 ________。
   a. 国防部长　　b. 外交部长
   c. 教育部长　　d. 工业部长

二、改错 CORRECTING MISTAKES

1. 国家无道，行为和说话都要谦虚谨慎。
2. 儒家提倡隐居，不提倡做官。
3. 君子当官是为了升官发财。
4. 苏轼在黄州兴修水利，疏浚西湖。
5. 苏轼在一首诗中写道：“用舍由时，行藏在我”。

三、问答题 ANSWERING QUESTIONS

1. 孔子在鲁国从政，做过什么官？
2. 孔子周游列国多少年？
3. 孔子晚年专注于什么工作？
4. 苏轼在哪些方面取得了登峰造极的成就？
5. 苏轼几岁中进士？
6. 苏轼为什么会被捕入狱？
7. 苏轼在给皇帝当秘书的两年中，起草了多少件诏令？
8. 苏轼在朝廷中当过哪些高官？
9. 苏轼晚年被贬到哪里？
10. 苏轼词中的“用舍由时，行藏在我”的出典在哪里？

四、讨论题 QUESTIONS FOR DISCUSSION

1. 为什么很多儒家学者在顺境和逆境中都能保持积极乐观的态度？
2. 苏轼在他的政治生涯中经历了三起三落，请具体说明。

五、故事复述 RETELLING THE STORY

《苏东坡仰俯皆宽》

六、用本课的成语改写句子 REWRITING SENTENCES USING IDIOMS FROM THE CHAPTER

1. 我昨天晚上看的中国杂技表演精彩极了，他们的技巧之高是没人超得过的。
2. 现代社会科学技术发达了，即使你的朋友去了很远的地方，你也可以跟他随时联系，距离一下子就缩短了。

3. 人生的道路不会是又平又直的，我们应该学会怎么面对生活中的困难和挫折。
4. 贾主任为人正直，心胸开阔，虽然工作很忙，他总是高高兴兴的。

七、选词 WORD CHOICE

1. 由于汽油价格不断上升，现在我国的经济前景黯淡，(危急存亡、危在旦夕、危机四伏)。
2. 小明，你每天在饭店里端盘子，念书的时间都没有了，这不是(舍生忘死、舍本逐末、舍近就远)吗？
3. 严老师的书房里（收藏、储藏、珍藏）着数以千计的书，简直像个小图书馆了。
4. 你今天怎么了？一付茶饭无心的样子，一定有什么事对我(隐藏、隐瞒、隐患)着吧？
5. 小李找到了一个很好的工作，可是有个（使用、适用、试用）期，表现好才能转正。

八、中译英 TRANSLATION FROM CHINESE INTO ENGLISH

苏东坡吃鱼

苏东坡和高僧佛印①是好朋友。和尚应该吃素，可是佛印却吃肉喝酒。一天中午，佛印刚把做好的一条鱼端上桌，就听到小和尚禀报：东坡居士来访。佛印怕暴露吃鱼的秘密，就急忙把鱼扣在一口磬中。苏东坡进屋后，闻到阵阵鱼香，又见到桌上反扣的磬，心中有数了。

佛印说："居士今日光临，不知有何见教？" 苏东坡装着一本正经的样子说："我今日遇到一难题，特来请教。" 佛印连忙说："阿弥陀佛②，岂敢，岂敢。"

苏东坡笑了笑说："今日友人出了一对联，上联是：向阳门第春常在。我一时对不出下联，望长老赐教。" 佛印不知是计，脱口而出："居士是大学问家，今日怎么这么健忘，这是一副老对联，下联是：积善人家庆有馀。"

苏东坡不由得哈哈大笑："既然长老明示磬(庆)有鱼(余)，就让我来大饱口福吧！"

【注释】①佛印(1032–1089)：北宋高僧。②阿弥陀佛Ēmítuófó (Amitābha Buddha)：和尚表示祝愿的常用语。

九、英译中 TRANSLATION FROM ENGLISH INTO CHINESE

DONGPO'S PORK (东坡肉)

It is said that once, out of boredom, Su Dongpo decided to make stewed pork during his free time. Then an old friend visited him while he was cooking and challenged him to a game of *weiqi* 围棋. Su totally forgot about the stew during the game, until a very fragrant aroma came from his kitchen and he was reminded of it. Thus, Dongpo's Pork, a dish famous in Chinese cuisine, was created by accident.

十、讲故事 STORYTELLING (根据下面的提示在网上找资料)

【题目】东坡和佛印斗智的故事

【提示】苏东坡和佛印有很多斗智的故事，请你再讲一个。

15. Careers for Scholars 禄在其中

《论语》选段 *Analects* Passages

15-1. 子曰："君子谋道不谋食。耕也，馁在其中矣。学也，禄在其中矣。君子忧道不忧贫。" (15.31)

孔子说："君子只谋求行道，不谋求衣食。耕田，就会挨饿；学习，俸禄会随之而来。君子只担心不能行道，不担心贫穷。"

15-2. 樊迟请学稼。子曰："吾不如老农。"请学为圃。曰："吾不如老圃。"樊迟出。子曰："小人哉，樊须也！上好礼，则民莫敢不敬；上好义，则民莫敢不服；上好信，则民莫敢不用情。夫如是，则四方之民襁负其子而至矣，焉用稼？" (13.4)

樊迟向孔子请教如何种庄稼。孔子说："我不如老农。"樊迟又请教如何种菜。孔子说："我不如老菜农。"樊迟退出以后，孔子说："樊迟真是小人。君主只要重视礼，老百姓就不敢不敬畏；君主只要重视义，老百姓就不敢不服从；君主只要重视信，老百姓就不敢不用真心实情来对待你。要是做到这样，四面八方的老百姓就会背着自己的小孩来投奔，哪里用得着自己去种庄稼呢？"

15-3. 子张学干禄。子曰："多闻阙疑，慎言其余，则寡尤。多见阙殆，慎行其余，则寡悔。言寡尤，行寡悔，禄在其中矣。" (2.18)

子张学谋取官职的办法。孔子说："要多听，保留疑问，其余的也要谨慎地说出来，就能减少过失。要多看，搁置疑难，其余的也要谨慎地去做，就能减少后悔。说话少过失，做事少后悔，官职俸禄就在这里了。"

词汇一 VOCABULARY I

1.	禄	lù	an official's salary
2.	耕	gēng	to plow, to till
3.	馁	něi	饿
4.	俸禄	fènglù	an official's salary
5.	稼	jià	to sow (grain), crops
6.	圃	pǔ	garden, gardener
7.	四方	sìfāng	all quarters, everywhere
8.	襁	qiǎng	swaddling clothes, to swaddle
9.	负	fù	to carry on the back or shoulder
10.	投奔	tóubèn	to go to a friend or place for shelter or support

11. 庄稼 zhuāngjià crops
12. 干 gān 求
13. 阙 quē 空缺
14. 疑 yí 疑问
15. 尤 yóu fault, wrongdoing
16. 殆 dài 不安、疑难
17. 保留 bǎoliú to hold back, to reserve
18. 搁置 gēzhì to shelve, to lay aside
19. 疑难 yínán difficult, knotty problem

虚词 FUNCTION WORDS

1. 夫 fú (to initiate a sentence) (夫如是，则四方之民襁负其子而至矣，焉用稼)
2. 焉 yān 何必（同上）

专名 PROPER NAMES

1. 樊迟 Fán Chí 名须，字子迟，孔子的学生
2. 子张 Zǐzhāng 姓颛 (Zhuān) 孙名师 (b. 503 BCE), 孔子的学生

解读 Exegeses

孔子在本章中的头两段话常常受到误解甚至批判。

我们先来看第一段。受到批评较多的是中间两句："耕也，馁在其中矣。学也，禄在其中矣。"有人据此就断定孔子鄙视农民，鼓吹读书做官。他们的错误在于忽略了这一段的第一句："君子谋道不谋食"和最后一句："君子忧道不忧贫"。这两句分别是中间两句的前提和结论。孔子说的是君子努力学习，为国家作贡献，为人民谋福利，自己的生活自然会好的。反之，如果只想着赚钱，比如种地，那倒是可能会饿肚子的。我们还需要知道的是孔子的时代农民的地位并不太低。当时的排列顺序是"士农工商"，农民在工人和商人之上。孔子用农民来做生产、赚钱的代表，并无轻视的意思。这段话就是现在也可以作为人生格言。

本章第二段也常被误解和批判。其实，孔子说自己种田不如老农是很实事求是的。孔子的要点是一个君主只要做到礼、义、信，国家就搞好了，为什么一定要学种田呢？

词汇二 VOCABULARY II

1. 误解 wùjiě to misunderstand
2. 批判 pīpàn to criticize

3.	据	jù	according to, on the grounds of
4.	断定	duàndìng	to conclude, to form a judgment, to determine
5.	鄙视	bǐshì	to despise, to disdain, to look down upon
6.	鼓吹	gǔchuī	to advocate, to preach, to advertise
7.	忽略	hūlüè	to neglect, to overlook
8.	前提	qiántí	premise, prerequisite, presupposition
9.	结论	jiélùn	conclusion
10.	福利	fúlì	material benefits, welfare
11.	赚钱	zhuànqián	to make money
12.	排列	páiliè	to arrange, to put in order
13.	顺序	shùnxù	sequence, order
14.	轻视	qīngshì	to look down upon, to underestimate

事例 An Illustrative Story

A STATESMAN OF FOUR REIGNS 司马光四朝元老

司马光是北宋时期著名的政治家、史学家和文学家。

司马光二十岁就考中进士。步人仕途后，他仍然好学不倦，力求博古通今。他睡觉时用一段圆木当枕头，头稍一动，圆木就要转动。他惊醒了，就能起来读书。这就是有名的"警枕"。

司马光在学术上最主要的成就是编撰史书《资治通鉴》。这是中国最大的一部编年史，全书共二百九十四卷，上起战国初期（公元前403年），下迄五代末年（公元960年），共一千三百六十二年。司马光费时十九年写成此书。他自己说："日力不足，继之以夜"，"精力尽于此书"。

当时北宋建国近百年，已出现种种危机。作为一个坚定的儒家学者，司马光积极参与政事，力图为国家作贡献。虽然经过许多政治风浪，他晚年官至宰相，成为四朝元老。

词汇三 VOCABULARY III

1.	四朝元老	sìcháo yuánlǎo	a veteran statesman who stays in power under four successive emperors or regimes
2.	警	jǐng	alert, vigilant
3.	编年史	biānnián shǐ	chronological history
4.	迄	qì	until, up to
5.	危机	wēijī	crisis

专名 PROPER NAMES

1.	司马光	Sīmǎ Guāng	Song statesman and historian (1019–1086)
2.	资治通鉴	Zīzhì tōngjiàn	*Comprehensive Mirror to Aid in Government*, a chronological history written by Sima Guang
3.	五代	Wǔdài	the Five Dynasties period (907–960)

成语 Idioms

1. 禄在其中
   【课文】学也，禄在其中矣。
2. 谋道不谋食
   【课文】君子谋道不谋食。
3. 忧道不忧贫
   【课文】君子忧道不忧贫。
4. 随之而来
   【课文】学习，俸禄会随之而来。
5. 多闻阙疑
   【课文】多闻阙疑，慎言其余，则寡尤。
6. 多见阙殆
   【课文】多见阙殆，慎行其余，则寡悔。
7. 寡尤寡悔
   【课文】言寡尤，行寡悔，禄在其中矣。
8. 博古通今
   【课文】步入仕途后，他仍然好学不倦，力求博古通今。

词汇扩展 Vocabulary Expansion

1. 谋
   【课文】君子谋道不谋食。
   【例词】谋求、谋生、谋反、谋害、计谋、参谋、阴谋、密谋、同谋、谋财害命
2. 农
   【课文】樊迟请学稼。子曰：“吾不如老农。”
   【例词】农业、农民、农村、农田、农场、农活、农具、农历、农药、农学院
3. 礼
   【课文】上好礼，则民莫敢不敬。

【例词】礼节、礼貌、礼堂、婚礼、葬礼、典礼、礼仪之邦、礼尚往来、礼贤下士、礼轻情意重

4. 信

【课文】上好信，则民莫敢不用情。

【例词】信心、信念、信誉、信仰、信服、信赖、信息、自信、诚信、信用卡

5. 情

【课文】同上。

【例词】情感、情谊、情绪、情人、情歌、情投意合、情深意长、情不自禁、情景交融、情同手足

6. 方

【课文】夫如是，则四方之民襁负其子而至矣，焉用稼？

【例词】方向、方面、方言、地方、前方、远方、对方、双方、各方、四面八方

7. 疑

【课文】多闻阙疑，慎言其余，则寡尤。

【例词】疑问、疑心、疑惑、疑难、疑点、疑虑、猜疑、可疑、怀疑、疑神疑鬼

练习 Exercises

一、选择题 MULTIPLE CHOICE

1. 孔子关于"耕也，馁在其中"的话常常受到 ________。
   a. 批评　　b. 批判
   c. 批准　　d. 批示
2. 有人根据孔子的这句话就断定孔子 ________ 农民。
   a. 鄙视　　b. 轻视
   c. 重视　　d. 藐视
3. "君子忧道不忧贫"是孔子这段话的 ________。
   a. 结尾　　b. 结局
   c. 结果　　d. 结论
4. 这段话就是现在也可以作为人生 ________。
   a. 成语　　b. 短语
   c. 格言　　d. 名言

二、改错 CORRECTING MISTAKES

1. 君子谋求行道，也要谋求衣食。
2. 君主也要学习种庄稼和种菜。

3. 一个人要大胆地发表自己的意见，就能减少过失。
4. 在孔子的时代农民的地位在工人和商人之下。

三、问答题 ANSWERING QUESTIONS

1. 有名的“警枕”是个什么样的东西？
2. 《资治通鉴》是一部什么体裁的史书？
3. 《资治通鉴》写了哪个时期的历史？
4. 司马光费时多少年写成《资治通鉴》？
5. 为什么说司马光是四朝元老？

四、讨论题 QUESTIONS FOR DISCUSSION

1. 应该怎样理解孔子说的“耕也，馁在其中矣。学也，禄在其中矣”？
2. 为什么孔子说“小人哉，樊须也”？

五、故事复述 RETELLING THE STORY

《司马光四朝元老》

六、用本课的成语改写句子 REWRITING SENTENCES USING IDIOMS FROM THE CHAPTER

1. 天空中突然乌云密布，远处传来隆隆的雷声，接着就下起倾盆大雨来了。
2. 周教授的学问广博极了，你随便问他古代的或是现在的问题，他都能对答如流。
3. 许先生职务提升得很快，年纪轻轻就当上了局长。他说：“只要你努力工作，官帽子自己会来的。”
4. 如果你讲话多动动脑子，做事手脚勤快些，你就能少犯错误少后悔了。

七、选词 WORD CHOICE

1. 小明一个人在看电视，突然（情投意合、情不自禁、情景交融）地叫了起来，把我吓了一跳。
2. 上次你请我吃饭，这次该轮到我请你了，（礼仪之邦、礼贤下士、礼尚往来）嘛。
3. 那家餐馆的（信誉、信用、信息）好，所以生意兴隆，每天都是座无虚席。
4. 你有什么（疑问、疑心、疑虑）可以去办公室问老师，不要一个人坐着苦思冥想了。
5. 今年暑假我去我叔叔的（农村、农田、农场）帮他收玉米，我很喜欢乡下的生活。

八、文译白 TRANSLATION FROM CLASSICAL CHINESE INTO MODERN CHINESE

司马光背书①

司马温公②幼时，患记问③不若人。群居讲习，众兄弟既成诵，游息矣；独下帷绝编④，迨能倍诵⑤乃止。用力多者收功远，其所精诵，乃终身不忘也。温公尝言："书不可不成诵，或在马上，或中夜不寝时，咏其文，思其义，所得多矣。"

【注释】①选自《三朝名臣言行录》。②温公：司马光封温国公。③记问：记诵书本。④绝编：形容勤读。编是古时串连竹简的皮条或绳子。⑤倍诵：即背诵。

九、英译中 TRANSLATION FROM ENGLISH INTO CHINESE

1. The material covered in the civil service examinations (科举考试) was largely Confucian in nature. Therefore, as examinations became a determining factor in one's social status, the profound influence of Confucianism on the traditional Chinese cultural bedrock was far reaching.
2. Social mobility was the major impact of the imperial examinations. Even the lowest born could become a member of the ruling class by acquiring an education and passing the examinations.
3. To ensure that coveted government positions went to individuals with talent, poetry was included as a compulsory subject in the civil service examinations during the Tang dynasty.
4. Since all candidates practiced poetry composition as part of their preparation for the examinations, the Tang dynasty was known as the golden age of Chinese poetry.
5. The Qing dynasty, in the midst of modernization attempts, finally abolished the examination system in 1905.

十、作文 COMPOSITION

【题目】《求职记事》

【提示】讲讲你找工作的经历，成功的或失败的都可以。在求职时，你在学校里的成绩重要吗？用人单位注重哪些方面？毕业时具备什么条件才能找到理想的工作？孔子关于"禄在其中"的说法在今日美国有没有现实意义？

PART IV

Government 为政篇

16. Governing with Virtue 为政以德

《论语》选段 *Analects* Passages

16-1. 子曰："为政以德，譬如北辰，居其所而众星共之。" (2.1)

孔子说："以道德来治理政事，就会像北极星那样，安居在自己的位置上，而群星都环绕在它的周围。"

16-2. 子曰："无为而治者，其舜也与？夫何为哉？恭己正南面而已矣。" (15.5)

孔子说："能无为而治的，大概是舜吧？他做了些什么呢？只是恭敬、端正地朝南坐着而已。"

16-3. 子曰："道之以政，齐之以刑，民免而无耻；道之以德，齐之以礼，有耻且格。" (2.3)

孔子说："用法制引导百姓，用刑法约束他们，人民可免于犯罪受罚却失去了羞耻之心。用道德引导百姓，用礼教约束他们，人民不仅会有羞耻之心，而且也会端正自己的行为了。"

词汇一 VOCABULARY I

1.	为政	wéizhèng	治理国家
2.	譬如	pìrú	比如、好像
3.	共	gǒng	拱、 to encircle
4.	环绕	huánrào	to surround, to encircle, to revolve around
5.	无为而治	wúwéi érzhì	to achieve peace and order without action
6.	治	zhì	to govern, state of peace and order
7.	夫	fú	他
8.	南面	nánmiàn	面南, facing south
9.	道	dǎo	导、引导、 to guide, to lead
10.	刑	xíng	penalty, punishment
11.	免	miǎn	to be excused, exempted
12.	耻	chǐ	sense of shame
13.	格	gé	standard, norm
14.	法制	fǎzhì	legal system
15.	刑法	xíngfǎ	penal code, criminal law
16.	礼教	lǐjiào	ethical code
17.	约束	yuēshù	to restrain, to bind

虚词 FUNCTION WORDS

1. 而已 éryǐ (used to connote limited scope) (恭己正南面而已矣)

专名 PROPER NAMES

1. 北辰 Běichén 北极星, Polaris (North Star)
2. 舜 Shùn legendary ruler said to have ruled around 2200 BCE

解读 Exegeses

孔子主张“为政以德”，表明儒家治国的基本原则是德治，而非严刑峻法。春秋后期，各诸侯国之间战争不断，各国国内经常发生流血政变。为了维护自己的统治，许多国君依靠严酷的刑法作为统治手段，使百姓处于水深火热之中。为了纠正这种局面，孔子提出了“为政以德”的治国策略。

作为治国以德的方法，孔子提倡“无为而治”。他举出舜为例子，似乎君主只要朝南坐好，就天下太平了。有这么容易吗？从《论语》的其他章节中，我们能看到，孔子所说的“无为而治”至少有三层意思。一是君主要修己正身， 二是要启用贤才，三是不要用坏的政策来扰乱百姓。比如，《论语》中多次讲到舜用能臣治国：“舜有臣五人，而天下治”，“舜有天下，选于众，举皋陶，不仁者远矣”。可见，“无为而治”并非什么事都不做，而是一种高级的领导艺术，只是不做小事，不做坏事罢了。

词汇二 VOCABULARY II

1. 严刑峻法 yánxíng jùnfǎ severe punishment and draconian law
2. 政变 zhèngbiàn coup
3. 维护 wéihù to safeguard, to defend, to uphold
4. 严酷 yánkù harsh, bitter, grim
5. 纠正 jiūzhèng to correct, to rectify
6. 扰乱 rǎoluàn to harass, to disturb

专名 PROPER NAMES

1. 皋陶 Gāoyáo a minister of Shun

事例 An Illustrative Story

A PALACE WITHOUT A TERRACE 汉文帝休养生息

汉文帝在位的二十三年，是汉朝从国家初定走向繁荣昌盛的过渡时期。

他推行休养生息的政策。他把田赋减为三十税一，甚至十二年免收全国田赋，大大减轻了农民的负担。他还亲自耕作，做天下之表率，对当时农业生产的迅速恢复与发展，起了积极的推动作用。

他节俭朴素，严以律己。在位期间，宫室、苑圃、车骑、衣服等很少增添。有一次他想造一座供宴游用的露台，但看到工匠的预算，要用“百金”，就说道：“这等于十个中等人家的财产，我本来用先帝的宫殿就觉得很奢侈了，露台就不用建了。”

他反对厚葬。他的坟墓修在长安附近灞水的旁边，称做灞陵。修筑时顺着山陵形势挖掘洞穴，不再加高，陪葬品全用陶器，不准用金银等贵重金属。也可能正因为如此，没人盗墓，灞陵一直到现在都保存得很好。

词汇三 VOCABULARY III

1.	休养生息	xiūyǎng shēngxī	to recuperate and grow in population
2.	昌盛	chāngshèng	prosperous
3.	过渡	guòdù	transition
4.	田赋	tiánfù	taxes on agricultural lands
5.	税	shuì	tax
6.	严以律己	yányǐ lǜjǐ	to be strict with oneself, to exercise strict self-discipline
7.	律	lǜ	to restrain, to keep under control
8.	苑圃	yuànpǔ	gardens, parks
9.	露台	lùtái	balcony, deck
10.	预算	yùsuàn	budget
11.	先帝	xiāndì	deceased emperors
12.	奢侈	shēchǐ	luxurious, extravagant
13.	厚葬	hòuzàng	an elaborate funeral
14.	坟墓	fénmù	grave, tomb
15.	陵	líng	imperial tomb, mausoleum
16.	形势	xíngshì	terrain, topographical features
17.	挖掘	wājué	to dig, to excavate
18.	穴	xué	cave, hole
19.	陪葬	péizàng	to be buried with the deceased

20. 陶器 táoqì pottery, earthenware
21. 金属 jīnshǔ metal
22. 盗墓 dàomù to rob a grave

专名 PROPER NAMES

1. 汉文帝 Hàn Wéndì Emperor Wen of the Han (r. 180–157 BCE)
2. 长安 Cháng'ān Han dynasty capital, in present-day Xi'an 西安
3. 灞水 Bàshuǐ river flowing through the eastern part of Chang'an

成语 Idioms

1. 为政以德
   【课文】为政以德，譬如北辰，居其所而众星共之。
2. 无为而治
   【课文】无为而治者，其舜也与？
3. 严刑峻法
   【课文】儒家治国的基本原则是德治，而非严刑峻法。
4. 水深火热
   【课文】许多国君依靠严酷的刑法作为统治手段，使百姓处于水深火热之中。
5. 修己正身
   【课文】君主要修己正身。
6. 休养生息
   【课文】汉文帝休养生息
7. 繁荣昌盛
   【课文】汉文帝在位的二十三年，是汉朝从国家初定走向繁荣昌盛的过渡时期。
8. 节俭朴素
   【课文】他节俭朴素，严以律己。
9. 严以律己
   【课文】同上。

词汇扩展 Vocabulary Expansion

1. 为
   【课文】为政以德，譬如北辰，居其所而众星共之。
   【例词】为数不多、为期不远、为时过早、为时已晚、为所欲为、为富不仁、为非作歹、为数甚微、为人师表、好为人师、处世为人

2. 政
【课文】同上。
【例词】政治、政策、政党、政局、政权、政客、政变、行政、参政、财政
3. 以
【课文】同上。
【例词】以德报德、以牙还牙、以毒攻毒、以讹传讹、以攻为守、以寡敌众、以卵击石、以假乱真、以逸待劳、以貌取人
4. 德
【课文】同上。
【例词】德行、德政、德育、品德、道德、德才兼备、德高望重、以德报怨、感恩戴德、功德无量
5. 无
【课文】无为而治者，其舜也与？
【例词】无法无天、无边无际、无穷无尽、无依无靠、无忧无虑、无影无踪、无缘无故、无怨无仇、无时无刻、无声无息
6. 治
【课文】同上。
【例词】治理、治国、治安、治疗、治学、政治、统治、自治、治病救人、分而治之
7. 面
【课文】恭己正南面而已矣。
【例词】面不改色、面无惧色、面无人色、面有菜色、面有得色、面有难色、面有喜色、面红耳赤、面目全非、面目一新

练习 Exercises

一、选择题 MULTIPLE CHOICE

1. ________ 治国的基本原则是德治。
   a. 道家　　b. 儒家
   c. 法家　　d. 佛家
2. 许多国君依靠严酷的刑法作为统治 ________。
   a. 方法　　b. 手法
   c. 方针　　d. 手段
3. 孔子提出“为政以德”的治国 ________。
   a. 策略　　b. 政策
   c. 战略　　d. 计策

4. “无为而治”是一种高级的领导 ________。
   a. 技术　　b. 战术
   c. 艺术　　d. 手术

二、改错 CORRECTING MISTAKES

1. 孔子提倡“无为而治”，举出尧为例子。
2. “无为而治”就是什么事都不做。
3. 汉文帝在位的二十三年，是汉朝繁荣昌盛的时期。
4. 汉文帝的墓中的陪葬品全用金银等贵重金属。

三、问答题 ANSWERING QUESTIONS

1. 为什么各国百姓在春秋后期处于水深火热之中？
2. 古代君主是朝哪个方向坐的？
3. 汉文帝是怎样做天下之表率的？
4. 汉文帝是怎样节俭朴素，严以律己的？
5. 为什么汉文帝停止建造供宴游用的露台？

四、讨论题 QUESTIONS FOR DISCUSSION

1. “无为而治”至少有哪三层意思？
2. 汉文帝是怎样推行休养生息政策的？

五、故事复述 RETELLING THE STORY

《汉文帝休养生息》

六、用本课的成语改写句子 REWRITING SENTENCES USING IDIOMS FROM THE CHAPTER

1. 这位亿万富翁还经常去麦当劳吃汉堡包，他对生活一点都不讲究，从不浪费钱。
2. 你这个做爸爸的，一回来就坐在电视机前看球赛，自己要求不严，还想让儿子好好做功课？
3. 这个国家已经打了好几年的仗了，到处断电缺水，老百姓过着痛苦的生活。
4. 我好多年没回我的家乡小镇了，这次回去一看真是大变样了。街道上高楼林立，商店里东西琳琅满目，一派繁华的景象。

七、选词 WORD CHOICE

1. 今年的毕业典礼，学校请来了一位（德才兼备、德高望重、功德无量）的著名教授来为学生做演讲。
2. 老周特别能喝酒，不管喝多少都（面无惧色、面无人色、面不改色），人们都称他为“大酒缸”。

3. 小城市的（治安、治理、统治）比大城市好多了，我的车从来不上锁的。
4. 这幅模仿齐白石的画真是像极了，把它拿到市场上去卖的话，还真能（以寡敌众、以假乱真、以貌取人）呢。
5. 我家的后院里有一个鹿妈妈和她的几个孩子在悠闲地吃着草，听到我开门的声音，一下子就跑得（无声无息、无穷无尽、无影无踪）了。

八、中译英 TRANSLATION FROM CHINESE INTO ENGLISH

缇萦救父①

汉文帝的时候，有个小姑娘名叫缇萦。她的父亲是个县官。有一次，他被人告了，被判处肉刑，②要把他押解到长安去受刑。

缇萦的父亲有五个女儿，但没有儿子。他被押解离家的时候，说："唉，可惜我没有男孩，遇到急难，一个有用的也没有。" 最小的女儿缇萦非常悲伤，就陪父亲一起去长安。

缇萦到了长安，就写了一封奏章给汉文帝。 那奏章上写道："我父亲做官的时候，当地的人都说他是个清官。这回儿他犯了罪，被判处肉刑。死者不可再生，伤者无法康复。以后就是想改过自新，也没有办法了。我情愿给官府当奴婢，替父亲赎罪，好让他有个改过自新的机会。"

汉文帝看了信，十分同情这个小姑娘，又觉得她说的有道理，就下诏书说："现在有三种肉刑而罪犯仍不断，是什么问题呢？是不是我的德教做得不够呢？我很惭愧。现在有人犯了错误，不加教育就上刑，使人无法改过自新，我很可怜他们。脸上刺字或砍断手脚，使人终身痛苦，是多么不道德！这样做，怎么能称得上为民父母呢！从今以后，废除肉刑。"

【注释】①根据《史记·孝文本纪》改写。②当时的肉刑有脸上刺字、割去鼻子，及砍去左足或右足等三种。

九、英译中 TRANSLATION FROM ENGLISH INTO CHINESE

1. Confucius's political philosophy is rooted in the belief that a ruler should learn self-discipline, govern by example, and treat subjects with love and concern.
2. For Confucius, what characterized superior leadership was the possession of virtue. Conceived of as a kind of moral power that allows one to gain a following without resorting to physical force, virtue also enables a ruler to maintain good order in his state without troubling himself.
3. The Confucian ideal of "government through virtue" was strongly criticized by another school of thought: Legalism 法家. According to the Legalists, an ethical code will not make a state strong. A system of harsh punishments and rewards, regulated through laws and enforced without exception, should guarantee good behavior within the state.

十、辩论 DEBATING

【题目】《以德治国还是以法治国?》

【提示】儒家主张以德治国，认为“德”是治理国家、取得民心的主要方法，德也是区分“仁君”与“暴君”的标准，是执政、司法的指导方针。法家主张用刑法来约束百姓的行为，惩罚违法之人。儒家要人为善，法家要人不作恶。你觉得哪种治国的方法更好、更有效?

17. Sovereigns and Subjects 君君臣臣

《论语》选段 *Analects* Passages

17-1. 齐景公问政於孔子。孔子对曰："君君，臣臣，父父，子子。"公曰："善哉！信如君不君，臣不臣，父不父，子不子，虽有粟，吾得而食诸？" (12.11)

齐景公问孔子如何治理国家。孔子说："君主要像个君主，臣子要像个臣子，父亲要像个父亲，儿子要像个儿子。"齐景公说："讲得好呀！如果君不像君，臣不像臣，父不像父，子不像子，虽然有粮食，我能吃得上吗？"

17-2. 定公问："君使臣，臣事君，如之何？"孔子曰："君使臣以礼，臣事君以忠。" (3.19)

鲁定公问："君主使用臣子，臣子为君主服务，应该怎么样呢？"孔子回答说："君主应该按照礼的要求来使用臣子，臣子应该忠心地为君主服务。"

17-3. 子曰："道千乘之国：敬事而信，节用而爱人，使民以时。" (1.5)

孔子说："治理一个拥有一千辆兵车的国家，办事要认真而又守信用，节约开支而又爱护人民，役使百姓要不违农时。"

词汇一 VOCABULARY I

1.	粟	sù	millet, also a general term for grain
2.	事	shì	to serve, to attend
3.	乘	shèng	a carriage pulled by four horses
4.	敬事	jìngshì	敬业, to respect work
5.	节	jié	to economize, to save
6.	用	yòng	consumption, spending
7.	时	shí	农时; the proper season for planting, harvesting, etc.
8.	开支	kāizhī	expenses, spending
9.	役使	yìshǐ	to employ as a servant, to make someone work
10.	役	yì	labor, service
11.	违	wéi	to disobey, to violate

虚词 FUNCTION WORDS

1. 信如 xìnrú 假如(信如君不君，臣不臣，父不父，子不子，虽有粟，吾得而食诸)
2. 得而 dé'ér 能够(同上)
3. 诸 zhū 之乎(同上)
4. 如之何 rúzhīhé 怎样才好(君使臣，臣事君，如之何)

专名 PROPER NAMES

1. 齐景公 Qí Jǐnggōng 齐国国君 (r. 547–490 BCE)
2. 定公 Dìnggōng Duke Ding of Lu 鲁 (r. 509–495)

解读 Exegeses

孔子在第一段中讲的"君君臣臣"就是要把名分弄清楚。春秋时代，是历史学家所称的乱世。据司马迁统计，在那个时代，"弑君三十六，亡国五十二。"至于国君被臣子赶下台、赶出国的更是不计其数。孔子到齐国时，齐国的大权落在姓陈的家族手中。所以当齐景公问政於孔子时，孔子对症下药，提出了"君君臣臣"的办法。景公听了虽加赞美，可惜他不能实行，以致在他死后乱了几代，终使齐国由吕姓改变为陈姓。

名分是儒家伦理的基础。一个人有什么样的名，就要尽什么样的分。君主对臣下要待之以礼，臣下对君主要忠心耿耿。这是儒家对于君臣关系的基本要求。

词汇二 VOCABULARY II

1. 名分 míngfèn a person's title/position and duty
2. 弑 shì regicide or patricide
3. 下台 xiàtái to fall out of power, to leave office
4. 家族 jiāzú clan, family
5. 症 zhèng disease, symptoms of a disease
6. 以致 yǐzhì consequently, as a result

事例 An Illustrative Story

THREE VISITS TO A STRATEGIST 刘备三请诸葛亮

汉朝末年，天下大乱，刘备、曹操和孙权成了三股最强大的势力。刘备听人介绍说，隐居在山中的诸葛亮是个天才的军事家，就决定请他出山相助。

一天，刘备和他的两个结义兄弟关羽、张飞带着礼物去诸葛亮的家中拜访。不巧诸葛亮这天出去了，刘备只得失望地回去。

不久，刘备等三人顶风冒雪第二次去请。不料诸葛亮又出外闲游去了。张飞本不愿意再来，见诸葛亮不在家，就催着要回去。刘备只得留下一封信，表达自己对诸葛亮的敬佩和请他出来帮助自己、挽救国家危险局面的意思。

又过了几天，刘备准备再去请诸葛亮。关羽说诸葛亮也许并没有真才实学，不用去了。张飞却主张由他一个人去，如请不来，就用绳子把他捆来。刘备把张飞责备了一顿，又和他俩第三次登门拜访诸葛亮。他们到的时候，诸葛亮正在睡午觉。刘备不敢惊动他，一直站到诸葛亮醒来，才一起坐下谈话。

诸葛亮为刘备的诚心所感动，就出来全力帮助刘备打天下。刘备死后，诸葛亮继续忠心地辅佐他的儿子，直至自己病逝。

词汇三 VOCABULARY III

1.	股	gǔ	(measure word) group, cluster, faction
2.	势力	shìlì	force, power
3.	结义	jiéyì	to become sworn brothers
4.	不巧	bùqiǎo	unluckily, unfortunately
5.	顶	dǐng	to go against
6.	不料	bùliào	unexpectedly, to one's surprise
7.	闲游	xiányóu	to take a stroll, to go on an outing
8.	催	cuī	to hurry, to urge
9.	敬佩	jìngpèi	to esteem, to admire
10.	挽救	wǎnjiù	to save, to remedy
11.	捆	kǔn	to tie, to bundle
12.	打天下	dǎ tiānxià	to struggle to seize state power, to establish an enterprise
13.	病逝	bìngshì	to die of illness

专名 PROPER NAMES

1.	刘备	Liú Bèi	king of Shu 蜀 (161–223)
2.	关羽	Guān Yǔ	a general of Shu (d. 220)
3.	张飞	Zhāng Fēi	a general of Shu (d. 221)

成语 Idioms

1. 君君臣臣
   【课文】君君，臣臣，父父，子子。
2. 使臣以礼
   【课文】君使臣以礼，臣事君以忠。
3. 事君以忠
   【课文】同上。
4. 敬事而信
   【课文】道千乘之国：敬事而信，节用而爱人，使民以时。
5. 节用爱人
   【课文】同上。
6. 使民以时
   【课文】同上。
7. 对症下药
   【课文】孔子对症下药，提出了"君君臣臣"的办法。
8. 待之以礼
   【课文】君主对臣下要待之以礼，臣下对君主要忠心耿耿。
9. 忠心耿耿
   【课文】同上。
10. 天下大乱
    【课文】汉朝末年，天下大乱。
11. 顶风冒雪
    【课文】不久，刘备等三人顶风冒雪第二次去请。
12. 真才实学
    【课文】关羽说诸葛亮也许并没有真才实学，不用去了。

词汇扩展 Vocabulary Expansion

1. 君
【课文】君君，臣臣，父父，子子。
【例词】国君、暴君、昏君、夫君、郎君、君圣臣贤、君辱臣死、君子固穷、君子之交、正人君子
2. 臣
【课文】同上。
【例词】臣子、臣下、臣民、臣服、君臣、大臣、功臣、忠臣、奸臣、权臣
3. 父
【课文】同上。
【例词】祖父、伯父、继父、养父、岳父、慈父、国父、父老兄弟、父慈子孝、严父慈母
4. 子
【课文】同上。
【例词】长子、独生子、私生子、子弟兵、浪子回头、子孙满堂、子孙万代、子子孙孙、子承父业、妻离子散
5. 使
【课文】君使臣，臣事君，如之何？
【例词】使用、使唤、使劲、使馆、使命、使女、天使、大使、假使、即使
6. 千
【课文】道千乘之国：敬事而信，节用而爱人，使民以时。
【例词】千山万水、千变万化、千言万语、千秋万代、千军万马、千恩万谢、千辛万苦、千差万别、千头万绪、千叮万嘱
7. 爱
【课文】同上。
【例词】博爱、宠爱、恋爱、疼爱、爱财如命、爱才如命、爱憎分明、爱莫能助、爱不释手、恩爱夫妻

练习 Exercises

一、选择题 MULTIPLE CHOICE

1. 当齐景公问政於孔子时，孔子 ________，提出了“君君臣臣”的办法。
   a. 对号入座　　b. 对症下药
   c. 对牛弹琴　　d. 对答如流

2. 汉朝末年，刘备、曹操和孙权成了三股最强大的 ________。
   a. 势力　　b. 权力
   c. 能力　　d. 动力
3. 诸葛亮正在睡午觉。刘备不敢 ________ 他。
   a. 惊奇　　b. 惊吓
   c. 惊喜　　d. 惊动
4. 诸葛亮为刘备的诚心所 ________。
   a. 感化　　b. 感动
   c. 感谢　　d. 感恩

二、改错 CORRECTING MISTAKES

1. 孔子到齐国时，齐国的大权落在姓吕的家族手中。
2. 刘备一请诸葛亮的时候，诸葛亮正在睡午觉。
3. 刘备二请诸葛亮的那天，天气很好，所以诸葛亮出去闲游了。
4. 刘备三请诸葛亮的时候，张飞用绳子把诸葛亮捆来了。

三、问答题 ANSWERING QUESTIONS

1. 孔子说如何才能治理好国家？
2. 孔子说君主应该如何对待臣子，臣子应该如何对待君主？
3. 孔子说役使百姓要注意什么？
4. 在春秋时代，有多少君主给杀了？有多少国家被灭了？
5. 刘备的两个结义兄弟叫什么名字？

四、讨论题 QUESTIONS FOR DISCUSSION

1. 孔子为什么要提出“君君臣臣”的原则？

五、故事复述 RETELLING THE STORY

《刘备三请诸葛亮》

六、用本课的成语改写句子 REWRITING SENTENCES USING IDIOMS FROM THE CHAPTER

1. 你别看老王平时沉默寡言，肚子里的学问可多着呢，我们叫他“活字典”。
2. 我们的城市冬天天气常常很糟糕，常常刮大风下大雪，可是无论多大的风雪大家还得去上班。
3. 小华，你怎么能对客人这么没有礼貌呢？就是你不喜欢他，你也要对他有礼貌啊。
4. 中国历史上每个朝代的末年都有很多战争，最后一个强者统一中国，建立一个新的朝代。

七、选词 WORD CHOICE

1. 秦始皇焚书坑儒，是中国历史上有名的（国君、暴君、昏君）。
2. 孙先生和他的太太二十年前开了一个小店，经历了（千变万化、千秋万代、千辛万苦），现在已经是一家大公司的老板了。
3. 哥哥给妹妹买了一个高级照相机作为她的生日礼物，妹妹看了高兴得（爱不释手、爱莫能助、爱财如命），到哪儿都带在身边，看到什么都要照一下。
4. 这个电脑已经用了五年了，（使劲、使唤、使用）的时候有很多问题，得买个新的了。
5. 过年的时候，顾老先生的七个子女都带了他们的孩子来看他。顾老先生看着（子孙满堂、子孙万代、子承父业）的样子，开心得合不拢嘴。

八、文译白 TRANSLATION FROM CLASSICAL CHINESE INTO MODERN CHINESE

诸葛亮《出师表》①节选

臣本布衣，躬耕于南阳，苟全性命于乱世，不求闻达于诸侯。先帝不以臣卑鄙，猥自枉屈，三顾臣于草庐之中，咨臣以当世之事，由是感激，遂许先帝以驱驰。后值倾覆，受任于败军之际，奉命于危难之间，尔来二十有一年矣。

先帝知臣谨慎，故临崩寄臣以大事也。受命以来，夙夜忧叹，恐托付不效，以伤先帝之明。故五月渡泸②，深入不毛③。今南方已定，兵甲已足，当奖率三军，北定中原④，庶竭驽钝，攘除奸凶，兴复汉室，还于旧都。此臣所以报先帝而忠陛下之职分也。

【注释】①《出师表》：诸葛亮写于227年出师攻打魏国之前。②泸：泸水，即金沙江。③不毛：不长草木，此处指不毛之地，即荒蛮的地方。④中原：指当时魏国所在的地方。

九、英译中 TRANSLATION FROM ENGLISH INTO CHINESE

1. Often depicted wearing a robe and holding a fan made of crane feathers, Zhuge Liang is recognized as one of the greatest and most accomplished strategists in Chinese history.
2. The wisdom and achievements of Zhuge Liang were popularized by *Romance of the Three Kingdoms,* written more than a millennium after the end of the Three Kingdoms era.
3. Zhuge Liang's "On Dispatching the Troops" 出师表, written before his first Northern Expedition, was considered so moving it was said that if one read it and shed no tears, the reader was a disloyal person.

十、讲故事 STORYTELLING (根据下面的提示在网上找资料)

【题目】诸葛亮的故事

【提示】诸葛亮有很多有名的故事，比如“草船借箭”、“借东风”、“空城计”、“七擒孟获”等，选讲一个。

18. Exemplary Leaders 身正令行

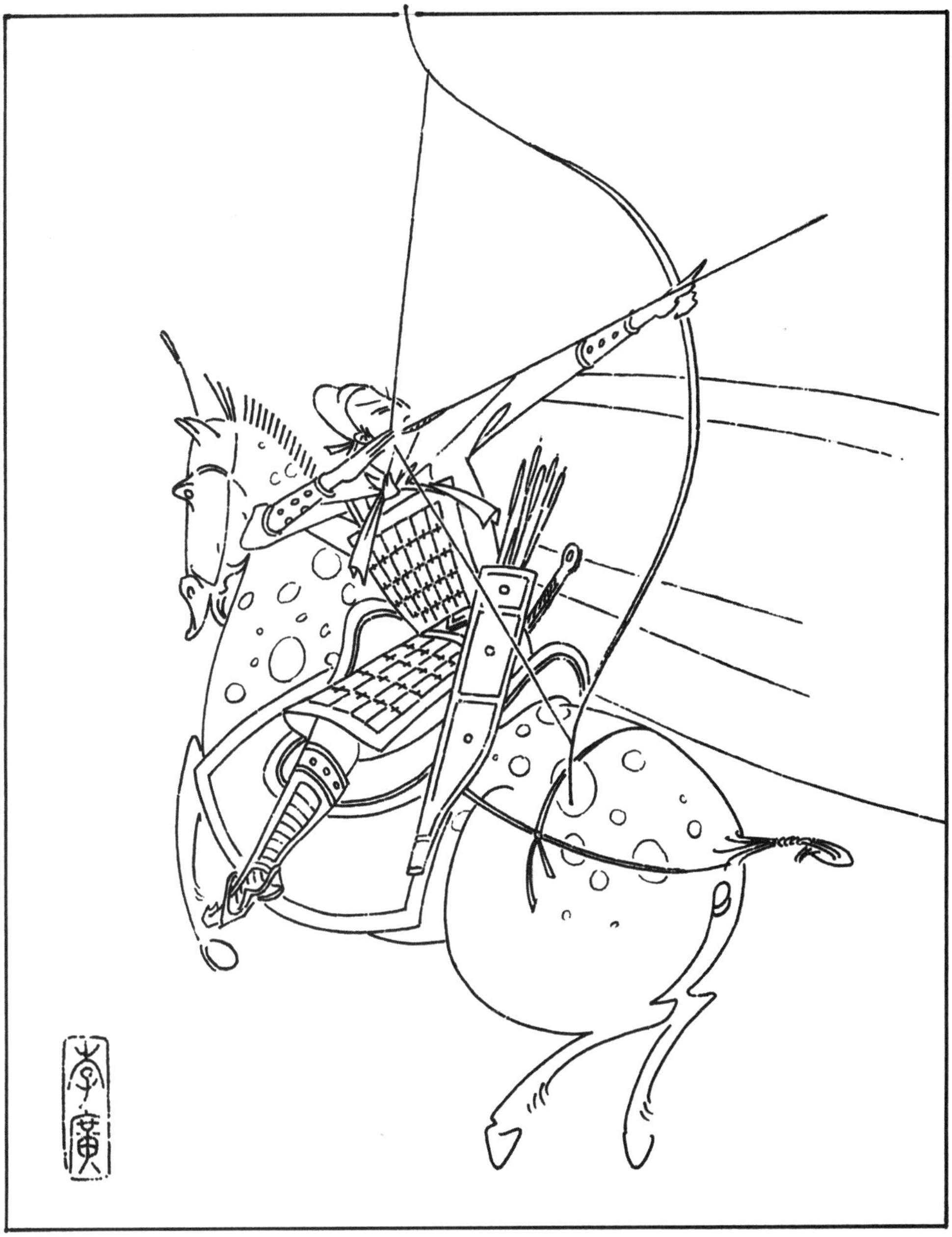

《论语》选段 *Analects* Passages

18-1. 季康子问政于孔子。孔子对曰："政者正也。子帅以正，孰敢不正？"(12.17)

季康子问孔子如何治理国家。孔子回答说："政就是正的意思。您本人带头做事正派，谁敢不正派呢？"

18-2. 子曰："其身正，不令而行；其身不正，虽令不从。"(13.6)

孔子说："自身正了，即使不发布命令，老百姓也会去做。自身不正，即使发布命令，老百姓也不会服从。"

18-3. 子曰："苟正其身矣，于从政何有乎？不能正其身，如正人乎？"(13.13)

孔子说："如果端正了自身的行为，管理政事还有什么困难呢？如果不能端正自身的行为，怎能使别人端正呢？"

18-4. 季康子患盗，问于孔子。孔子对曰："苟子之不欲，虽赏之不窃。"(12.18)

季康子担忧盗窃，就向孔子请教。孔子回答说："假如你自己没有贪欲，即使悬赏，也没有人会偷盗。"

18-5. 子路问政。子曰："先之，劳之。"请益。曰："无倦。"(13.1)

子路问怎样治理政事。孔子说："做在老百姓之前，并使老百姓勤劳地工作。"子路请求多讲一点。孔子说："不要懈怠。"

词汇一 VOCABULARY I

1.	令	lìng	command, order
2.	帅	shuài	to lead, to command
3.	正派	zhèngpài	upright, honest, decent
4.	发布	fābù	to issue, to release
5.	盗	dào	thief, robber
6.	赏	shǎng	to grant a reward, to award
7.	窃	qiè	to steal
8.	担忧	dānyōu	to worry, to be anxious
9.	即使	jíshǐ	even, even if, even though
10.	悬赏	xuánshǎng	to offer (or post) a reward (for the capture of a criminal, etc.)

11. 先 xiān to lead, to go ahead of
12. 劳 láo to labor, to make people work hard
13. 益 yì to add, to increase
14. 懈怠 xièdài slack, sluggish

虚词 FUNCTION WORDS

1. 虽 suī 虽然（其身不正，虽令不从）
2. 苟 gǒu 假如（苟正其身矣，于从政何有乎）
3. 乎 hū 呢（苟正其身矣，于从政何有乎）
4. 如 rú 如何，怎样（不能正其身，如正人乎）

专名 PROPER NAMES

1. 季康子 Jì Kāngzi a powerful minister of Lu

解读 Exegeses

无论为人还是为官，首先在一个“正”字。这个“正”字的内容非常丰富：思想要纯正，品行要端正，办事要公正。孔子十分重视为官者的个人修养，正人先正己。只要身居要职的人能够正己，那么手下的各级官员和平民百姓就都会归于正道。

孔子说：“其身正，不令而行。”俗话说： “上梁不正下梁歪”。讲的角度不同，道理是一个：领导人的德行、好恶会为下面的人仿效，会形成社会风气。所以古人说：“吴王好剑客，百姓多创瘢；楚王好细腰，宫中多饿死。”

唐太宗能把国家治理好，就因为他懂得上行下效这个道理。他曾说过：“流水是清是浊，取决于它的源头。君王就像那源头，臣民就像是流水。做君王的自己行诈，却指望臣民们正道直行，就好比是源头污浊，却指望流水清澈，没有这个道理。”

词汇二 VOCABULARY II

1. 纯 chún pure
2. 品行 pǐnxíng conduct, behavior
3. 端正 duānzhèng upright, proper, correct
4. 要职 yàozhí important post
5. 仿效 fǎngxiào to imitate, to follow the example of
6. 剑客 jiànkè swordsman
7. 创瘢 chuāngbān scar
8. 细 xì thin, slender

9. 腰 yāo waist
10. 效 xiào 仿效, to imitate, to follow the example of
11. 浊 zhuó turbid, muddy
12. 源头 yuántóu fountainhead, source
13. 诈 zhà to cheat, to swindle
14. 污 wū dirty, filthy
15. 指望 zhǐwàng 希望
16. 清澈 qīngchè limpid, clear

专名 PROPER NAMES

1. 楚 Chǔ State of Chu

事例 An Illustrative Story

THE FLYING GENERAL 李广身先士卒

李广，西汉名将。当时汉朝经常跟匈奴作战。李广英勇善战，屡建奇功，人称“飞将军”。

公元前一二一年夏季，汉朝又跟匈奴发生了大战。李广率领四千精锐先行，不料被四万匈奴骑兵团团包围。强敌当前，将士们都心惊胆战。李广想，应该趁敌人阵脚未稳，派人冲击，打他个措手不及。让谁去完成这个危险的任务呢？他让自己的儿子李敢率队去冲锋陷阵。

李敢带着一队骑兵直插敌阵，突入重围，又杀回自己的阵地。一归队，李敢就大声说：“匈奴骑兵没什么可怕的！”汉军听了士气大振。

激战了一天，李广始终身先士卒，英勇杀敌。他爱兵如子，等到士兵们个个有水喝，人人吃饱饭，自己才喝水吃饭。因此士兵都决心死战。

第二天，正在危急关头，汉朝大军赶到。匈奴见大势已去，匆忙撤退。

司马迁在《史记·李广传》中引用孔子的话评论说：“‘其身正，不令而行；其身不正，虽令不从’。其李将军之谓也！”

词汇三 VOCABULARY III

1. 身先士卒 shēnxiān shìzú to lead one’s men in a charge
2. 士卒 shìzú 士兵
3. 善 shàn to be good at, to be an expert
4. 屡 lǚ repeatedly, time and again
5. 精锐 jīngruì elite troops
6. 团团 tuántuán all around
7. 心惊胆战 xīnjīng dǎnzhàn to tremble with fear

8.	战	zhàn	to tremble, to shiver
9.	趁	chèn	to take advantage of, to avail oneself of
10.	阵脚	zhènjiǎo	military position, battle formation
11.	冲击	chōngjī	to charge, to assault
12.	措手不及	cuòshǒu bùjí	to be caught unprepared
13.	冲锋陷阵	chōngfēng xiànzhèn	to charge the enemy lines
14.	冲锋	chōngfēng	to charge, to assault
15.	陷	xiàn	to crush (the enemy), to capture (a city, etc.)
16.	插	chā	to stick into, to insert
17.	突	tū	to dash forward, to charge
18.	重围	chóngwéi	tight encirclement
19.	归队	guīduì	to rejoin one's unit
20.	士气	shìqì	morale
21.	振	zhèn	to rouse to action, to raise, to boost
22.	激战	jīzhàn	fierce fighting
23.	死战	sǐzhàn	to fight to the death
24.	大势已去	dàshì yǐqù	the situation is beyond salvation, irretrievable, hopeless
25.	匆忙	cōngmáng	急忙
26.	撤退	chètuì	to withdraw, to retreat

专名 PROPER NAMES

1.	李广	Lǐ Guǎng	a Han general (d. 119 BCE)
2.	李敢	Lǐ Gǎn	Li Guang's third son, also a valiant general (d. 119 BCE)

成语 Idioms

1. 身正令行
   【课文】其身正，不令而行。
2. 先之劳之
   【课文】子路问政。子曰："先之，劳之。"
3. 品行端正
   【课文】思想要纯正，品行要端正，办事要公正。
4. 身居要职
   【课文】只要身居要职的人能够正己，那么手下的各级官员和平民百姓就都会归于正道。

5. 上行下效
【课文】唐太宗能把国家治理好，就因为他懂得上行下效这个道理。
6. 身先士卒
【课文】李广身先士卒。
7. 英勇善战
【课文】李广英勇善战，屡建奇功，人称“飞将军”。
8. 屡建奇功
【课文】同上。
9. 团团包围
【课文】李广率领四千精锐先行，不料被四万匈奴骑兵团团包围。
10. 心惊胆战
【课文】强敌当前，将士们都心惊胆战。
11. 措手不及
【课文】应该趁敌人阵脚未稳，派人冲击，打他个措手不及。
12. 冲锋陷阵
【课文】他让自己的儿子李敢率队去冲锋陷阵。
13. 士气大振
【课文】汉军听了士气大振。
14. 爱兵如子
【课文】他爱兵如子，等到士兵们个个有水喝，人人吃饱饭，自己才喝水吃饭。
15. 大势已去
【课文】匈奴见大势已去，匆忙撤退。

词汇扩展 Vocabulary Expansion

1. 问
【课文】季康子问政于孔子。
【例词】问候、问世、学问、提问、反问、顾问、审问、问长问短、问寒问暖、问心无愧
2. 正
【课文】政者正也。子帅以正，孰敢不正？
【例词】正面、正直、正派、正确、正宗、正大光明、正人君子、一本正经、正中下怀、正中要害
3. 身
【课文】其身正，不令而行。
【例词】身强力壮、身经百战、身先士卒、身居要职、身不由己、身败名裂、身无分文、身外之物、心身疲劳、言传身教

4. 患

【课文】季康子患盗，问于孔子。

【例词】忧患、后患、隐患、外患、患病、患得患失、患难之交、患难与共、有备无患、防患未然

5. 赏

【课文】苟子之不欲，虽赏之不窃。

【例词】赏花、赏月、赏识、赏赐、赏析、欣赏、鉴赏、奖赏、赏罚分明、赏心悦目

6. 先

【课文】先之，劳之。

【例词】先礼后兵、先斩后奏、先来后到、先苦后甜、先人后己、先见之明、先睹为快、先入为主、先知先觉、先声夺人

7. 劳

【课文】同上。

【例词】劳动、劳作、劳役、劳碌、劳累、劳苦功高、劳民伤财、劳逸结合、劳心劳力、劳而无功

练习 Exercises

一、选择题 MULTIPLE CHOICE

1. 假如你自己没有贪欲， ________ 悬赏，也没有人会偷盗。
   - a. 如果　　c. 即使
   - b. 要是　　d. 假使
2. 无论为人还是为官，办事要 ________。
   - a. 端正　　c. 纯正
   - b. 公正　　d. 方正
3. 领导人的德行、好恶会为下面的人仿效，会形成社会 ________。
   - a. 风貌　　c. 风格
   - b. 风景　　d. 风气
4. 这好比是源头污浊，却指望流水 ________，没有这个道理。
   - a. 清净　　b. 清澈
   - c. 清白　　d. 清纯
5. 强敌当前，将士们都 ________。
   - a. 心慌意乱　　c. 心惊胆战
   - b. 心领神会　　d. 心平气和

二、改错 CORRECTING MISTAKES

1. 自身不正，但发布了命令，老百姓还是会服从的。
2. 即使端正了自身的行为，管理政事还是有困难的。
3. 就是你自己没有贪欲，也还是有人会偷盗的。
4. 只要身居要职的人能够正人，那么手下的各级官员就都会归于正道。
5. 公元一二一年夏季，唐朝又跟匈奴发生了大战。
6. 李广率领四千精锐先行，不料被四万匈奴步兵团团包围。
7. 李广爱兵如子，跟士兵一起喝水吃饭。
8. 匈奴被李广打败，匆忙撤退。

三、问答题 ANSWERING QUESTIONS

1. 无论为人还是为官，首先要注意一个什么字？
2. 这个“正”字包含哪些内容？
3. 怎样才能使各级官员和平民百姓都会归于正道？
4. 古人说的“楚王好细腰，宫中多饿死”是什么意思？
5. 唐太宗用了什么作比喻来说明君主要正己的道理的？
6. 李广有个什么外号？
7. 李广的军队被多少匈奴骑兵包围了？
8. 李广派谁去冲击敌人的阵地？
9. 李广是怎样爱兵如子的？
10. 司马迁是怎样评论李广的？

四、讨论题 QUESTIONS FOR DISCUSSION

1. “上行下效”这句成语一般是用在消极意义上的，就是说上面的人做了不好的事，下面的人会学样。请结合现实社会中的事例加以讨论。
2. 李广以英勇善战和箭法闻名，可是司马迁却把李广作为身正令行的典型。请以本课的小故事中的事例来说明司马迁的论点。

五、故事复述 RETELLING THE STORY

《李广身先士卒》

六、用本课的成语改写句子 REWRITING SENTENCES USING IDIOMS FROM THE CHAPTER

1. 王先生是公司的总裁，虽然地位很高，每天都非常忙，但他总在百忙中找出时间跟自己的孩子玩。
2. 昨天那场拳击赛真是太残酷了，双方都打得头破血流，看得我害怕极了。
3. “什么？你下个月就要结婚？”姐姐突如其来的通知让爸妈觉得根本来不及准备。

4. 开车时弟弟把一张糖纸往窗外一扔，爸爸很生气。妈妈说："你上次不是把一个烟头扔到窗外了吗？小孩儿学大人的样么。"

七、选词 WORD CHOICE

1. 虽然你觉得自己年轻力壮，不会生病，但我还是要劝你买健康保险，总得(防患未然、有备无患、患难与共）吧。
2. "这个周末我们一起去看一个新电影，怎么样？""对不起，老李，我是一个(身无分文、身不由己、身居要职）的人，凡事都得请示一下我的老婆。"
3. 这次我能考上好大学，最(劳而无功、劳民伤财、劳苦功高）的是我的妈妈。没有她的精心照顾，我怎么考得好呢？
4. 拳击比赛开始前，双方先伸出带着手套的手碰一下，互相致意，这叫(先礼后兵，先苦后甜，先斩后奏）。
5. 这首李白诗的(赏识、赏析、赏赐）我不太懂，你帮我解释一下，好吗？

八、文译白 TRANSLATION FROM CLASSICAL CHINESE INTO MODERN CHINESE (以身作则小故事两则)

1. 曾子杀猪①

曾子之妻之市，其子随之而泣。其母曰："女还，顾反②为女杀彘③。"妻适市来，曾子欲捕彘杀之。妻止之曰："特与婴儿戏耳。"曾子曰："婴儿非与戏也。婴儿非有知也，待父母而学者也，听父母之教。今子欺之，是教子欺也。母欺子，子而不信其母，非所以成教也。"遂烹彘也。

【注释】①选自《韩非子》。②顾反：回来。③彘zhì：猪。

2. 曹操割发①

太祖②尝出军，行经麦中，令"卒士无败麦，犯者死"。骑士皆下马，扶麦以相持。于是太祖马腾入麦中。敕主簿③请罪。主簿对以《春秋》之义，罚不加于尊。太祖曰："制法而自犯之，何以帅下？然孤④为军帅，不可自杀，请自刑。"因援剑，割发以置地。

【注释】①选自《三国志》。②太祖：三国时魏太祖曹操 (155–220)。③主簿：官名。④孤：君主自称。

九、英译中 TRANSLATION FROM ENGLISH INTO CHINESE (李广故事两则)

1. A Tiger-Stone

   Li Guang was famous for his strength and archery skills. Legend has it that one evening Li Guang was out on patrol. Out of the corner of his eye he saw movement in the tall grass and a tiger-like form. Li Guang drew his bow and fired an arrow with all his might. All was quiet. In the morning, Li Guang and his troops returned to investigate. In the tall grass they found his arrow lodged deep inside a large rock!

2. A Great Escape

   The Xiongnu admired Li Guang so much that there was a standing order in battle that he was to be taken alive. Once, badly outnumbered, Li Guang was wounded and captured. His captors placed him in a hammock between two horses. Li Guang faked unconsciousness to lower his captors' suspicions and bide his time. After traveling a distance, an opportunity presented itself when a rider on a fast horse came by. Li Guang leaped onto the horse, pushed the rider off, and took his bow. He headed back and rejoined the Han forces. Along the way he killed a number of his pursuers with the stolen bow and arrows.

十、讲故事 STORYTELLING (根据下面的提示在网上找资料)

【题目】清官名将的故事。

【提示】中国历史上有很多身正令行的清官，也有很多身先士卒的名将。请讲一个清官或者名将的故事。下面这些名字供你参考。清官：西门豹、狄仁杰、包拯、况钟、海瑞、于成龙、林则徐。名将：李牧、霍去病、薛仁贵、狄青、岳飞、常遇春、戚继光。

19. The Upright above the Crooked
举直错枉

《论语》选段 *Analects* Passages

19-1. 哀公问曰："何为则民服？"孔子对曰："举直错诸枉，则民服；举枉错诸直，则民不服。"(2.19)

鲁哀公问："怎样才能使百姓服从呢？"孔子回答说："选拔正直的人，放在邪恶的人之上，百姓就服从了；选拔邪恶的人，放在正直的人之上，百姓就不服从了。"

19-2. 樊迟问仁。子曰："爱人。"问知。子曰："知人。"樊迟未达。子曰："举直错诸枉，能使枉者直。"樊迟退，见子夏曰："乡也，吾见于夫子而问知；子曰：'举直错诸枉，能使枉者直。'何谓也？"子夏曰："富哉言乎！舜有天下，选于众，举皋陶，不仁者远矣；汤有天下，选于众，举伊尹，不仁者远矣。"(12.22)

樊迟问什么是仁。孔子说："爱人。"樊迟问什么是智，孔子说："了解人。"樊迟还不明白。孔子说："选拔正直的人，放在邪恶的人之上，能使邪恶的人归正。"樊迟退出来，见到子夏说："刚才我见到老师，问他什么是智，他说'选拔正直的人，放在邪恶的人之上，能使邪恶的人归正。"这是什么意思？子夏说："这话说得多么深刻呀！舜有天下，在众人中挑选人才，把皋陶选拔出来，不仁的人就远离了。汤有天下，在众人中挑选人才，把伊尹选拔出来，不仁的人就远离了。"

19-3. 子贡问为仁。子曰："工欲善其事，必先利其器。居是邦也，事其大夫之贤者，友其士之仁者。"(15.9)

子贡问怎样实行仁德。孔子说："工匠想把活儿做好，必须先把工具磨得锋利。住在这个国家，就要为大夫中的贤者服务，与士人中的仁者交朋友。"

词汇一 VOCABULARY I

1.	直	zhí	straight, honest, and upright
2.	错	cuò	措、放, to place
3.	枉	wǎng	crooked, devious
4.	服	fú	to obey, to submit oneself to
5.	选拔	xuǎnbá	to select, to choose
6.	邪恶	xié'è	evil, wicked
7.	达	dá	明白

8. 乡 xiàng 过去、从前、刚才
9. 富 fù 丰富
10. 深刻 shēnkè deep, profound
11. 利 lì sharp
12. 器 qì 工具
13. 大夫 dàfu senior official
14. 锋利 fēnglì sharp

虚词 FUNCTION WORDS

1. 于 yú 被（乡也，吾见于夫子而问知）
2. 乎 hū 啊（富哉言乎）

专名 PROPER NAMES

1. 汤 Tāng founder of the Shang dynasty (1600–1046 BCE)
2. 伊尹 Yī Yǐn a Shang dynasty minister

解读 Exegeses

举直错枉是关系到国家兴亡的大事。选用直臣、忠臣，政治就清明，国家就强大。反之，把权力交给奸臣，政治就腐败、国家就衰亡。子夏举了舜和汤作为正面例子。历史上，正反两方面的例子不胜枚举。

唐太宗李世民作了皇帝后，重用一批能臣，其中就包括有名的直臣魏征。他经常对太宗直谏，像他自己所说的，“知无不言，言无不尽”。即使唐太宗有时非常生气，他也据理力争。唐太宗甚至对魏征有了敬畏之心，但对他的意见总能认真地听取。有一天，唐太宗问他：“什么是明君？什么是暗君？”魏征说：“兼听则明，偏信则暗。尧、舜听取各方面的意见，所以是明君。秦朝的秦二世只听信奸臣赵高，最终导致亡国。”魏征死的时候，太宗很伤心，说魏征是我的一面镜子，使我看到自己的得失，现在这面镜子没了。

可惜的是，在历史上举枉错直的事要多得多。下面讲的就是一个例子。

词汇二 VOCABULARY II

1. 兴亡 xīngwáng rise and fall (of a nation)
2. 清明 qīngmíng clear and just (administration)
3. 奸臣 jiānchén treacherous courtier
4. 腐败 fǔbài corrupt
5. 不胜枚举 bùshèng méijǔ too numerous to mention individually
6. 重用 zhòngyòng to put somebody in an important position

7. 能臣 néngchén capable courtier
8. 兼听则明，偏听则暗 jiāntīng zémíng, piāntīng zéàn listen to both sides and you will be enlightened
9. 偏 piān to lean to one side

专名 PROPER NAMES

1. 李世民 Lǐ Shìmín Emperor Taizong's name
2. 秦 Qín the Qin dynasty (221–206 BCE)
3. 秦二世 Qín Èrshì Second Emperor of the Qin (r. 210–207 BCE)
4. 赵高 Zhào Gāo a Qin dynasty courtier (d. 207 BCE)

事例 An Illustrative Story

A TATTOOED GENERAL 岳飞精忠报国

岳飞是南宋名将、民族英雄。他少年丧父，由母亲养育成人。当时正逢金兵入侵，其母在岳飞的背上刺了“精忠报国”四个字，鼓励他保家卫国。

岳飞在抗金战场上屡建战功。他组建了纪律严明、英勇善战的岳家军，多次打败金兵主力。他廉洁奉公、武艺高强、令出如山、出生入死，要求“文官不爱钱，武将不怕死”。他指挥了一百二十六仗，未尝一败，是名副其实的常胜将军。金军发出了“撼山易，撼岳家军难”的哀叹。

但是，外敌难以撼动的岳家军，却遭到了南宋朝廷内部投降派的摧残。就在抗金战争取得辉煌胜利的时刻，宋高宗与他重用的丞相秦桧密谋全线撤军。秦桧不但是个奸臣，还是金人安插在南宋朝廷里的奸细。他们连下十二道金牌，急令岳飞“班师”。岳飞愤慨地说；“十年之功，废于一旦！”

岳飞回到南宋的首都临安（现在的杭州），秦桧竟诬告他谋反，把他杀害，年仅三十九岁。

谁忠谁奸，谁直谁枉，公道自在人心。在杭州西湖边的岳王庙里，有一个秦桧的跪像，放在岳飞的墓前，承受世人的唾骂。

词汇三 VOCABULARY III

1. 刺 cì to tattoo
2. 廉洁 liánjié incorruptible, to be honest in performing one's official duties
3. 未尝 wèicháng 不曾、没有

4.	名副其实	míngfù qíshí	the name matches the reality, to be worthy of the name
5.	撼	hàn	to shake
6.	摧残	cuīcán	to wreck, to destroy, to devastate
7.	安插	ānchā	to plant (a person)
8.	奸细	jiānxì	spy, enemy agent
9.	金牌	jīnpái	gold plaque that represents an emperor's edict
10.	班师	bānshī	triumphant return of the army
11.	愤慨	fènkǎi	(righteous) indignation
12.	一旦	yīdàn	in a single day, in a very short time
13.	诬告	wūgào	to bring a false charge against
14.	谋反	móufǎn	to plot a rebellion
15.	承受	chéngshòu	to bear, to endure
16.	唾骂	tuòmà	to spit on and revile

专名 PROPER NAMES

1.	岳飞	Yuè Fēi	a Southern Song general (1103–1142)
2.	金	Jīn	the Jin Dynasty (1115–1234)
3.	高宗	Gāozōng	first Southern Song emperor (r. 1127–1162)
4.	秦桧	Qín Huì	Gaozong's chief minister (1095–1155)

成语 Idioms

1. 举直错枉
   【课文】举直错诸枉，则民服。
2. 工欲善其事，必先利其器
   【课文】子曰：“工欲善其事，必先利其器。”
3. 不胜枚举
   【课文】历史上，正反两方面的例子不胜枚举。
4. 知无不言，言无不尽
   【课文】他经常对太宗直谏，像他自己所说的，“知无不言，言无不尽”。
5. 据理力争
   【课文】即使唐太宗有时非常生气，他也据理力争。
6. 兼听则明，偏信则暗
   【课文】魏征说：“兼听则明，偏信则暗。”
7. 精忠报国
   【课文】岳飞母亲在他的背上刺了“精忠报国”四个字，鼓励他保家卫国。

8. 保家卫国
【课文】同上。
9. 廉洁奉公
【课文】他廉洁奉公、武艺高强、令出如山、出生入死。
10. 令出如山
【课文】同上。
11. 出生入死
【课文】同上。
12. 名副其实
【课文】他指挥了一百二十六仗，未尝一败，是名副其实的常胜将军。
13. 常胜将军
【课文】同上。

词汇扩展 Vocabulary Expansion

1. 直
【课文】举直错诸枉，则民服。
【例词】直译、正直、朴直、刚直、直话直说、直来直去、直升飞机、直达快车、理直气壮、横冲直撞
2. 民
【课文】同上。
【例词】民主、民族、民乐、公民、移民、民贵君轻、民穷财尽、民心所向、民间艺术、国计民生
3. 服
【课文】同上。
【例词】服从、服输、服老、佩服、信服、说服、征服、服务员、服务台、心服口服
4. 达
【课文】樊迟未达。
【例词】达到、达成、表达、传达、转达、到达、发达、达官贵人、通情达理、词不达意
5. 选
【课文】舜有天下，选于众，举皋陶，不仁者远矣。
【例词】选择、选举、选手、选修、选本、选题、选读、选集、选曲、选贤任能
6. 远
【课文】同上。

【例词】远洋、远东、远征、远亲、远景、永远、遥远、远隔重洋、远走高飞、远近闻名、远道而来、远见卓识

7. 器

【课文】工欲善其事，必先利其器。

【例词】器官、器材、器皿、器乐、器量、器重、武器、兵器、乐器、大器晚成

练习 Exercises

一、选择题 MULTIPLE CHOICE

1. 举直错枉是 ________ 到国家兴亡的大事。
   a. 关系　　b. 关于
   c. 关心　　d. 关照
2. 尧、舜能 ________，所以是明君。
   a. 知无不言　　b. 言无不尽
   c. 兼听则明　　d. 偏信则暗
3. 岳飞的时代，正逢 ________ 兵入侵。
   a. 元　　b. 清
   c. 辽　　d. 金
4. 南宋的首都在 ________。
   a. 北京　　b. 西安
   c. 开封　　d. 杭州

二、改错 CORRECTING MISTAKES

1. 舜有天下，在众人中选拔了伊尹。
2. 唐太宗有时对魏征非常生气，对他的意见也就不能认真地听取了。
3. 秦始皇只听信奸臣赵高，最终导致亡国。
4. 在抗金战争失败的时候，宋高宗与秦桧密谋全线撤军。
5. 秦桧的坐像放在岳飞的墓前，承受世人的唾骂。

三、问答题 ANSWERING QUESTIONS

1. 为什么唐太宗说魏征是他的一面镜子？
2. 为什么说岳飞是名副其实的常胜将军？
3. 金军是怎么评论岳家军的？
4. 秦桧是个什么样的人？
5. 宋高宗和秦桧连下几道金牌，急令岳飞撤兵？
6. 岳飞死时几岁？
7. 岳王庙在哪里？

四、讨论题 QUESTIONS FOR DISCUSSION

1. 从正反两方面举例说明举直错枉是关系到国家兴亡的大事。
2. 岳飞抗金节节胜利是对南宋有利的大好事，为什么宋高宗和秦桧却要杀害他（需要做一点研究）？

五、故事复述 RETELLING THE STORY

《岳飞精忠报国》

六、用本课的成语改写句子 REWRITING SENTENCES USING IDIOMS FROM THE CHAPTER

1. 小安的车被人撞了，警察却给了他一张罚单。他去了法庭为自己辩护，总算赢了。
2. 麦克的爸爸是个越战老兵。他常常跟我们讲起他爸爸好几次差点儿死去的故事，真感动人。
3. 老听人说“月星”中国餐馆的菜特别好，昨晚去吃了一下，觉得真是不错。
4. 我的邻居张大妈是个热心肠的好人，她帮助别人的故事多得说不完。

七、选词 WORD CHOICE

1. 微软和雅虎两家公司商讨合并的事，因为价钱谈不拢，最终没能（达到、到达、达成）协议。
2. 白教授已经七十多岁了，可是每天还来学校上课、做研究。她的不（服输、服老、服从）的精神令人佩服。
3. “下个学期你打算（选读、选修、选举）哪些课程？”“我还没想好呢。”
4. 那个人寿保险推销员因为业绩出色而受到公司的（器量、器重、器材）。
5. 老金家的三个孩子都（远走高飞、远隔重洋、远近闻名）去外国留学了，他打算以后多抽些时间和太太去各地旅游。

八、文译白 TRANSLATION FROM CLASSICAL CHINESE INTO MODERN CHINESE

岳飞《满江红》

怒发冲冠，凭阑处、潇潇雨歇。抬望眼，仰天长啸，壮怀激烈。三十功名尘与土，八千里路云和月。莫等闲、白了少年头，空悲切。

靖康①耻，犹未雪；臣子恨，何时灭？驾长车、踏破贺兰山②缺。壮志饥餐胡虏肉，笑谈渴饮匈奴血。待从头、收拾旧山河，朝天阙③。

【注释】①靖康：宋钦宗年号。靖康元年（1126），金兵攻陷开封；次年掳徽宗、钦宗北去，北宋灭亡。②贺兰山：在今宁夏西，此处借指金人所在地。③天阙：宫门，指朝廷。

九、英译中 TRANSLATION FROM ENGLISH INTO CHINESE

1. In 1126, several years before Yue Fei became a general, the Jin army invaded the north of the country, forcing the Song out of their capital, Kaifeng 开封, and capturing the emperor Qinzong 钦宗. This marked the end of the Northern Song and the beginning of the Southern Song dynasty, under Emperor Gaozong.
2. Yue Fei fought a long campaign against the invading Jin in an effort to retake the north of the country. Just as he was threatening to attack and retake Kaifeng, corrupt officials advised Emperor Gaozong to recall Yue Fei to the capital and sue for peace with the Jin. Fearing that a defeat at Kaifeng might cause the Jin to release Qinzong and threaten his claim to the throne, the emperor followed their advice.
3. Twenty years after Yue Fei's death, Emperor Xiaozong 孝宗 recognized the general's loyalty and had a tomb and temple complex built to honor him. Today it is a memorial to General Yue's spirit of loyalty and patriotism. The tomb and the tomb sculptures date from the twelfth century and have been meticulously restored.
4. One story says that after Yue Fei was executed, a pastry vendor kneaded a piece of dough into two human shapes representing Qin Hui and his wife. He then twisted them together and put them in boiling hot oil. The local people all came, bought the fried dough, and had bites of it. This is said to be the origin of today's *youtiao* 油条, a common breakfast food in China.

十、讲故事 STORYTELLING (根据下面的提示在网上找资料)

【题目】岳飞的故事

【提示】岳飞廉洁奉公、严以律己、事母至孝、爱民如子、令出如山、赏罚分明、武艺高强、身先士卒、出生入死、军功卓著。选其中一个主题，讲一个故事。

20. Economy and Education 富之教之

《论语》选段 *Analects* Passages

20-1. 子适卫，冉有仆。子曰："庶矣哉！"冉有曰："既庶矣，又何加焉？"曰："富之。"曰："既富矣，又何加焉？"曰："教之。"(13.9)

孔子到卫国，冉有为他驾车。孔子说："人口真多呀！"冉有说："人口已经多了，还要再做什么呢？"孔子说："使他们富起来。"冉有说："富了以后又还要再做什么？"孔子说："教育他们。"

20-2. 哀公问于有若曰："年饥，用不足，如之何？"有若对曰："盍彻乎？"曰："二，吾犹不足，如之何其彻也？"对曰："百姓足，君孰与不足？百姓不足，君孰与足？"(12.9)

鲁哀公问有若道："遭了饥荒，国用不足，怎么办？"有若回答说："为什么不实行什一税法呢？"哀公说："现在抽十分之二的税，我还不够，怎么能实行什一税法呢？"有若回答说："如果百姓的用度够，您怎么会不够呢？如果百姓的用度不够，您又怎么会够呢？"

20-3. 孔子曰："丘也闻有国有家者，不患贫而患不均，不患寡而患不安。盖均无贫，和无寡，安无倾。"(16.1)

孔子说："我听说，对于诸侯和大夫，不怕贫穷，而怕财富不均；不怕人口少，而怕不安定。因为财富平均了，也就没有所谓贫穷；大家和睦，就不会感到人少；安定了，也就没有倾覆的危险了。"

词汇一 VOCABULARY I

1.	适	shì	to go, to arrive at
2.	仆	pú	to drive a horse-drawn carriage
3.	庶	shù	人口多
4.	年	nián	年成, harvest, crops
5.	饥	jī	famine, crop failure
6.	用	yòng	finances, funds
7.	彻	chè	tithe, a tax of one-tenth
8.	二	èr	two-tenths, 20 percent
9.	遭	zāo	to meet with, to suffer
10.	饥荒	jīhuāng	farming
11.	抽	chōu	to levy or collect taxes
12.	用度	yòngdù	expenditure, expense
13.	什一	shíyī	十分之一, one-tenth

14. 均 jūn 平均, equal
15. 倾 qīng to incline, to collapse
16. 倾覆 qīngfù to overturn, to topple

虚词 FUNCTION WORDS

1. 既 jì 已经（既庶矣，又何加焉）
2. 焉 yān 呢（同上）
3. 盍 hé 何不（盍彻乎）
4. 犹 yóu 还（二，吾犹不足，如之何其彻也）
5. 如之何 rúzhīhé 怎么能（二，吾犹不足，如之何其彻也）
6. 孰与 shúyǔ 怎么会（百姓足，君孰与不足）

专名 PROPER NAMES

1. 卫 Wèi State of Wei, in present-day Henan Province
2. 冉有 Rǎnyǒu 名求，孔子的学生 (522–489 BCE)

解读 Exegeses

这一章讲的是了孔子的经济思想，首先是他的“富民”理论。鲁国所征的田税是十分之二的税率，即使如此，国家的财政仍然十分拮据。有若提出改行“彻税”即什一税率，使百姓减轻经济负担。只要百姓富足了，国家就不可能贫穷。反之，如果对百姓征收太多，必将造成民不聊生，国家经济也就随之衰退了。这种“藏富于民”的思想至今仍有现实意义。

与收入的增加相比，孔子更重视分配的均衡。“不患寡而患不均，不患贫而患不安。”这段文字，是孔子经济思想的核心，对于现代国家的经营之道，也是极有启示的。现在世界上很多国家，都注重提高国民生产总值，而对于分配问题则并没有实行有效的政策。因此，贫富悬殊、两极分化的现象严重，造成社会阶层之间的隔阂和矛盾，成为社会的不安定因素。

词汇二 VOCABULARY II

1. 征 zhēng to levy or collect taxes
2. 税率 shuìlǜ tax rate
3. 财政 cáizhèng finance, financial administration
4. 拮据 jiéjū financial constraints
5. 民不聊生 mín bù liáoshēng the people have no means to earn a living
6. 分配 fēnpèi to distribute, to assign
7. 均衡 jūnhéng balanced, proportionate
8. 经营 jīngyíng to manage, to run

9.	启示	qǐshì	enlightenment, inspiration
10.	注重	zhùzhòng	to stress, to pay attention to
11.	悬殊	xuánshū	great disparity, wide gap
12.	两极分化	liǎngjí fēnhuà	polarization, division (of a group, society, etc.)
13.	阶层	jiēcéng	(social) stratum
14.	隔阂	géhé	estrangement, misunderstanding
15.	矛盾	máodùn	contradiction

事例 An Illustrative Story

THE EMPEROR'S DICTIONARY 康熙帝好学勤政

清朝的康熙皇帝八岁登基，在位六十一年，是中国历史上统治时间最长的皇帝。

康熙是清政权入关后的第二位皇帝。在他即位之初，百废待兴。他不但在政治和军事上统一了国家，而且还采取了一系列有利于国计民生的政策。他积极鼓励垦荒，下令整修黄河和淮河的水利工程。他还决定“永不加赋”，取消新增人口的人头税。这些措施有力地促进了耕地面积的迅速扩大和粮食产量的提高，推动了经济的发展。

康熙对文化建设也非常重视。他优待汉族知识分子，发展科举制度，并亲临曲阜拜谒孔庙。他下令编撰了《明史》、《全唐诗》、《康熙字典》和《古今图书集成》等大型图书。同时他对西方科学也有浓厚的兴趣，毕生学习天文学、数学、物理学、化学、药学、医学等方面的知识。

他的雄才大略和文治武功，开创了“康乾盛世”的局面。

词汇三 VOCABULARY III

1.	勤政	qínzhèng	to govern the country diligently
2.	登基	dēngjī	to ascend to the throne
3.	在位	zàiwèi	to be on the throne
4.	入关	rùguān	to enter the pass—here referring to Qing troops entering the Shanhai Pass 山海关 in 1644 and starting to rule China proper
5.	国计民生	guójì mínshēng	national economy and the people's livelihood
6.	垦荒	kěnhuāng	to open up virgin soil
7.	人头税	réntóushuì	head tax, tax according to population
8.	耕地	gēngdì	cultivated land
9.	迅速	xùnsù	rapid, swift, speedy, prompt

10.	优待	yōudài	preferential treatment
11.	科举	kējǔ	civil service examinations (in ancient China)
12.	临	lín	to arrive, to be present
13.	拜谒	bàiyè	to pay a formal call, to pay respects
14.	集成	jíchéng	collection (of books)
15.	浓厚	nónghòu	dense, strong, profound
16.	毕生	bìshēng	all one's life, lifetime
17.	天文学	tiānwénxué	astronomy
18.	雄才大略	xióngcái dàlüè	great talent and bold strategy
19.	文治武功	wénzhì wǔgōng	political and military achievements
20.	局面	júmiàn	situation, phase

专名 PROPER NAMES

1.	康熙	Kāngxī	Emperor Kangxi (r. 1661–1722)
2.	淮河	Huáihé	the Huai River
3.	孔庙	Kǒngmiào	Temple of Confucius
4.	康乾盛世	Kāng Qián shèngshì	the heyday of Kangxi and Qianlong 乾隆 (r. 1736–1795)

成语 Idioms

1. 富之教之
   【课文】冉有曰："既庶矣，又何加焉？"曰："富之。"曰："既富矣，又何加焉？"曰："教之。"
2. 民不聊生
   【课文】如果对百姓征收太多，必将造成民不聊生，国家经济也就随之衰退了。
3. 藏富于民
   【课文】这种"藏富于民"的思想至今仍有现实意义。
4. 贫富悬殊
   【课文】因此，贫富悬殊、两极分化的现象严重，造成社会阶层之间的隔阂和矛盾，成为社会的不安定因素。
5. 两极分化
   【课文】同上。
6. 百废待兴
   【课文】在他即位之初，百废待兴。

7. 国计民生
【课文】他不但在政治和军事上统一了国家，而且还采取了一系列有利于国计民生的政策。
8. 雄才大略
【课文】他的雄才大略和文治武功，开创了“康乾盛世”的局面。
9. 文治武功
【课文】同上。

词汇扩展 Vocabulary Expansion

1. 加
【课文】既庶矣，又何加焉？
【例词】加班、加薪、加倍、加工、加固、加紧、加快、加强、加深、加油
2. 富
【课文】未若贫而乐道，富而好礼者也。
【例词】富豪、富贵、富裕、富强、富庶、富国强兵、富丽堂皇、荣华富贵、丰富多彩、为富不仁
3. 教
【课文】“既富矣，又何加焉？”曰：“教之。”
【例词】教育、教学、教导、教诲、教材、教练、教训、教科书、教学相长、有教无类
4. 年
【课文】年饥，用不足，如之何？
【例词】年代、年号、成年、晚年、丰年、年富力强、年轻力壮、年幼无知、年复一年、年华似水
5. 足
【课文】同上。
【例词】足够、富足、满足、实足、足智多谋、足食足兵、丰衣足食、知足常乐、鼓足勇气、不足之处
6. 百
【课文】百姓足，君孰与不足？
【例词】百战百胜、百发百中、百花齐放、百家争鸣、百里挑一、百年大计、百年好合、百依百顺、百川归海、百鸟朝凤
7. 倾
【课文】盖均无贫，和无寡，安无倾。
【例词】倾倒、倾覆、倾盆大雨、倾家荡产、倾囊相助、倾国倾城、倾巢而出、倾耳而听、倾诉衷情、倾心交谈

练习 Exercises

一、选择题 MULTIPLE CHOICE

1. 如果对百姓征收太多，必将造成 ________。
   a. 贫富悬殊 b. 两极分化
   c. 民不聊生 d. 藏富于民
2. 与收入的增加相比，孔子更重视分配的 ________。
   a. 均衡 b. 均匀
   c. 均等 d. 均势
3. 这段文字，对于现代国家的经营之道，也是极有 ________ 的。
   a. 教训 b. 启示
   c. 道理 d. 说明
4. 两极分化的现象成为社会的不 ________ 因素。
   a. 安全 b. 安稳
   c. 安心 d. 安定

二、改错 CORRECTING MISTAKES

1. 税率越高，征税越多，国家就越富足。
2. 百姓虽然富足，国家仍可能贫穷。
3. 康熙下令整修长江的水利工程。
4. 康熙下令编撰了《全明诗》。
5. 《康熙字典》是康熙皇帝亲自编写的。

三、问答题 ANSWERING QUESTIONS

1. 什么叫“彻税”？
2. 与收入的增加相比，孔子更重视什么？
3. 康熙皇帝几岁登基？在位多少年？
4. 康熙采取了哪些有利于国计民生的政策？
5. 康熙下令编撰了哪些大型图书？
6. 康熙学习了哪些西方科学知识？

四、讨论题 QUESTIONS FOR DISCUSSION

1. 结合当今世界上的例子，讨论“藏富于民”的思想的现实意义。
2. 孔子说的“不患寡而患不均，不患贫而患不安”这段文话对于现代国家的经营之道有什么启示？

五、故事复述 RETELLING THE STORY

《康熙帝好学勤政》

六、用本课的成语改写句子 REWRITING SENTENCES USING IDIOMS FROM THE CHAPTER

1. 这个城市被地震彻底破坏了，一切都得重新建立起来，工作将会多艰巨啊！
2. 那个国家的富强是非常表面的，因为它国内的穷人和富人的距离相差太大了。
3. 不管国家利益和人民生活的总统是得不到人民的拥护的。
4. 中国历史上有几位在政治和军事上都很有建树的皇帝，唐朝的太宗和清朝的康熙就是两个例子。

七、选词 WORD CHOICE

1. 小东，你可不能再酒后开车了，别忘了上次车祸差点儿送命的(教诲、教导、教训)。
2. 那个做房地产的商人在房价疯涨时大量买进房产，现在房价暴跌，他因付不出银行的贷款而(倾国倾城、倾家荡产、倾囊相助)了。
3. 你去过小英的家吗？她家可真是(丰富多彩、富丽堂皇、荣华富贵)啊。
4. 唐太太对孩子(百发百中、百战百胜、百依百顺)，要什么给什么，结果孩子的独立性都不强。
5. 小牛，你(年轻力壮、年幼无知、年华似水)，看那个老先生一个人在搬电视机，还不快过去帮忙！

八、中译英 TRANSLATION FROM CHINESE INTO ENGLISH

1. 《康熙字典》是三十多位著名学者奉康熙圣旨编撰的一部具有深远影响的汉字辞书。该书的编撰工作始于康熙四十九年(1711)，成书于康熙五十五年(1716)，历时六年。字典采用部首分类法，共收录汉字四万七千零三十五个，在很长一个时期内是中国字数最多的一部字典。
2. 《全唐诗》是康熙下令编撰的唐代诗歌的总集，于康熙四十六年(1707)出版。这部书共收诗四万九千四百零三首，作者共二千八百七十三人。康熙亲自为此书作了序。他在序中说："于是唐三百年诗人之菁华，咸采撷荟萃于一编之内，亦可云大备矣"。
3. 康熙生前，他的很多儿子争夺皇位。传说康熙在他的遗诏中原来写的是"传位十四子"，可是他的第四个儿子派人偷偷地在"十"字上加了一横，变成"于"字。等康熙死后，打开遗诏，就变成了"传位于四子"。于是，第四个儿子即位，就是雍正皇帝。

九、英译中 TRANSLATION FROM ENGLISH INTO CHINESE

1. Kangxi once visited the Confucian temple in Qufu, Shandong Province, and paid his respects to Confucius. He wrote the four characters "wan shi shi biao"

(万世师表) on a banner to show his determination to rule the nation as a Confucian.

2. *Collected Works, Ancient and Modern* (*Gujin tushu jicheng* 古今图书集成), one of the world's largest book projects, originated as a private undertaking but was adopted as an imperial enterprise by Kangxi. Completed just before the emperor's death, this vast encyclopedia of 5,020 volumes and some 800,000 pages was published during the reign of Kangxi's successor.
3. Emperor Kangxi was a passionate calligrapher, and numerous examples of his work have survived. The importance he placed on this art is reflected in a portrait of him at an early age, in which he pointedly wields his writing brush.
4. Emperor Kangxi's six inspection tours to southern China sent an impressive message throughout the empire about his vitality, personal commitment, and imperial splendor, and at the same time familiarized him with regions that had different geology, climates, cultures, and history.
5. During Kangxi's reign, society accumulated great wealth and most of the time enjoyed peace. The period of Kangxi and Qianlong's reigns has been called "Kang-Qian shengshi"; prosperity lasted for more than one hundred years, and never again has there been a more prosperous period in Chinese history.

十、辩论 DEBATING

【题目】《藏富于国还是藏富于民?》

【提示】正方：人民富足是国家富强的基础和保障，也是社会和谐安定的基本条件。

反方：政府有充分的资金才能兴办大型企业、发展经济建设，从而造福于人民。

Appendix 附录

ENGLISH TRANSLATIONS OF THE *ANALECTS* PASSAGES
《论语》选段英译

1-1. 子曰："学而时习之，不亦说乎？有朋自远方来，不亦乐乎？人不知而不愠，不亦君子乎？"(1.1)

The Master said, "To learn and then to practice at due times—is this not also a pleasure? To have friends come from afar—is this not also a joy? A person unacknowledged by others but not resentful—is this not also a gentleman?"

1-2. 子夏曰："百工居肆以成其事，君子学以致其道。"(19.7)

Zixia said, "The many artisans stay in their workshops to master their trades; the gentleman engages in learning so as to attain the Way."

1-3. 子夏曰："博学而笃志，切问而近思，仁在其中矣。"(19.6)

Zixia said, "Extensive study with a serious purpose, earnest inquiry combined with reflection on things at hand—therein lies humanity."

2-1. 子曰："十室之邑，必有忠信如丘者焉，不如丘之好学也。"(5.28)

The Master said, "In any town of ten households, there are bound to be those who are as dutiful or as trustworthy as I am, but there is no one who matches my love for learning."

2-2. 哀公问："弟子孰为好学？"孔子对曰："有颜回者好学，不迁怒，不贰过。不幸短命死矣。今也则亡，未闻好学者也。"(6.3)

Duke Ai asked, "Which of your disciples love learning?" Confucius replied, "There was one Yan Hui who loved learning. He did not vent his anger, nor make the same mistake twice. Unfortunately, he died young. Now there is none. I have not heard of anyone who loves learning."

2-3. 子曰："君子食无求饱，居无求安，敏于事而慎于言，就有道而正焉，可谓好学也已。"(1.14)

The Master said, "The gentleman does not seek satiety in eating, nor comfort in lodging. He is brisk in action and careful in speech and approaches those who know the Way for rectification. Such a man may be said to love learning."

2-4. 子夏曰："日知其所亡，月无忘其所能，可谓好学也已矣。"(19.5)

Zixia said, "Aware every day of what he still lacks, and not forgetting, in the course of a month, what he has already mastered—a person like this can be said to love learning indeed."

2-5. 子曰："温故而知新，可以为师矣。"(2.11)

The Master said, "Reviewing the old to know the new—such a person can be considered a teacher."

3-1. 子曰："由！诲女知之乎！知之为知之，不知为不知，是知也。"(2.17)

The Master said, "Zilu, I will teach you what is to know! To take what you know for what you know, and what you do not know as what you do not know—that is to know."

3-2. 子曰："盖有不知而作之者，我无是也。"(7.28)

The Master said, "There may be those who try to innovate without possessing knowledge, but I am not one of them."

3-3. 子绝四：毋意、毋必、毋固、毋我。(9.4)

The Master eschewed four things: he had no need for conjecture, arbitrariness, obstinacy, or egoism.

3-4. 曾子曰："以能问于不能，以多问于寡，有若无，实若虚，犯而不校—昔者吾友尝从事于斯矣。"(8.5)

Master Zeng said, "Able himself yet asking those who are not so; having much himself yet asking those who have little. Having as if having not, substantial as if empty. Offended but not minding. In the old days, a friend of mine did thus."

4-1. 子曰："不愤不启，不悱不发。举一隅不以三隅反，则不复也。"(7.8)

The Master said, "I do not inspire those who do not strive; I do not express things to the inarticulate. If on showing students one corner they do not come back with the other three, I will not repeat myself."

4-2. 子谓子贡曰："女与回也孰愈？"对曰："赐也何敢望回？回也闻一以知十，赐也闻一以知二。"子曰："弗如也。吾与女，弗如也。"(5.8)

The Master said to Zigong, "Who is better, you or Yan Hui?" Zigong replied, "How dare I hope to compare myself with Hui? Hui learns one thing and thereby knows ten. I learn one thing and thereby know two." The Master said, "You are not his match. I agree with you: You are not his match."

4-3. 子贡曰："贫而无谄，富而无骄，何如？"子曰："可也。未若贫而乐道，富而好礼者也。"子贡曰："《诗》云：'如切如磋，如琢如磨'，其斯之谓与？"子曰："赐也！始可与言《诗》已矣，告诸往而知来者。"(1.15)

Zigong said, "Poor without servility, rich without arrogance—how is that?" The Master replied, "Not bad, but better still: Poor yet delighting in the Way, rich yet loving ritual." Zigong said, "The *Classic of Poetry* says, 'As if cut, as if polished; / As if carved, as if ground.' Is this what it means?" The Master said, "Zigong, it is only with you that I can talk about the *Classic of Poetry*. Informed what has gone before, you know what is yet to come."

5-1. 子曰："知之者不如好之者，好之者不如乐之者。"(6.20)

The Master said, "To know it is not comparable to loving it; to love it is not comparable to enjoying it."

5-2. 子曰："默而识之，学而不厌，诲人不倦，何有於我哉？"(7.2)

The Master said: "To memorize silently, learn insatiably, and instruct others indefatigably—what else do I need?"

5-3. 子曰："饭疏食、饮水、曲肱而枕之，乐亦在其中矣。不义而富且贵，于我如浮云。"(7.16)

The Master said, "To eat coarse food, drink water, and rest one's head in the crook of one's bent arm—joy also lies therein. Wealth and rank attained through unrighteous means are like floating clouds to me."

5-4. 叶公问孔子於子路，子路不对。子曰："女奚不曰：'其为人也，发愤忘食，乐以忘忧，不知老之将至'云尔。"(7.18)

The Duke of She asked Zilu about Confucius. Zilu did not reply. The Master said, "Why did you not say: 'He is so passionate that he forgets to eat, his joy makes him forget his worries, and he is not aware that old age is upon him' and the like?"

5-5. 子曰："贤哉，回也！一箪食，一瓢饮，在陋巷，人不堪其忧，回也不改其乐。贤哉，回也！" (6.11)

The Master said, "How worthy Hui is! A bamboo basket of rice, a ladle of water, and living in a meager alley—other people could not bear such misery, yet Hui never abandons his joy. How worthy Hui is!"

6-1. 有子曰："其为人也孝弟，而好犯上者，鲜矣；不好犯上，而好作乱者，未之有也。君子务本，本立而道生。孝弟也者，其为仁之本欤！" (1.2)

Master You said, "There are indeed few men who are filial to their parents and obedient to their elder brothers and have the inclination to transgress against his superiors; and there has never been a case of someone disinclined to transgress against his superiors stirring up rebellion. The gentleman attends to his roots. Once the roots are established, the Way will grow. Filial piety and brotherly obedience are the roots of humanity."

6-2. 子曰："弟子入则孝，出则弟，谨而信，汎爱众，而亲仁，行有余力，则以学文。" (1.6)

The Master said, "A young man should be filial at home and respectful of his elders in public. Discreet and truthful, he should love the multitudes all and keep close to humane men. If he has energy to spare, he should employ it to study culture."

6-3. 子夏问孝。子曰："色难。有事，弟子服其劳；有酒食，先生馔，曾是以为孝乎？" (2.8)

Zixia asked about filial piety. The Master said: "Facial expressions are most difficult. When there are chores, the juniors render their services; when there is wine and food, the elders drink and eat. Can this be considered filial piety?"

7-1. 子曰："君子喻于义，小人喻于利。" (4.16)

The Master said, "The gentleman knows righteousness; the small man knows profit."

7-2. 子曰："君子周而不比，小人比而不周。" (2.14)

The Master said, "The gentleman enters into associations but not cliques; the small man enters into cliques but not associations."

7-3. 子曰："君子和而不同，小人同而不和。" (13.23)

The Master said, "The gentleman seeks harmony, not sameness. The small man seeks sameness, not harmony."

7-4. 子曰："君子成人之美，不成人之恶；小人反是。" (12.16)

The Master said, "The gentleman helps others achieve worthy ends; he does not help them carry out evil deeds. The small man does the opposite."

7-5. 子曰："君子坦荡荡，小人长戚戚。" (7.36)

The Master said, "The gentleman is open-hearted and composed; the small man is perpetually full of worry."

7-6. 子曰："君子道者三，我无能焉：仁者不忧，知者不惑，勇者不惧。"子贡曰："夫子自道也！" (14.28)

The Master said, "The gentleman's Way has three facets, all of which are beyond me: The humane have no worries, the wise have no delusions, and the courageous have no fear." Zigong said, "This is the Master's own way."

8-1. 曾子曰："吾日三省吾身：为人谋而不忠乎？与朋友交而不信乎？传不习乎？" (1.4)

Master Zeng said, "I examine myself thrice daily. In my undertakings on behalf of others, have I not been trustworthy? In my interactions with friends, have I not been truthful? Have I not put into practice what has been imparted to me?"

8-2. 子曰："三人行，必有我师焉：择其善者而从之，其不善者而改之。" (7.21)

The Master said, "When three men walk together, I can surely find teachers. I choose merits to emulate and faults to correct."

8-3. 子曰："见贤思齐焉，见不贤而内自省也。" (4.17)

The Master said, "On seeing a worthy man, think of equaling him; on seeing an unworthy man, look inside yourself."

8-4. 子曰："过而不改，是谓过矣。" (15.30)

The Master said, "A fault that is not amended is a fault indeed!"

8-5. 子贡曰："君子之过也，如日月之食焉。过也，人皆见之；更也，人皆仰之。" (19.21)

Zigong said, "The gentleman's errors are like the eclipses of the sun and moon. When he makes one, everyone sees it; when he reforms, everyone looks up to him."

8-6. 子夏曰："小人之过也必文。" (19.8)

Zixia said, "When the small man makes a mistake, he is sure to cover it up."

9-1. 在陈绝粮。从者病，莫能兴。子路愠见曰："君子亦有穷乎？"子曰："君子固穷；小人穷斯滥矣。" (15.2)

In the State of Chen, provisions were exhausted. The followers became sick and could not rise. Resentful, Zilu appeared before the Master and said, "Is the gentleman also susceptible to adversity?" The Master said, "The gentleman is steadfast in adversity; the small man, once reduced to adversity, becomes reckless."

9-2. 子曰："岁寒然后知松柏之后凋也。" (9.28)

The Master said, "When the year turns cold, only then do we realize that the pine and cypress are the last to fade."

9-3. 子曰："士志于道，而耻恶衣恶食者，未足与议也。" (4.9)

The Master said: "A scholar-official who aspires to the Way but is ashamed of shabby clothes and coarse food is not worth discoursing with."

9-4. 子曰："衣敝缊袍，与衣狐貉者立，而不耻者，其由也与？" (9.27)

The Master said, "Clad only in a shabby quilted gown, and yet unashamed to stand together with those dressed in fox and badger furs—is this perhaps You?"

9-5. 子欲居九夷。或曰："陋，如之何？"子曰："君子居之，何陋之有！" (9.14)

The Master wanted to settle among the nine barbarian tribes of the east. Someone said, "It is crude. How can we go?" The Master said, "If a gentleman were to dwell there, what crudeness could there be?"

10-1. 曾子曰："士，不可以不弘毅，任重而道远。仁以为己任，不亦重乎？死而后已，不亦远乎？" (8.7)

Master Zeng said, "A scholar-official cannot do without strength and stamina, for his burden is heavy and the road is long. He takes up humanity as his burden—is it not heavy? He will not stop until death—is that not long?"

10-2. 子曰："志士仁人，无求生以害仁，有杀身以成仁。" (15.9)

The Master said, "Lofty-minded scholar-officials and humane men do not seek to preserve their lives at the expense of humanity; there are instances where they give their lives in the aid of humanity."

10-3. 子曰："三军可夺帅也，匹夫不可夺志也。" (9.26)

The Master said, "The three armies may be deprived of their commander-in-chief, but a common man cannot be deprived of his will."

10-4. 曾子曰："可以托六尺之孤，可以寄百里之命，临大节而不可夺也。君子人与？君子人也。" (8.6)

Master Zeng said, "A man who can be entrusted with an orphan six *chi* tall and charged with the fate of a state one hundred *li* square, and who in approaching great matters of life and death cannot be robbed of his integrity—is he a gentleman? A gentleman indeed!"

11-1. 子曰："君子求诸己，小人求诸人。" (15.20)

The Master said, "The gentleman seeks within himself; the small man looks to others."

11-2. 子曰："不患人之不己知，患不知人也。" (1.16)

The Master said, "Do not worry about not being understood by others; worry about not understanding them."

11-3. 子曰："君子病无能焉，不病人之不己知也。" (15.18)

The Master said, "The gentleman worries about his own inabilities; he does not worry about the failure of others to appreciate him."

11-4. 子曰："躬自厚，而薄责于人，则远怨矣。" (15.14)

The Master said, "Be more critical of yourself, and less so of others, and you shall keep enmity at a distance."

11-5. 司马牛忧曰："人皆有兄弟，我独亡！"子夏曰："商闻之矣：'死生有命，富贵在天'。君子敬而无失，与人恭而有礼；四海之内皆兄弟也。君子何患乎无兄弟也？" (12.5)

Sima Niu said, sadly, "Everyone has brothers; I alone have none." Zixia said, "I have heard this: 'Life and death lie with Fate; wealth and rank rest upon Heaven.' If the gentleman is reverent and does nothing amiss, if he treats others with respect and courtesy, all within the four seas are his brothers. Why should the gentleman grieve over having no brothers?"

12-1. 孔子曰："益者三友，损者三友。友直，友谅，友多闻，益矣。友便辟，友善柔，友便佞，损矣。" (16.4)

Confucius said, "Three types of friends are beneficial and three types of friends are harmful. To befriend the upright, the truthful, and the erudite is beneficial. To befriend the devious, the obsequious, and the glib is harmful."

12-2. 孔子曰："益者三乐，损者三乐。乐节礼乐，乐道人之善，乐多贤友，益矣。乐骄乐，乐佚游，乐宴乐，损矣。" (16.5)

Confucius said, "Three types of delight are beneficial and three types of delight are harmful. To delight in conducting oneself in tune with rites and music, in talking about other men's goodness, and in having many worthy friends is beneficial. To delight in extravagant pleasure, in dissolute diversions, and in the pleasures of carousing is harmful."

12-3. 子曰："群居终日，言不及义，好行小慧，难矣！" (15.17)

The Master said, "Those who herd together all day without touching on righteousness in their conversation and love to display their petty cleverness are sure to have difficulty!"

12-4. 子贡问曰："有一言而可以终身行之者乎？"子曰："其恕乎！己所不欲，勿施于人。" (15.23)

Zigong asked, "Is there one single word that one can practice throughout one's life?" The Master said, "It is perhaps magnanimity. Do not impose on others what you yourself do not desire."

13-1. 宰予昼寝。子曰："朽木不可雕也，粪土之墙不可圬也，于予与何诛？"子曰："始吾于人也，听其言而信其行；今吾于人也，听其言而观其行。于予与改是。"(5.10)

Zaiyu slept during the day. The Master said, "Rotten wood cannot be carved, nor a wall of filthy soil be troweled. As for Yu, what is the use of reprimanding him?" The Master said, "At first, my attitude toward people was to hear their words and believe in their deeds. Now my attitude toward people is to hear their words and observe their deeds. It was because of Yu that I have changed this."

13-2. 子曰："众恶之，必察焉。众好之，必察焉。"(15.28)

The Master said, "If the multitudes loathe him, it must be looked into; if the multitudes love him, it must be looked into."

13-3. 子贡问曰："乡人皆好之，何如？"子曰："未可也。""乡人皆恶之，何如？"子曰："未可也。不如乡人之善者好之，其不善者恶之。"(13.24)

Zigong asked, "All the villagers love him—what do you think?" The Master said, "That won't do." "All the villagers hate him—what do you think?" The Master said, "That won't do. Best of all would be that the village's good people love him and its evil people hate him."

13-4. 子曰："君子不以言举人，不以人废言。"(15.23)

The Master said, "The gentleman does not recommend a man on account of his words; nor does he dismiss words on account of their speaker."

13-5. 子路曰："子行三军，则谁与？"子曰："暴虎冯河，死而不悔者，吾不与也。必也临事而惧，好谋而成者也。"(7.11)

Zilu said: "If you were to command the Three Armies, who would you take with you?" The Master said, "I would not take a man who wrestles a tiger barehanded, or walks across a river, and dies without regret. It must be someone who is apprehensive before a task, and who is good not only at making stratagems but also implementing them."

14-1. 子谓颜渊曰："用之则行，舍之则藏，惟我与尔有是夫。"(7.11)

The Master said to Yan Yuan, "To go forward when used, and to stay hidden when dismissed—perhaps only you and I are capable of this."

14-2. 子曰："邦有道，危言危行；邦无道，危行言孙。" (14.3)

The Master said, "When the state possesses the Way, speak uprightly and act uprightly; when the state loses the Way, act uprightly but speak modestly."

14-3. 子曰："宁武子，邦有道则知，邦无道则愚。其知可及也，其愚不可及也。" (5.21)

The Master said, "Ning Wuzi—when the state possessed the Way, he was wise; when the state lost the Way, he was foolish. His wisdom was within the reach of others, but not his foolishness."

14-4. 子曰："天下有道则见，无道则隐。邦有道，贫且贱焉，耻也，邦无道，富且贵焉，耻也。" (8.13)

The Master said, "When the world possesses the Way, reveal yourself. When it loses the Way, conceal yourself. When the state possesses the Way, there is shame in poverty and obscurity. When the state loses the Way, there is shame in wealth and renown."

15-1. 子曰："君子谋道不谋食。耕也，馁在其中矣。学也，禄在其中矣。君子忧道不忧贫。" (15.31)

The Master said, "The gentleman seeks the Way and not food. If he tills the land, hunger lies therein. If he learns, an official salary lies therein. The gentleman worries about the Way and not poverty."

15-2. 樊迟请学稼。子曰："吾不如老农。"请学为圃。曰："吾不如老圃。樊迟出。子曰："小人哉，樊须也！上好礼，则民莫敢不敬；上好义，则民莫敢不服；上好信，则民莫敢不用情。夫如是，则四方之民襁负其子而至矣，焉用稼？" (13.4)

Fan Chi asked to be taught how to grow crops. The Master said, "I am not as good as an old farmer." He asked to be taught how to grow a garden. The Master said, "I am not as good as an old gardener." Fan Chi left. The Master said, "What a small man Fan Chi is! If the sovereign loves ritual, the people dare not be irreverent; if the sovereign loves righteousness, the people dare not be disobedient; if the sovereign loves truthfulness, the people dare not be dishonest. In that case, people from all directions will come with their children swaddled on their backs. What need is there to grow crops?"

15-3. 子张学干禄。子曰："多闻阙疑，慎言其余，则寡尤。多见阙殆，慎行其余，则寡悔。言寡尤，行寡悔，禄在其中矣。"(2.18)

Zizhang was studying in order to obtain an official position. The Master said, "If you listen much, leave what is doubtful, and speak discreetly on the rest, you shall make fewer mistakes. If you do a lot of looking, leave what is knotty, and act discreetly on the rest, you shall have fewer regrets. If you make fewer mistakes in speech and have fewer regrets in action, therein lies an official position."

16-1. 子曰："为政以德，譬如北辰，居其所而众星共之。"(2.1)

The Master said, "He who conducts government with virtue may be likened to the North Star, which, seated in its place, is surrounded by a multitude of other stars."

16-2. 子曰："无为而治者，其舜也与？夫何为哉？恭己正南面而已矣。"(15.5)

The Master said, "The one who achieved good government through nonaction was perhaps Shun! For what did he do? He conducted himself respectfully and took his proper position facing south, that is all."

16-3. 子曰："道之以政，齐之以刑，民免而无耻；道之以德，齐之以礼，有耻且格。"(2.3)

The Master said, "If you govern them with decrees and regulate them with punishments, the people will evade trouble but will have no sense of shame. If you govern them with virtue and regulate them with ritual, they will have a sense of shame and will rectify themselves."

17-1. 齐景公问政於孔子。孔子对曰："君君，臣臣，父父，子子。"公曰："善哉！信如君不君，臣不臣，父不父，子不子，虽有粟，吾得而食诸？"(12.11)

Duke Jing of Qi asked Confucius about government. Confucius replied, "Let the sovereign be a sovereign, the subject a subject, the father a father, and the son a son." The Duke said, "Excellent! If indeed the sovereign is not a sovereign, the subject not a subject, the father not a father, and the son not a son, even if there were millet, how would I get to eat?"

17-2. 定公问："君使臣，臣事君，如之何？"孔子曰："君使臣以礼，臣事君以忠。"(3.19)

Duke Ding asked, "The sovereign employing his subjects, the subjects serving their sovereign—how should it be done?" Confucius replied, "The sovereign should employ his subjects with ritual; the subjects should serve their sovereign with loyalty."

17-3. 子曰："道千乘之国：敬事而信，节用而爱人，使民以时。"(1.5)

The Master said, "In guiding a state of a thousand chariots, respect your duties and be truthful, economize on consumption and love people, and employ the people only in due season."

18-1. 季康子问政于孔子。孔子对曰："政者正也。子帅以正，孰敢不正？"(12.17)

Ji Kangzi asked Confucius about government. Confucius replied, "Government means uprightness. If you take the lead in being upright, who would dare not to straighten up?"

18-2. 子曰："其身正，不令而行；其身不正，虽令不从。"(13.6)

The Master said, "If the ruler himself is upright, all will go well even if he does not give orders. If he himself is not upright, even if he gives orders, they will not be obeyed."

18-3. 子曰："苟正其身矣，于从政何有乎？不能正其身，如正人乎？"(13.13)

The Master said, "If you can set yourself upright, what difficulty do you have in conducting state affairs? If you cannot set yourself upright, how can you make others upright?"

18-4. 季康子患盗，问于孔子。孔子对曰："苟子之不欲，虽赏之不窃。"(12.18)

Ji Kangzi was troubled by theft and consulted with Confucius. Confucius replied, "If only you were free from desire, no one would steal even if stealing were rewarded."

18-5. 子路问政。子曰："先之，劳之。"请益。曰："无倦。"(13.1)

Zilu asked about government. The Master said, "Lead by example, and make the people toil." Zilu asked him to elaborate. The Master said, "Indefatigably."

19-1. 哀公问曰："何为则民服？"孔子对曰："举直错诸枉，则民服；举枉错诸直，则民不服。"(2.19)

Duke Ai asked, "What must we do to make the people obedient?" Confucius replied, "Promote the upright, place them above the crooked, and the people shall be obedient. Promote the crooked, place them above the upright, and the people shall be disobedient."

19-2. 樊迟问仁。子曰："爱人。"问知。子曰："知人。"樊迟未达。子曰："举直错诸枉，能使枉者直。"樊迟退，见子夏曰："乡也，吾见于夫子而问知；子曰：'举直错诸枉，能使枉者直。'何谓也？"子夏曰："富哉言乎！舜有天下，选于众，举皋陶，不仁者远矣；汤有天下，选于众，举伊尹，不仁者远矣。"(12.22)

Fan Chi asked about humanity. The Master said, "Love people." When asked about wisdom, the Master said, "Know people." Fan Chi did not quite understand. The Master said, "Promote the upright, place them above the crooked, and you shall make the crooked upright." Fan Chi withdrew, and, on meeting Zixia, said, "A moment ago, I went to see the Master and asked him about wisdom. The Master said, 'Promote the upright, place them above the crooked, and you shall make the crooked upright.' What does it mean?" Zixia said, "Rich words indeed! When Shun was in possession of the empire, he selected from among the multitudes and promoted Gao Yao, thus distancing inhumane men. When Tang was in possession of the empire, he selected from among the multitudes and promoted Yi Yin, thus distancing inhumane men."

19-3. 子贡问为仁。子曰："工欲善其事，必先利其器。居是邦也，事其大夫之贤者，友其士之仁者。"(15.9)

Zigong asked how to cultivate humanity. The Master said, "If an artisan wishes to do good work, he must first sharpen his tools. Living in this state, one must serve the worthy among the ministers and befriend the humane among the scholar-officials."

20-1. 子适卫，冉有仆。子曰："庶矣哉！"冉有曰："既庶矣，又何加焉？"曰："富之。"曰："既富矣，又何加焉？"曰："教之。"(13.9)

The Master journeyed to Wei, with Ran You driving. The Master said, "How populous!" Ran You said, "Now that it is populous, what is to be done next?" The Master said, "Enrich them." Ran You said, "When they are rich, what is to be done next?" The Master said, "Educate them."

20-2. 哀公问于有若曰："年饥，用不足，如之何？"有若对曰："盍彻乎？"曰："二，吾犹不足，如之何其彻也？"对曰："百姓足，君孰与不足？百姓不足，君孰与足？"(12.9)

Duke Ai asked You Ruo, "The year is lean, and revenues are insufficient. What is to be done?" You Ruo replied, "Why not levy a tithe?" Duke Ai said, "Even two-tenths is not enough for us. How could we manage with tithing?" You Ruo replied, "If your people have enough, how can you not have enough? If your people do not have enough, how can you have enough?"

20-3. 孔子曰："丘也闻有国有家者，不患贫而患不均，不患寡而患不安。盖均无贫，和无寡，安无倾。"(16.1)

Confucius said, "I have heard that the head of a state or of a noble house worries not about poverty but about inequality, and not about scarcity but about instability. For where there is equality, there is no poverty; where there is harmony, there is no scarcity; where there is stability, there is no collapse."

Vocabulary Index 词汇索引

The three numbers in the last column of this table represent chapter, section, and item, respectively. For example, 19.3.7 refers to chapter 19, vocabulary list 3, item 7. Chapter 0 refers to "Confucius and the *Analects*," which precedes chapter 1.

A

安插	ānchā	to plant (a person)	19.3.7
安逸	ānyì	easy and comfortable	11.3.18
傲	ào	proud, haughty	5.3.22

B

罢（官）	bà	to be removed from office	7.3.22
罢了	bàle	merely, only, that's all (used at the end of a sentence)	2.1.5
柏	bǎi	cypress	9.1.8
百科全书	bǎikē quánshū	encyclopedia	3.3.28
拜	bài	to make obeisance	4.3.14
拜	bài	to appoint (a government official)	13.3.11
拜谒	bàiyè	to pay a formal call, to pay respects	20.3.13
班师	bānshī	triumphant return of the army	19.3.10
邦	bāng	feudal state	14.1.4
帮补	bāngbǔ	to help, to supply	14.3.12
绑	bǎng	to bind, to tie	2.3.15
包围	bāowéi	to surround, to encircle	13.3.20
宝库	bǎokù	treasure house	0.1.27
保留	bǎoliú	to hold back, to reserve	15.1.17
报仇	bàochóu	to avenge	11.3.7
报答	bàodá	to repay another's kindness	6.2.2
报效	bàoxiào	to render a service to, to repay somebody's kindness by working hard for him	6.2.9
抱负	bàofù	aspiration, ambition	14.2.2
暴虎	bàohǔ	to fight a tiger barehanded	13.1.17
备	bèi	fully, in every possible way	6.3.4
狈	bèi	a kind of wolf with short forelegs	6.3.17

被动	bèidòng	passive	5.2.7
本	běn	stem, root, origin, basis, foundation	6.1.8
本来	běnlái	original	8.2.7
本来面目	běnlái miànmù	one's true colors	8.2.6
比	bǐ	collusion	7.1.4
鄙视	bǐshì	to despise, to disdain, to look down upon	15.2.5
敝	bì	破旧	9.1.19
弊病	bìbìng	malady, evil	3.1.9
避免	bìmiǎn	to avoid, to refrain from	11.1.9
毕生	bìshēng	all one's life, lifetime	20.3.16
陛下	bìxià	Your Majesty	8.3.17
编订	biāndìng	to edit, to compile	0.1.23
编年史	biānnián shǐ	chronological history	15.3.3
编撰	biānzhuàn	to compile and write	9.3.11
辨	biàn	to differentiate, to distinguish	2.1.23
便	biàn	就, then, in that case	2.1.28
遍	biàn	all over, everywhere	0.1.5
变更	biàngēng	change, alteration	14.3.29
标本	biāoběn	specimen, sample	3.3.13
表	biǎo	a memorial to the emperor	6.3.8
表（率）	biǎo (shuài)	example, model	0.1.36
表述	biǎoshù	表达和陈述	7.1.24
别号	biéhào	alias, byname, cognomen	14.3.14
兵部	bīngbù	the Ministry of War	14.3.21
兵书	bīngshū	books on military strategy	13.3.9
秉承	bǐngchéng	to act on orders	3.2.5
病	bìng	to worry	11.1.2
病逝	bìngshì	to die of illness	17.3.13
薄	bó	light, slight	11.1.5
搏斗	bódòu	to wrestle, to fight	13.1.24
博取	bóqǔ	to seek, to try to win	1.2.20
捕	bǔ	to catch, to arrest	14.3.8
部	bù	measure word for books, films, etc.	9.3.20
不计其数	bùjì qíshù	countless, innumerable	7.3.16
不料	bùliào	unexpectedly, to one's surprise	17.3.6
不巧	bùqiǎo	unluckily, unfortunately	17.3.4
不求甚解	bùqiú shènjiě	not to seek to understand things thoroughly	8.2.11
不屈	bùqū	unbending, unyielding	9.2.7

不胜枚举	bùshèng méijǔ	too numerous to mention individually	19.2.5
步入	bùrù	走进，走上	1.3.15
不足	bùzú	deficiency, inadequacy	8.2.15

C

猜测	cāicè	to guess, to surmise	3.1.10
材	cái	material, talent, aptitude	5.2.14
才干	cáigàn	ability, competence	10.2.6
财政	cáizhèng	finance, financial administration	20.2.3
残	cán	deficient, remaining	11.3.11
残兵败将	cánbīng bàijiàng	remnants of a routed army	11.3.10
藏	cáng	to hide, to conceal	14.1.2
操	cāo	a type of qin music	4.3.11
草鞋	cǎoxié	straw sandals	3.3.7
插	chā	to stick into, to insert	18.3.16
差错	chācuò	mistake, error	11.1.16
察	chá	to examine, to scrutinize	13.1.8
柴	chái	firewood	3.3.15
柴草	cháicǎo	firewood	11.3.16
阐述	chánshù	to expound, to elaborate	5.2.9
谄	chǎn	to flatter, to fawn over	4.1.17
谄媚	chǎnmèi	to flatter, to fawn over	4.1.26
昌盛	chāngshèng	prosperous	16.3.2
长	cháng	常	7.1.18
偿还	chánghuán	to repay	7.3.12
朝堂	cháotáng	imperial court	8.3.20
彻	chè	tithe, a tax of one-tenth	20.1.7
撤退	chètuì	to withdraw, to retreat	18.3.26
臣	chén	official under a sovereign, subject	6.2.10
陈	chén	to state	6.3.1
陈述	chénshù	to state	6.3.9
趁	chèn	to take advantage of, to avail oneself of	18.3.9
称道	chēngdào	to speak approvingly of, to commend	12.1.17
成	chéng	to help somebody to accomplish his goals	7.1.11
成全	chéngquán	to help somebody to accomplish his goals	7.1.13
惩处	chéngchǔ	to penalize, to punish	8.3.11
承受	chéngshòu	to bear, to endure	19.3.15
丞相	chéngxiàng	prime minister	10.3.4
持	chí	to hold	3.2.9

持久	chíjiǔ	lasting, enduring, protracted	13.3.1
尺	chǐ	unit of length measuring one-third of a meter today, but a shorter length in ancient times	10.1.16
耻	chǐ	to feel ashamed of	9.1.12
		sense of shame	16.1.12
耻辱	chǐrǔ	shame, disgrace, humiliation	9.1.16
赤	chì	红	12.2.2
赤手空拳	chìshǒu kōngquán	barehanded, unarmed	13.1.22
冲锋	chōngfēng	to charge, to assault	18.3.14
冲锋陷阵	chōngfēng xiànzhèn	to charge the enemy lines	18.3.13
冲击	chōngjī	to charge, to assault	18.3.11
充实	chōngshí	substantial	3.1.21
重	chóng	layer	1.2.5
重围	chóngwéi	tight encirclement	18.3.18
抽	chōu	to levy or collect taxes	20.1.11
仇	chóu	hatred, enmity	11.3.8
绸缎	chóuduàn	silks and satins	7.3.15
出处	chūchù	source (of a quotation or allusion)	4.2.1
出仕	chūshì	to take a government office	6.3.26
锄	chú	hoe, to hoe	12.3.3
处方	chǔfāng	prescription	3.3.22
处世	chǔshì	to conduct one's life, philosophy of life	11.1.1
处死	chǔsǐ	to execute, to put to death	8.3.13
触犯	chùfàn	to offend, to violate, to go against	8.3.25
传	chuán	to teach, to pass on (knowledge, skills, etc.)	8.1.6
传人	chuánrén	disciple, exponent	14.2.4
传诵	chuánsòng	to be widely read about; to be admired	1.3.25
创瘢	chuāngbān	scar	18.2.7
创始人	chuàngshǐ rén	founder	0.1.3
垂	chuí	to hang down, to hand down	9.3.13
纯	chún	pure	18.2.1
慈	cí	kind, benevolent, loving	6.2.16
词	cí	a poetic genre	14.3.30
刺	cì	to tattoo	19.3.1
刺	cì	to stab, to prick	2.3.6

次日	cìrì	第二天	10.3.12
匆忙	cōngmáng	急忙	18.3.25
从容	cōngróng	calm, unhurried	10.3.16
从	cóng	跟从, to follow	8.1.8
从事	cóngshì	to do, to be engaged in	3.1.20
从政	cóngzhèng	to have a political career	0.1.11
粗粮	cūliáng	coarse grains such as corn and millet as (distinct from wheat and rice)	5.1.14
粗心大意	cūxīn dàyì	careless, negligent	8.2.14
催	cuī	to hurry, to urge	17.3.8
摧残	cuīcán	to wreck, to destroy, to devastate	19.3.6
磋	cuō	to grind and polish	4.1.20
错	cuò	措，放, to place	19.1.2
措手不及	cuòshǒu bùjí	to be caught unprepared	18.3.12

D

达	dá	successful, prominent	14.2.6
达	dá	明白	19.1.7
打盹儿	dǎ dǔnr	to doze off	2.3.16
打瞌睡	dǎ kēshuì	to doze off, take a nap	2.3.20
打天下	dǎ tiānxià	to struggle to seize state power, to establish an enterprise	17.3.12
打猎	dǎliè	to go hunting	3.3.16
大夫	dàfu	senior official	19.1.13
大节	dàjié	political integrity	10.1.22
大举进攻	dàjǔ jìngōng	to mount a large-scale offensive	10.3.3
大势已去	dàshì yǐqù	the situation is beyond salvation, irretrievable, hopeless	18.3.24
殆	dài	不安、疑难	15.1.16
代理宰相	dàilǐ zǎixiàng	acting chief minister	0.1.13
丹	dān	红色	10.3.23
箪	dān	a bamboo vessel for holding cooked rice	5.1.18
担心	dānxīn	to worry	11.1.18
担忧	dānyōu	to worry, to be anxious	18.1.8
胆	dǎn	gallbladder, gall	11.3.2
当差	dāngchāi	to do a duty (as a clerk or servant)	5.3.14
当众	dāngzhòng	in the presence of all, in public	7.3.14
荡	dàng	level	7.1.17

道	dǎo	导、引导、 to guide, to lead	16.1.9
道	dào	真理, the Way, the ultimate principle of the universe	1.1.15
盗	dào	thief, robber	18.1.5
盗墓	dàomù	to rob a grave	16.3.22
登峰造极	dēngfēng zàojí	to reach the summit, to reach the height of perfection	14.3.4
登基	dēngjī	to ascend to the throne	20.3.2
堤坝	dībà	dikes and dams	14.3.20
敌	dí	敌手、对手、 rivals of equal strength	13.3.10
抵御	dǐyù	to resist	1.3.21
弟子	dìzǐ	disciple	0.1.9
弟子	dìzǐ	年轻人	6.1.17
典范	diǎnfàn	model, example	0.1.31
雕	diāo	to carve	13.1.2
凋	diāo	to wither	9.1.9
凋谢	diāoxiè	to wither and fall	9.1.10
叮嘱	dīngzhǔ	to enjoin and urge repeatedly	13.3.13
顶	dǐng	measure word for things that serve as (or might have) a top cover, such as hats, etc.	12.3.13
顶	dǐng	to go against	17.3.5
定义	dìngyì	definition	7.2.1
动摇	dòngyáo	to vacillate, to waver	10.1.24
毒	dú	poison	3.3.18
独	dú	lonely, alone	11.1.11
笃	dǔ	sincere, earnest	1.1.20
睹	dǔ	to see	12.3.5
杜绝	dùjué	to stop (a bad practice, etc.)	3.1.8
端	duān	upright, proper	10.3.15
端正	duānzhèng	upright, proper, correct	18.2.3
断定	duàndìng	to conclude, to form a judgment, to determine	15.2.4
夺	duó	to take by force	10.1.12
舵	duò	rudder, helm	12.2.5

E

阿谀	ēyú	to fawn over	12.1.10
恶	è	坏	9.1.13

恩	ēn	kindness, favor, grace	6.2.4
尔	ěr	你	14.1.3
二	èr	two-tenths, 20 percent	20.1.8
贰	èr	二	2.1.11
贰过	èrguò	to repeat errors	2.1.10

F

发	fā	to initiate, to enlighten	4.1.4
发兵	fābīng	to dispatch troops	11.3.3
发布	fābù	to issue, to release	18.1.4
发愤	fāfèn	to make a determined effort, to strive resolutely	2.3.18
发挥	fāhuī	to fully utilize (one's abilities)	14.2.5
发泄	fāxiè	to give vent to, to let out	2.1.14
罚	fá	punishment	8.3.16
法制	fǎzhì	legal system	16.1.14
番	fān	次	13.3.3
凡	fán	ordinary	5.3.25
繁茂	fánmào	lush, luxuriant	5.3.15
烦恼	fánnǎo	to be vexed, worried	5.1.23
返	fǎn	to return	0.1.20
反	fǎn	to infer, to analogize	4.1.7
反省	fǎnxǐng	introspection, self-examination	8.2.5
汎	fàn	广泛, broadly, extensively	6.1.13
饭	fàn	吃	5.1.7
犯	fàn	to violate, to offend	2.1.15
犯上	fànshàng	to go against one's superior	6.1.3
犯颜	fànyán	to incur the displeasure of an elder or superior by one's words	8.3.21
纺线	fǎngxiàn	to spin cotton into yarn	11.3.20
仿效	fǎngxiào	to imitate, to follow the example of	18.2.5
放牛	fàngniú	to herd cattle	5.3.2
放纵	fàngzòng	self-indulgent, undisciplined, unmannered	12.1.18
非	fēi	不是	8.2.1
非...不可	fēi . . . bùkě	必须、一定要、一定得	1.2.17
悱	fěi	inarticulate, unable to express one's emotion	4.1.3
废	fèi	to abandon	13.1.13
废弃	fèiqì	to discard, to abandon	13.1.15
分配	fēnpèi	to distribute, to assign	20.2.6

分歧	fēnqí	difference, divergence	0.1.15
分手	fēnshǒu	to separate, to part company with	12.3.20
芬芳	fēnfāng	fragrance	5.3.30
纷纷	fēnfēn	numerous and disorderly	13.3.21
焚	fén	to burn	7.3.1
坟墓	fénmù	grave, tomb	16.3.14
粉刷	fěnshuā	to whitewash, to plaster	13.1.7
粪	fèn	manure, dirty	13.1.3
愤	fèn	anger, resentment	4.1.1
愤慨	fènkǎi	(righteous) indignation	19.3.11
封地	fēngdì	fief	7.3.4
锋利	fēnglì	sharp	19.1.14
逢	féng	to meet, to come across, to happen upon	11.3.15
奉承	fèngchéng	to flatter	12.1.11
俸禄	fènglù	an official's salary	15.1.4
奉献	fèngxiàn	to devote, to dedicate	6.2.8
奉行	fèngxíng	to pursue, to practice	12.1.26
佛寺	fósì	Buddhist temple	1.3.8
肤浅	fūqiǎn	superficial, shallow	1.2.3
服	fú	to serve	6.1.18
服	fú	to obey, to submit oneself to	19.1.4
服丧	fúsāng	to be in mourning (for the death of a kinsman, etc.)	6.3.25
服侍	fúshi	to wait upon, to attend	6.3.5
浮	fú	floating	5.1.13
夫	fú	他	16.1.7
扶	fú	to support with the hand	7.3.24
俘	fú	to capture, to take prisoner	10.3.5
幅	fú	measure word for paintings, etc.	3.3.24
福利	fúlì	material benefits, welfare	15.2.10
抚养	fúyǎng	to provide subsistence, to bring up	6.3.3
俯	fǔ	to bow (one's head)	14.3.1
腐败	fǔbài	corrupt	19.2.4
腐朽	fǔxiǔ	rotten	13.1.6
辅佐	fǔzuǒ	to assist a ruler in governing a country	10.2.7
负	fù	to carry on the back or shoulder	15.1.9
复	fù	再	4.1.8
赴	fù	去、到	6.3.11
赴宴	fùyàn	to attend a banquet	7.3.10
富	fù	丰富	19.1.9

富裕	fùyù	rich, wealthy, prosperous	4.1.27
附和	fùhè	to echo, to chime in with, to parrot another's opinions	7.2.6
妇孺	fùrú	妇女和孩子	1.2.1
附图	fùtú	attached map or drawing, figure	3.3.23

G

该	gāi	这	3.3.27
改嫁	gǎijià	(of a woman) to remarry	6.3.2
盖	gài	to build (a house)	5.3.12
概括	gàikuò	to summarize, to generalize	1.2.8
概念	gàiniàn	concept	1.2.21
干	gān	求	15.1.12
感	gǎn	sense, feeling	6.2.6
感慨	gǎnkǎi	deep feeling, thoughts	7.3.27
纲目	gāngmù	detailed outline (often used in a book title)	3.3.1
刚毅	gāngyì	resolute and steadfast	10.1.5
割	gē	to cut, to slash	12.2.1
胳膊	gēbo	arm	5.1.15
搁置	gēzhì	to shelve, to lay aside	15.1.18
格	gé	standard, norm	16.1.13
格言	géyán	motto	1.3.26
隔阂	géhé	estrangement, misunderstanding	20.2.14
各行各业	gèháng gèyè	all trades and professions	1.1.16
更	gēng	改	8.1.11
耕	gēng	to plow, to till	15.1.2
耕地	gēngdì	cultivated land	20.3.8
耕耘	gēngyún	to till and weed	5.3.11
肱	gōng	forearm	5.1.10
恭	gōng	respectful	11.1.14
躬	gōng	身体、亲自	11.1.3
躬身	gōngshēn	to bend at the waist, to bow	4.3.13
工匠	gōngjiàng	craftsman, artisan	1.1.18
功名	gōngmíng	official rank and academic degree (determined by performance in the imperial examinations)	5.3.9
宫刑	gōngxíng	punishment by castration	9.3.8
公余	gōngyú	spare time after work	14.3.10
共	gǒng	拱, to encircle	16.1.3

供养	gòngyǎng	to offer provisions (especially to one's parents)	6.2.19
勾结	gōujié	to collude, to gang up on	7.1.6
孤	gū	solitary, isolated, alone	5.3.21
孤	gū	orphan	10.1.17
孤傲	gū'ào	proud and aloof	5.3.20
孤苦伶仃	gūkǔ língdīng	lonely and helpless	6.3.20
股	gǔ	thigh	2.3.7
股	gǔ	(measure word) group, cluster, faction	17.3.1
鼓吹	gǔchuī	to advocate, to preach, to advertise	15.2.6
古籍	gǔjí	ancient books	0.1.22
故	gù	旧	2.1.26
固	gù	stubborn	3.1.7
固	gù	firm	9.1.1
固然	gùrán	虽然	8.3.15
固执	gùzhí	stubborn	3.1.12
寡	guǎ	少	3.1.14
观	guān	outlook, view	10.2.4
关键	guānjiàn	key, crux	8.2.2
观念	guānniàn	sense, concept, mentality	6.2.18
关头	guāntóu	juncture, moment	10.2.9
光芒	guāngmáng	rays of light, radiance	4.3.7
归队	guīduì	to rejoin one's unit	18.3.19
归顺	guīshùn	to submit, to surrender	11.3.13
跪	guì	to kneel	10.3.14
国计民生	guójì mínshēng	national economy and the people's livelihood	20.3.5
国君	guójūn	monarch, king	0.1.14
过	guò	过错, fault, error	2.1.12
过程	guòchéng	course, process	5.2.6
过渡	guòdù	transition	16.3.3
过失	guòshī	过错	2.1.16

H

害	hài	to do harm to, to impair	10.1.7
含义	hányì	meaning, implication	1.2.7
颔	hǎn	chin	8.3.22
撼	hàn	to shake	19.3.5
汗青	hànqīng	(history) book	10.3.24

行	háng	trade, profession	1.1.17
毫不	háobù	not at all	12.3.4
好不	hǎobù	非常、十分	12.3.15
号	hào	alias, byname, cognomen	14.3.2
好	hào	喜爱	2.1.7
貉	hé	raccoon dog	9.1.23
和	hé	harmony, to mingle	7.1.7
和睦	hémù	harmony, concord	6.2.14
和谐	héxié	harmony	7.1.10
核对	héduì	to check (the facts), to verify	7.3.11
核心	héxīn	core	0.1.26
弘	hóng	great, magnificent	10.1.2
鸿	hóng	wild goose	9.3.9
厚	hòu	深、重、 thick, deep	11.1.4
厚葬	hòuzàng	an elaborate funeral	16.3.13
后悔	hòuhuǐ	to regret	13.1.26
后世	hòushì	later generations	0.1.25
忽略	hūlüè	to neglect, to overlook	15.2.7
忽视	hūshì	to disregard, to neglect	6.2.15
狐	hú	fox	9.1.22
画	huà	划、划分、 to divide	1.3.3
话题	huàtí	topic (of a conversation or talk)	10.2.1
环绕	huánrào	to surround, to encircle, to revolve around	16.1.4
患	huàn	担心, to worry	7.2.8
悔	huǐ	to regret	13.1.19
诲	huì	教导	3.1.3
贿	huì	bribe	8.3.14
慧	huì	intelligence, wisdom	12.1.21
荤菜	hūncài	meat dishes	1.3.19
惑	huò	to be puzzled, bewildered	7.1.21

J

击	jī	to attack	9.3.4
齑	jī	chopped pickles	1.3.2
饥	jī	famine, crop failure	20.1.5
饥荒	jīhuāng	farming	20.1.10
积累	jīlěi	to accumulate	11.2.3
激励	jīlì	to encourage, to inspire	10.2.10
激战	jīzhàn	fierce fighting	18.3.22

即位	jíwèi	to ascend to the throne	8.3.5
即使	jíshǐ	even, even if, even though	18.1.9
急迫	jípò	urgent, pressing, imperative	6.3.14
集成	jíchéng	collection (of books)	20.3.14
集体	jítǐ	group, team	6.2.1
寄	jì	to consign	10.1.18
济	jì	to aid, to relieve	14.2.8
计	jì	stratagem, scheme, plot	13.3.18
计较	jìjiào	to mind, to care, to dispute, to haggle	3.1.23
计谋	jìmóu	scheme, stratagem	8.3.18
纪	jì	biographies of emperors	9.3.17
纪传体	jìzhuàntǐ	history presented in a series of biographies	9.3.16
技能	jìnéng	skill	1.2.9
技法	jìfǎ	skill, technique	4.3.4
既然	jìrán	since, this being the case	5.2.4
嘉奖	jiājiǎng	to commend, to cite	6.3.24
家境	jiājìng	family financial situation	1.3.6
家族	jiāzú	clan, family	17.2.4
甲	jiǎ	armor	13.3.17
甲兵	jiǎbīng	soldier in armor	1.3.23
驾	jià	to drive (a vehicle)	7.3.21
稼	jià	to sow (grain), crops	15.1.5
兼	jiān	concurrently, simultaneously	14.2.7
兼听则明，偏听则暗	jiāntīng zémíng, piāntīng zéàn	listen to both sides and you will be enlightened	19.2.8
奸臣	jiānchén	treacherous courtier	19.2.3
奸细	jiānxì	spy, enemy agent	19.3.8
肩负	jiānfù	to undertake, to shoulder	10.2.2
艰辛	jiānxīn	arduous and difficult	0.1.4
监狱	jiānyù	prison	9.3.7
捡	jiǎn	to pick up (from the ground)	12.3.6
检讨	jiǎntǎo	to examine oneself, to do some soul searching	8.2.10
检验	jiǎnyàn	to test, to examine, to inspect	2.2.4
简练	jiǎnliàn	succinct	13.2.1
谏	jiàn	admonition	8.3.3
箭	jiàn	arrow	11.3.4
贱	jiàn	lowly, humble	14.1.12

见风使舵	jiànfēng shǐduò	to act as the occasion dictates	12.2.3
剑客	jiànkè	swordsman	18.2.6
讲究	jiǎngjiu	to be particular about, to stress	2.2.3
讲求	jiǎngqiú	to stress, to strive for	7.1.9
交	jiāo	to associate with, to have friendly contact with	8.1.5
交战	jiāozhàn	to wage war, to be at war against each other	13.3.7
骄	jiāo	undisciplined, willful, arrogant	12.1.14
校	jiào	to be concerned, to dispute	3.1.17
轿子	jiàozi	sedan chair	12.3.14
皆	jiē	都	1.2.2
阶层	jiēcéng	(social) stratum	20.2.13
揭示	jiēshì	to reveal, to bring to light	1.2.4
截	jié	section	12.3.18
节	jié	to control, to be moderate in	12.1.12
节	jié	to economize, to save	17.1.5
节俭	jiéjiǎn	thrifty, frugal	1.3.18
节制	jiézhì	practice temperance in, to exercise moderation in	12.1.16
结党营私	jiédǎng yíngsī	to form a clique to pursue selfish interests	7.2.4
结论	jiélùn	conclusion	15.2.9
结义	jiéyì	to become sworn brothers	17.3.3
拮据	jiéjū	financial constraints	20.2.4
解	jiě	理解、了解	8.2.13
金牌	jīnpái	gold plaque that represents an emperor's edict	19.3.9
金属	jīnshǔ	metal	16.3.21
谨	jǐn	谨慎, prudent, circumspect	6.1.12
仅	jǐn	only, 差不多	10.3.18
尽管	jǐnguǎn	even though, despite	13.3.2
谨慎	jǐnshèn	prudent, careful	2.1.22
进谏	jìnjiàn	to present an admonition to the emperor	8.3.7
尽情	jìnqíng	to one's heart's content, as much as one likes	12.1.19
进士	jìnshì	one who has passed the highest-level imperial examinations	1.3.14
精练	jīngliàn	concise, succinct	0.1.30

K

开导	kāidǎo	to educate and enlighten, to help one straighten out wrong or muddled thinking	4.1.10
开荒	kāihuāng	to cultivate virgin soil	14.3.11
开支	kāizhī	expenses, spending	17.1.8
堪	kān	to bear, to stand	5.1.22
砍	kǎn	to cut, to chop	3.3.14
坎坷	kǎnkě	bumpy, rough	14.3.5
考察	kǎochá	to inspect, to examine	13.1.10
科举	kējǔ	civil service examinations (in ancient China)	20.3.11
可	kě	pretty good, not bad	4.1.18
可谓	kěwèi	可以说（是）	2.1.21
刻苦	kèkǔ	assiduous, hardworking, painstaking	4.2.3
垦荒	kěnhuāng	to open up virgin soil	20.3.6
恳切	kěnqiè	earnest, sincere	1.1.24
空前	kōngqián	unprecedented	3.3.25
苦于	kǔyú	to suffer (a disadvantage)	4.1.11
筐	kuāng	rectangular box woven from bamboo strips or wicker	3.3.8
矿物	kuàngwù	mineral	3.3.26
旷野	kuàngyě	wilderness, prairie	3.3.10
愧	kuì	to be ashamed, conscience-stricken	10.3.21
捆	kǔn	to tie, to bundle	17.3.11

L

滥	làn	reckless, unrestrained	9.1.5
狼	láng	wolf	6.3.16
狼狈	lángbèi	in a difficult position, in a dilemma	6.3.15
劳	láo	to labor, to make people work hard	18.1.12
类	lèi	kind, type, class	5.2.11
类型	lèixíng	type	13.2.7
李	lǐ	plum (blossoms)	5.3.28
里	lǐ	unit of length equal to half a kilometer	10.1.19
礼	lǐ	proprieties, rituals	1.2.10
礼部	lǐbù	the Ministry of Rites	14.3.23
礼教	lǐjiào	ethical code	16.1.16
礼节	lǐjié	courtesy, etiquette, protocol	11.1.17
理念	lǐniàn	ideas, concepts	1.2.15
利	lì	sharp	19.1.11

联	lián	a poetic couplet	10.3.22
廉洁	liánjié	incorruptible, to be honest in performing one's official duties	19.3.2
梁	liáng	roof beam	2.3.5
两极分化	liǎngjí fēnhuà	polarization, division (of a group, society, etc.)	20.2.12
谅	liàng	honest, sincere	12.1.3
鳞	lín	scale (of a fish, etc.)	8.3.24
临	lín	to face, to encounter	10.1.23
临	lín	to arrive, to be present	20.3.12
临终	línzhōng	on one's deathbed	13.3.12
陵	líng	imperial tomb, mausoleum	16.3.15
领会	lǐnghuì	to understand, to comprehend, to grasp	4.1.28
令	lìng	command, order	18.1.1
溜	liū	to go secretly and quietly	5.3.4
陋	lòu	narrow and small, ugly, mean	5.1.20
鲁莽	lǔmǎng	crude and rash	13.2.8
禄	lù	an official's salary	15.1.1
露台	lùtái	balcony, deck	16.3.9
屡	lǚ	repeatedly, time and again	18.3.4
屡次	lǚcì	多次	8.3.6
律	lǜ	to restrain, to keep under control	16.3.7
乱	luàn	disorder, chaos, upheaval, riot	6.1.6
伦理	lúnlǐ	ethics, moral principles	1.2.14
锣	luó	gong	12.3.9

M

埋头	máitóu	to immerse oneself in, to be engrossed in	4.3.3
卖弄	màinòng	to show off, to parade	12.1.22
盲目	mángmù	blind	7.2.5
矛盾	máodùn	contradiction	20.2.15
冒	mào	to risk, to brave	3.3.19
冒犯	màofàn	to offend	3.1.22
梅	méi	plum blossom	5.3.1
门客	ménkè	a hanger-on of an aristocrat	7.3.3
猛	měng	fierce, vigorous	13.3.16
迷惑	míhuò	to be puzzled, bewildered	7.1.22
免	miǎn	to be excused, exempted	16.1.11

免（职）	miǎn	to be removed from office	7.3.19
面目	miànmù	face, appearance	8.2.8
民不聊生	mín bù liáoshēng	the people have no means to earn a living	20.2.5
敏	mǐn	nimble, diligent	2.1.17
鸣	míng	to ring, to sound	12.3.12
鸣锣	míngluó	to beat gongs	12.3.11
名分	míngfèn	a person's title/position and duty	17.2.1
名副其实	míngfù qíshí	the name matches the reality, to be worthy of the name	19.3.4
命	mìng	fate, destiny	10.1.20
磨	mó	to grind and polish	4.1.23
默	mò	silent	5.1.2
莫	mò	不	9.1.3
莫非	mòfēi	难道	4.3.10
末年	mònián	last years of a dynasty or reign	10.3.1
谋	móu	to work for, to plot, to seek, to consult	8.1.4
谋反	móufǎn	to plot a rebellion	19.3.14
谋划	móuhuà	to plan, to scheme	13.1.27
谋取	móuqǔ	to try to gain, to seek	7.1.2
某	mǒu	certain (used to refer to a person or a thing)	7.2.2

N

纳	nà	to receive, to accept, to admit	8.3.2
纳谏	nàjiàn	(of an emperor) to accept an admonition	8.3.1
乃	nǎi	是	6.2.11
南面	nánmiàn	面南, facing south	16.1.8
囊	náng	bag	2.3.1
馁	něi	饿	15.1.3
能臣	néngchén	capable courtier	19.2.7
能否	néngfǒu	能不能	8.2.3
逆	nì	contrary, counter	8.3.23
逆境	nìjìng	unfavorable circumstances	14.3.28
年	nián	年成, harvest, crops	20.1.4
年成	niánchéng	the year's harvest	7.3.7
年迈	niánmài	年老	6.3.6

起草	qǐcǎo	to draft	14.3.15
起居	qǐjū	daily life	7.3.26
讫	qì	until, up to	15.3.4
器	qì	工具	19.1.12
气息奄奄	qìxī yǎnyǎn	at one's last gasp, at the point of death	6.3.22
牵	qiān	to pull, to drag	2.3.17
迁	qiān	to move, to change	2.1.9
迁怒	qiānnù	to vent one's anger at somebody else	2.1.8
千古	qiāngǔ	through the ages	1.3.24
谦恭	qiāngōng	modest and respectful	3.2.4
谦和	qiānhé	modest and amiable	3.2.7
谦虚	qiānxū	modest, humble	2.2.1
谦逊	qiānxùn	modest, unassuming	3.2.6
前提	qiántí	premise, prerequisite, presupposition	15.2.8
虔敬	qiánjìng	reverent	3.2.3
潜心	qiánxīn	to concentrate, to devote oneself to something	12.3.21
襁	qiǎng	swaddling clothes, to swaddle	15.1.8
切	qiē	to cut, to slice	4.1.19
切磋	qiēcuō	to improve oneself through discussion with another	4.1.21
切	qiè	earnestly, specifically	1.1.22
切近	qièjìn	近	1.1.25
窃	qiè	to steal	18.1.7
亲	qīn	亲近, to be close to	6.1.14
琴	qín	a seven-stringed, plucked instrument, similar to the zither	4.3.1
寝	qǐn	睡觉	13.1.1
倾	qīng	to incline, to collapse	20.1.15
倾覆	qīngfù	to overturn,to topple	20.1.16
轻视	qīngshì	to look down upon, to underestimate	15.2.14
清澈	qīngchè	limpid, clear	18.2.16
清苦	qīngkǔ	穷苦	1.3.11
清明	qīngmíng	clear and just (administration)	19.2.2
勤政	qínzhèng	to govern the country diligently	20.3.1
情操	qíngcāo	sentiment, value	9.2.1
情势	qíngshì	situation	6.3.13
穷	qióng	predicament	9.1.2
穷追	qióngzhuī	to pursue relentlessly	13.3.15

茕茕孑立	qióngqióng jiélì	standing all alone	6.3.18
求	qiú	to seek, to strive for	10.1.6
求和	qiúhé	to sue for peace	11.3.12
曲	qū	to bend	5.1.9
屈服	qūfú	to surrender, to yield	10.1.25
取代	qǔdài	to replace	13.3.14
拳	quán	fist	13.1.23
券	quàn	certificate, ticket	7.3.2
阙	quē	空缺	15.1.13
却	què	but, yet, however	12.3.17
确立	quèlì	to establish	0.1.32

R

然而	rán'ér	但是	0.1.18
扰乱	rǎoluàn	to harass, to disturb	16.2.6
人格	réngé	character, moral quality	5.2.2
人头税	réntóushuì	head tax, tax according to population	20.3.7
人云亦云	rényún yìyún	to parrot what another says	7.2.7
仁	rén	humanity, benevolence	1.1.23
忍	rěn	to bear, to endure	12.3.7
任	rèn	mission, task	10.1.1
日	rì	每天	8.1.2
日薄西山	rìbó xīshān	"the sun approaching the western hills"—old age	6.3.21
日食	rìshí	solar eclipse	8.1.13
日益	rìyì	(to advance) each day	8.2.16
融洽	róngqià	harmonious, on friendly terms	7.2.3
如此	rúcǐ	这样	5.2.5
儒家	rújiā	Confucianism	0.1.2
女	rǔ	汝，你	3.1.4
入关	rùguān	to enter the pass—here referring to Qing troops entering the Shanhai Pass 山海关 in 1644 and starting to rule China proper	20.3.4
蕊	ruǐ	flower bud	5.3.16

S

三军	sānjūn	the army (of a large state)	10.1.11
丧	sàng	to lose, to be deprived of	1.3.5

色	sè	脸色, facial expression	6.1.16
闪烁	shǎnshuò	to twinkle, to glisten	4.3.6
善	shàn	好	12.1.13
善	shàn	to be good at, to be an expert	18.3.3
善柔	shànróu	flattery	12.1.5
赏	shǎng	to grant a reward, to award	18.1.6
尚书	shàngshū	minister	14.3.22
奢侈	shēchǐ	luxurious, extravagant	16.3.12
蛇	shé	snake, serpent	3.3.17
舍	shě	to abandon, to give up	14.1.1
射	shè	archery	1.2.11
赦	shè	to pardon, to give amnesty	9.3.15
涉	shè	to wade	3.3.9
涉及	shèjí	to involve, to relate to, to touch upon	0.1.29
身	shēn	自身，自己	8.1.3
身先士卒	shēnxiān shìzú	to lead one's men in a charge	18.3.1
深刻	shēnkè	deep, profound	19.1.11
甚	shèn	很	8.2.12
慎	shèn	careful, cautious	2.1.18
生计	shēngjì	livelihood, means of livelihood	14.3.13
生气	shēngqì	life, vitality	5.3.19
绳之以法	shéngzhī yǐfǎ	to prosecute someone in accordance with the law	8.3.19
绳子	shéngzi	cord, rope, string	2.3.14
乘	shèng	a carriage pulled by four horses	17.1.3
圣人	shèngrén	sage	0.1.37
施	shī	to execute, to apply	5.2.15
施	shī	to give, to grant	12.1.25
施展	shīzhǎn	to put (a plan) into practice	14.2.1
失	shī	过失	11.1.13
失势	shīshì	to lose power and influence, to fall into disgrace	7.3.18
什一	shíyī	十分之一, one tenth	20.1.13
时	shí	按时, on schedule	1.1.5
时	shí	农时; the proper season for planting, harvesting, etc.	17.1.7
识别	shíbié	to distinguish, to discern, to judge	12.2.6
实	shí	substantial	3.1.15
实践	shíjiàn	practice	1.1.10

实事求是	shíshì qiúshì	to seek truth from facts, to be practical and realistic	3.2.1
食	shí	eclipse	8.1.10
使	shǐ	to use, to operate	12.2.4
史学家	shǐxuéjiā	historian	9.3.1
始终	shǐzhōng	from beginning to end, throughout	13.3.5
适	shì	to go, to arrive at	20.1.1
室	shì	household	2.1.1
弑	shì	regicide or patricide	17.2.2
士	shì	scholar-official	9.1.11
士气	shìqì	morale	18.3.20
士卒	shìzú	士兵	18.3.2
仕途	shìtú	official career	1.3.16
事	shì	to serve, to attend	17.1.2
事例	shìlì	example, case	1.3.1
是	shì	这	7.1.12
是非	shìfēi	对和错	2.1.24
势力	shìlì	force, power	17.3.2
手下	shǒuxià	subordinates	11.3.9
疏浚	shūjùn	to dredge	14.3.19
疏食	shūshí	coarse food	5.1.8
恕	shù	forgiveness, magnanimity	12.1.23
数	shù	几	1.3.22
庶	shù	人口多	20.1.3
庶几	shùjǐ	almost, nearly	10.3.20
衰落	shuāiluò	to decline, to be on the wane	1.3.7
衰亡	shuāiwáng	to decline and fall (as a nation)	13.3.23
帅	shuài	commander-in-chief	10.1.13
帅	shuài	to lead, to command	18.1.2
率	shuài	带领	0.1.16
税	shuì	tax	16.3.5
税率	shuìlǜ	tax rate	20.2.2
说法	shuōfa	statement, argument	0.1.28
顺境	shùnjìng	favorable circumstances	14.3.27
顺序	shùnxù	sequence, order	15.2.13
死记硬背	sǐjì yìngbèi	mechanical memorization	4.2.2
死战	sǐzhàn	to fight to the death	18.3.23
肆	sì	shop, workshop	1.1.13

四朝元老	sìcháo yuánlǎo	a veteran statesman who stays in power under four successive emperors or regimes	15.3.1
四方	sìfāng	all quarters, everywhere	15.1.7
松	sōng	pine tree	9.1.7
搜求	sōuqiú	to seek	3.3.11
俗	sú	vulgar, in poor taste	5.3.27
速	sù	快	10.3.11
粟	sù	millet, also a general term for grain	17.1.1
塑造	sùzào	to model, to mold, to portray	8.2.4
随波逐流	suíbō zhúliú	to go with the flow, to follow other people's views and actions	13.2.4
岁	suì	年	9.1.6
损	sǔn	harm, damage	12.1.2
损害	sǔnhài	to harm, to damage	10.1.9

T

泰然	tàirán	calm, composed	14.3.26
太史令	tàishǐlìng	title of the historian in the Han court	9.3.2
太守	tàishǒu	prefect	6.3.27
贪	tān	greedy	10.1.8
贪官污吏	tānguān wūlì	corrupt officials	8.3.8
贪污	tānwū	corruption, graft	8.3.9
坦	tǎn	(of a road, etc.) level and broad	7.1.16
坦荡	tǎndàng	bighearted, contented and composed	7.1.15
探讨	tàntǎo	to explore, to discuss	1.2.19
桃	táo	peach (blossoms)	5.3.26
陶器	táoqì	pottery, earthenware	16.3.20
讨	tǎo	to demand, to ask for	7.3.5
特质	tèzhì	special quality	2.2.2
题	tí	to inscribe (a poem, etc.)	5.3.24
提倡	tíchàng	to advocate, to promote, to encourage	5.2.1
体	tǐ	style, form	9.3.19
体会	tǐhuì	to know from experience	2.1.27
弟	tì	same as 悌, love and respect for one's elder brother	6.1.2
天文学	tiānwénxué	astronomy	20.3.17
天涯海角	tiānyá hǎijiǎo	the ends of the earth, the remotest corners of the world	14.3.24

W

为人	wéirén	behavior, character	4.3.5
为政	wéizhèng	治理国家	16.1.1
违	wéi	to disobey, to violate	17.1.11
围	wéi	to enclose, to surround	18.3.8
唯	wéi	only, alone	3.1.13
唯	wéi	因为	10.3.19
唯恐	wéikǒng	to worry	11.3.17
维护	wéihù	to safeguard, to defend, to uphold	16.2.3
委婉	wěiwǎn	mild and tactful	6.3.12
谓	wèi	（对什么人）说	4.1.13
未	wèi	没有	2.1.13
未尝	wèicháng	不曾、没有	19.3.3
温	wēn	温习	2.1.25
文	wén	to cover up, to paint over	8.1.15
文献	wénxiàn	documents	0.1.24
文治武功	wénzhì wǔgōng	political and military achievements	20.3.19
稳固	wěngù	firm, stable	6.2.13
圬	wū	trowel	13.1.4
污	wū	dirty, filthy	18.2.14
污垢	wūgòu	dirt, filth	8.2.9
诬告	wūgào	to bring a false charge against	19.3.13
诬陷	wūxiàn	to frame someone	14.3.7
吾	wú	我，我的	3.1.19
毋	wú	不要	3.1.1
无私	wúsī	selfless, unselfish	6.2.7
无为而治	wúwéi érzhì	to achieve peace and order without action	16.1.5
无影无踪	wúyǐng wúzōng	(to vanish or disappear) without a trace	5.3.6
武断	wǔduàn	arbitrary	3.1.11
武艺	wǔyì	martial arts	13.2.9
务	wù	to attend to, to devote one's efforts to	6.1.7
误解	wùjiě	to misunderstand	15.2.1

X

昔	xī	从前	3.1.18
牺牲	xīshēng	to sacrifice one's life, to die a martyr's death	10.1.10
稀有	xīyǒu	rare, unusual	7.3.17
席	xí	straw mat	12.2.2

习	xí	复习、练习、实习	1.1.6
习性	xíxìng	habits and characteristics	3.3.20
细	xì	thin, slender	18.2.8
细胞	xìbāo	cell	6.2.12
下台	xiàtái	to fall out of power, to leave office	17.2.3
先	xiān	to lead, to go ahead of	18.1.11
先帝	xiāndì	deceased emperors	16.3.11
先生	xiānsheng	父兄	6.1.10
咸菜	xiáncài	pickles	1.3.10
贤人	xiánrén	a person of virtue	0.1.10
闲游	xiányóu	to take a stroll, to go on an outing	17.3.7
显露	xiǎnlù	to become visible	14.1.8
鲜	xiǎn	少	6.1.4
见	xiàn	现, to emerge, to appear	14.1.10
陷	xiàn	to crush (the enemy), to capture (a city, etc.)	18.3.15
限度	xiàndù	limit	11.2.1
乡	xiāng	village, township	13.1.11
相传	xiāngchuán	according to legend	0.1.8
巷	xiàng	lane, alley	5.1.21
乡	xiàng	过去、从前、刚才	19.1.8
相	xiàng	宰相	7.3.23
象征	xiàngzhēng	to symbolize, to signify	9.2.6
消磨	xiāomó	to wear down, to sap	11.3.19
小辈	xiǎobèi	the younger generation	6.1.21
孝	xiào	filial piety	6.1.1
孝顺	xiàoshùn	filial piety	6.1.9
效	xiào	仿效, to imitate, to follow the example of	18.2.10
效法	xiàofǎ	to follow the model of, to learn from	9.3.10
携	xié	to take somebody by the hand	7.3.25
邪	xié	evil, heretical, irregular	12.1.9
邪恶	xié'è	evil, wicked	19.1.6
写照	xiězhào	portrayal	1.3.27
懈怠	xièdài	slack, sluggish	18.1.14
心惊胆战	xīnjīng dǎnzhàn	to tremble with fear	18.3.7
薪	xīn	firewood	11.3.1
信	xìn	faithful, honest	2.1.4
兴	xīng	起来	9.1.4
兴亡	xīngwáng	rise and fall (of a nation)	19.2.1

兴修	xīngxiū	to start construction (on a large project), to build	14.3.18
行	xíng	走	8.1.7
行	xíng	to do, to practice, to carry out	12.1.20
		to run, to administer	13.1.16
刑	xíng	penalty, punishment	16.1.10
刑场	xíngchǎng	execution ground	10.3.13
刑法	xíngfǎ	penal code, criminal law	16.1.15
形势	xíngshì	terrain, topographical features	16.3.16
形影相吊	xíngyǐng xiāngdiào	"body and shadow comforting each other"—extremely lonely	6.3.19
省	xǐng	to examine (oneself), to reflect, to be introspective	8.1.1
胸怀	xiōnghuái	mind, heart	3.2.8
雄才大略	xióngcái dàlüè	great talent and bold strategy	20.3.18
羞愧	xiūkuì	ashamed, abashed	11.3.22
修身	xiūshēn	to cultivate one's moral character	1.3.13
修养	xiūyǎng	cultivation, training	2.2.6
休养生息	xiūyǎng shēngxī	to recuperate and grow in population	16.3.1
朽	xiǔ	rotten, decayed	9.3.14
虚	xū	空	3.1.16
悬	xuán	to hang	2.3.4
悬赏	xuánshǎng	to offer (or post) a reward (for the capture of a criminal, etc.)	18.1.10
悬殊	xuánshū	great disparity, wide gap	20.2.11
旋涡	xuánwō	whirlpool, vortex	14.3.6
选拔	xuǎnbá	to select, to choose	19.1.5
穴	xué	cave, hole	16.3.18
学堂	xuétáng	学校 (old term)	5.3.5
学说	xuéshuō	theory, doctrine	0.1.34
雪耻	xuěchǐ	to avenge an insult, to wipe out a disgrace	11.3.14
孙	xùn	逊, respectful and compliant	14.1.6
迅速	xùnsù	rapid, swift, speedy, prompt	20.3.9

Y

押送	yāsòng	to send under escort, to escort	10.3.6
涯	yá	margin, limit	14.3.25
严	yán	strict, severe	8.3.10

意	yì	to guess, to speculate	3.1.2
意味	yìweì	to signify, to mean, to imply	6.2.20
佚游	yìyóu	unrestrained gaiety	12.1.15
因	yīn	on the basis of, in accordance with	5.2.13
因材施教	yīncái shījiào	to teach students according to their aptitudes	5.2.12
隐	yǐn	to hide, to retire, to live like a hermit	14.1.11
隐居	yǐnjū	to retire from public life, to live in seclusion	5.3.10
萤	yíng	firefly	2.3.2
萤火虫	yínghuǒchóng	firefly	2.3.11
映	yìng	to reflect	2.3.3
永垂不朽	yǒngchuí bùxiǔ	to be immortal (due to fame, accomplishment, etc.)	9.3.12
用	yòng	consumption, spending	17.1.6
用	yòng	finances, funds	20.1.6
用度	yòngdù	expenditure, expense	20.1.12
忧	yōu	worry, sorrow	11.1.10
优待	yōudài	preferential treatment	20.3.10
忧虑	yōulǜ	worry, anxiety	5.1.17
尤	yóu	fault, wrongdoing	15.1.15
有教无类	yǒujiào wúlèi	to provide education for all people without discrimination	5.2.10
有效	yǒuxiào	effective	1.3.20
黝黑	yǒuhēi	dark	4.3.8
幼	yòu	young, underage	2.3.8
诱导	yòudǎo	to guide, to lead, to induce	5.2.17
隅	yú	corner, nook	4.1.6
余	yú	more than, over	3.3.6
余力	yúlì	strength and energy to spare	6.1.15
愚	yú	foolish, stupid	14.1.7
愚昧	yúmèi	ignorant, dull	14.1.9
与	yǔ	同意	4.1.16
欲	yù	想要	12.1.24
狱	yù	prison, jail	14.3.9
御	yù	to drive (a carriage)	1.2.12
喻	yù	to understand, to know	7.1.1
愈	yù	better	4.1.14
源头	yuántóu	fountainhead, source	18.2.12

终身	zhōngshēn	lifelong	10.2.3
重伤	zhòngshāng	severe injury	11.3.5
重用	zhòngyòng	to put somebody in an important position	19.2.6
周	zhōu	circumference, unity, harmony	7.1.3
周游列国	zhōuyóu lièguó	to travel to many states	0.1.17
粥	zhōu	gruel	1.3.4
昼	zhòu	白天	1.3.9
朱	zhū	vermilion, bright red	12.2.1
诛	zhū	to reproach	13.1.5
逐	zhú	追	13.2.5
主动	zhǔdòng	taking the initiative	5.2.8
注重	zhùzhòng	to stress, to pay attention to	20.2.10
著称	zhùchēng	famous, celebrated	8.3.4
助长	zhùzhǎng	to encourage (a bad habit, etc.), to foment	7.1.14
专注	zhuānzhù	to concentrate on, to devote one's mind to	0.1.21
传	zhuàn	biography	9.3.18
馔	zhuàn	food, to eat and drink	6.1.20
赚钱	zhuànqián	to make money	15.2.11
庄稼	zhuāngjià	crops	15.1.11
状元	zhuàngyuán	title conferred on the top scorer in the highest-level imperial examination	10.3.2
追求	zhuīqiú	to seek, to pursue	2.2.7
追逐	zhuīzhú	to chase, to pursue, to seek	5.3.8
锥子	zhuīzi	awl	2.3.19
准	zhǔn	definitely, certainly	12.3.10
准则	zhǔnzé	standard, criterion	2.2.5
浊	zhuó	turbid, muddy	18.2.11
琢	zhuó	to chisel, to carve	4.1.22
琢磨	zhuómó	to carve and polish (jade), to refine and improve (literary works, moral status, etc.)	4.1.24
姿态	zītài	posture, pose	9.2.4
子	zǐ	master; used in the *Analects* to refer to Confucius	1.1.3
字	zì	style (name)	0.1.1
踪	zōng	footprint, trace	5.3.7
总结性	zǒngjiéxìng	conclusive	3.3.3
足	zú	to deserve	9.1.14

卒	zú	soldier	13.3.22
钻研	zuānyán	to study intensively, to dig into	4.2.4
遵命	zūnmìng	to obey orders	6.3.10
作	zuò	创造、建立（理论、学说）	3.1.5
作坊	zuòfáng	workshop	1.1.19
作乱	zuòluàn	to rebel	6.1.5

Proper Names Index 专名索引

The three numbers in the last column of this table represent chapter, section, and item, respectively. For example, 2.1.1 refers to chapter 2, proper name list 1, item 1. Chapter 0 refers to "Confucius and the Analects," which precedes chapter 1.

Z

Function Words Index 虚词索引

This is a concordance of all function words appearing in this textbook.

Word		Meaning/ Function	Example Sentences	Passage
必	bì	一定	小人之过也必文。	8.6
			众恶之，必察焉。	13.2
			众好之，必察焉。	13.2
			必也临事而惧，好谋而成者也。	13.5
尝	cháng	曾经	昔者吾友尝从事于斯矣。	3.4
得而	dé'ér	能够	虽有粟，吾得而食诸？	17.1
而	ér	又	博学而笃志	1.3
			切问而近思	1.3
			谨而信。	6.2
			汎爱众，而亲仁。	6.2
			任重而道远。	10.1
			君子敬而无失。	11.5
			与人恭而有礼。	11.5
		而且	学而时习之，不亦说乎？	1.1
			始吾于人也，听其言而信其行。	13.1
			今吾于人也，听其言而观其行。	13.1
			夫如是，则四方之民襁负其子而至矣，焉用稼？	15.2
			敬事而信，节用而爱人。	17.3
			乡也，吾见于夫子而问知。	19.2
		就、能	温故而知新。	2.5
			告诸往而知来者。	4.3
			君子务本，本立而道生。	6.1
			见不贤而内自省也。	8.3
			有一言而可以终身行之者乎？	12.4
			必也临事而惧，好谋而成者也。	13.5
			无为而治者，其舜也与？	16.2

Word		Meaning/ Function	Example Sentences	Passage
			其身正，不令而行。	18.2
		但是、却	人不知而不愠，不亦君子乎？	1.1
			犯而不校。	3.4
			贫而无谄，富而无骄。	4.3
			未若贫而乐道，富而好礼者也。	4.3
			学而不厌	5.2
			不义而富且贵。	5.3
			其为人也孝弟，而好犯上者。	6.1
			不好犯上，而好作乱者。	6.1
			君子周而不比，小人比而不周。	7.2
			君子和而不同，小人同而不和。	7.3
			为人谋而不忠乎？	8.1
			与朋友交而不信乎？	8.1
			过而不改，是谓过矣。	8.4
			士志于道，而耻恶衣恶食者，未足与议也。	9.3
			衣敝缊袍，与衣狐貉者立，而不耻者，其由也与？	9.4
			临大节而不可夺也。	10.4
			躬自厚，而薄责於人。	11.4
			暴虎冯河，死而不悔者，吾不与也。	13.4
			居其所而众星共之。	16.1
			道之以政，齐之以刑，民免而无耻。	16.3
			丘也闻有国有家者，不患贫而患均，不患寡而患不安。	20.3
		来、去	就有道而正焉。	2.3
而后	érhòu	然后	死而后已，不亦远乎。	10.1
而已	éryǐ	(used to connote limited scope)	夫何为哉？恭己正南面而已矣。	16.2
夫	fú	啊	惟我与尔有是夫。	14.1
		他	夫何为哉？	16.2

Word		Meaning/ Function	Example Sentences	Passage
		(to initiate a sentence)	夫如是，则四方之民襁负其子而至矣，焉用稼？	15.2
			夫何为哉？恭己正南面而已矣。	16.2
弗	fú	不	弗如也。吾与女，弗如也。	4.2
盖	gài	大概	盖有不知而作之者。	3.2
			盖均无贫，和无寡，安无倾。	20.3
苟	gǒu	假如	苟正其身矣，于从政何有乎？	18.3
			苟子之不欲，虽赏之不窃。	18.4
何	hé	什么	何有于我哉？	5.2
			君子居之，何陋之有！	9.5
			于予与何诛？	13.1
			夫何为哉？恭己正南面而已矣。	16.2
			苟正其身矣，于从政何有乎？	18.3
			何为则民服？	19.1
			既庶矣，又何加焉？	20.1
			既富矣，又何加焉？	20.1
		怎么	赐也何敢望回？	4.2
			“举直错诸枉，能使枉者直。”何谓也？	19.2
		何必	君子何患乎无兄弟也？	11.5
何如	hérú	怎么样	贫而无谄，富而无骄，何如？	4.3
			乡人皆好之，何如？	13.2
			乡人皆恶之，何如？	13.3
盍	hé	何不	盍彻乎？	20.2
乎	hū	吗	学而时习之，不亦说乎？	1.1
			有朋自远方来，不亦乐乎？	1.1
			人不知而不愠，不亦君子乎？	1.1
			曾是以为孝乎？	6.3

Word		Meaning/ Function	Example Sentences	Passage
			为人谋而不忠乎？	8.1
			与朋友交而不信乎？	8.1
			传不习乎？	8.1
			君子亦有穷乎？	9.1
			仁以为己任，不亦重乎？	10.1
			死而后已，不亦远乎？	10.1
			有一言而可以终身行之者乎？	12.4
		呢	苟正其身矣，于从政何有乎？	18.3
			不能正其身，如正人乎？	18.3
		吧	其恕乎！	12.4
		啊	富哉言乎！	19.2
		(to pause)	君子何患乎无兄弟也？	11.5
或	huò	有人	或曰："陋，如之何？"	9.5
既	jì	已经	既庶矣，又何加焉？	20.1
			既富矣，又何加焉？	20.1
皆，	jiē	都	过也，人皆见之。	8.5
			更也，人皆仰之。	8.5
			人皆有兄弟，我独亡！	11.5
			四海之内皆兄弟也。	11.5
			乡人皆好之，何如？	13.3
			乡人皆恶之，何如？	13.3
可	kě	能	三军可夺帅也。	10.3
			其知可及也，其愚不可及也。	14.3
		可以、行	未可也。	13.3
可以	kěyǐ	能	温故而知新，可以为师矣。	2.5
			可以托六尺之孤。	10.4
			可以寄百里之命。	10.4
		应当	士，不可以不弘毅。	10.1
莫	mò	不	从者病，莫能兴。	9.1
			上好礼，则民莫敢不敬。	15.2
			上好义，则民莫敢不服。	15.2

Word		Meaning/ Function	Example Sentences	Passage
			上好信，则民莫敢不用情。	15.2
其	qí	他（们）的、它（们）的	百工居肆以成其事。	1.2
			君子学以致其道。	1.2
			仁在其中矣。	1.3
			日知其所亡，月无忘其所能。	2.4
			乐亦在其中矣。	5.3
			人不堪其忧，回也不改其乐。	5.5
			始吾于人也，听其言而信其行。	13.1
			今吾于人也，听其言而观其行。	13.1
			不如乡人之善者好之，其不善者恶之。	13.3
			其知可及也，其愚不可及也。	14.3
			耕也，馁在其中矣。	15.1
			学也，禄在其中矣。	15.1
			夫如是，则四方之民襁负其子而至矣，焉用稼？	15.2
			多闻阙疑，慎言其馀，则寡尤。	15.3
			多见阙殆，慎行其馀，则寡悔。	15.3
			言寡尤，行寡悔，禄在其中矣。	15.3
			居其所而众星共之。	16.1
			其身正，不令而行。	18.2
			其身不正，虽令不从。	18.2
			苟正其身矣，于从政何有乎？	18.3
			不能正其身，如正人乎？	18.3
			工欲善其事，必先利其器。	19.3
			居是邦也，事其大夫之贤者，友其士之仁者。	19.3
		那个	有事，弟子服其劳。	6.3
		大概	其斯之谓与？	4.3
			衣敝缊袍，与衣狐貉者立，而不耻者，其由也与？	9.4
			其恕乎！	12.4
			无为而治者，其舜也与？	16.2
		如果	其为人也孝弟，而好犯上者，鲜矣。	6.1
		真是	孝弟也者，其为仁之本欤！	6.1

Word		Meaning/ Function	Example Sentences	Passage
且	qiě	而且	不义而富且贵。	5.3
			邦有道，贫且贱焉，耻也。	14.4
			邦无道，富且贵焉，耻也。	14.4
			道之以德，齐之以礼，有耻且格。	16.3
如	rú	像	十室之邑，必有忠信如丘者焉。	2.1
			如切如磋，如琢如磨。	4.3
			于我如浮云。	5.3
			君子之过也，如日月之食焉。	5.5
			夫如是，则四方之民襁负其子而至矣，焉用稼？	15.2
		及、比得上	不如丘之好学也。	2.1
			弗如也。吾与女，弗如也。	4.2
			吾不如老农。	15.2
			吾不如老圃。	15.2
		如何、怎样	不能正其身，如正人乎？	18.3
如之何	rúzhī hé	怎么办	或曰："陋，如之何？"	9.5
			哀公问于有若曰："年饥，用不足，如之何？"	20.2
		怎样才好	君使臣，臣事君，如之何？	17.2
		怎么能	二，吾犹不足，如之何其彻也？	20.2
若	ruò	像	有若无，实若虚。	3.4
是	shì	这、这个	我无是也。	3.2
			小人反是。	7.4
			过而不改，是谓过矣。	8.4
			于予与改是。	13.1
			惟我与尔有是夫。	14.1
			夫如是，则四方之民襁负其子而至矣，焉用稼？	15.2
			居是邦也，事其大夫之贤者，友其士之仁者。	19.3
孰	shú	谁	弟子孰为好学？	2.2
			女与回也孰愈？	4.2
			子帅以正，孰敢不正？	18.1

Word		*Meaning/ Function*	*Example Sentences*	*Passage*
孰与	shúyǔ	怎么会	百姓足，君孰与不足？	20.2
			百姓不足，君孰与足？	20.2
斯	sī	这、这个	昔者吾友尝从事于斯矣。	3.4
			其斯之谓与？	4.3
		则、就	小人穷斯滥矣。	9.1
虽	suī	虽然	其身不正，虽令不从。	18.2
			苟子之不欲，虽赏之不窃。	18.4
惟	wéi	只有	惟我与尔有是夫。	14.1
未	wèi	没有、不曾	未闻好学者也。	2.2
			不好犯上，而好作乱者，未之有也。	6.1
		不	未可也。	13.3
未若	wèiruò	不如	未若贫而乐道，富而好礼者也。	4.3
未足	wèizú	不值得	士志于道，而耻恶衣恶食者，未足与议也。	9.3
亡	wú	没有	今也则亡。	2.2
			日知其所亡。	2.4
			人皆有兄弟，我独亡！	11.5
无	wú	不	君子食无求饱，居无求安。	2.3
			月无忘其所能。	2.4
		没有	盖有不知而作之者，我无是也。	3.2
			无求生以害仁。	10.2
			君子病无能焉。	11.1
			君子何患乎无兄弟也？	11.5
毋	wú	不要	毋意、毋必、毋固、毋我。	3.3
勿	wù	不要	己所不欲，勿施于人。	12.4

Word		Meaning/ Function	Example Sentences	Passage
奚	xī	为什么	女奚不曰。	5.4
信如	xìnrú	假如	信如君不君，臣不臣，父不父，子不子，虽有粟，吾得而食诸？	17.1
焉	yān	了，啊	十室之邑，必有忠信如丘者焉。	2.1
			就有道而正焉。	2.3
			君子道者三，我无能焉。	7.6
			三人行，必有我师焉。	8.2
			见贤思齐焉。	8.3
			君子之过也，如日月之食焉。	5.5
			君子病无能焉。	11.3
			众恶之，必察焉。	13.2
			众好之，必察焉。	13.2
		(used to pause, and for emphasis)	邦有道，贫且贱焉，耻也。	14.4
		何必	夫如是，则四方之民襁负其子而至矣，焉用稼？	15.2
		呢	既庶矣，又何加焉？	20.1
			既富矣，又何加焉？	20.1
也	yě	了、啊	不如丘之好学也。	2.1
			未闻好学者也。	2.2
			可谓好学也已。	2.3
			可谓好学也已矣。	2.4
			知之为知之，不知为不知，是知也。	3.1
			我无是也。	3.2
			举一隅不以三隅反，则不复也。	4.1
			未若贫而乐道，富而好礼者也。	4.3
			贤哉，回也！	5.5
			不好犯上，而好作乱者，未之有也。	6.1
			夫子自道也！	7.6
			见不贤而内自省也。	8.3
			岁寒然后知松柏之后凋也。	9.2
			士志于道，而耻恶衣恶食者，未	9.3

Word	Meaning/ Function	Example Sentences	Passage
		足与议也。	
		三军可夺帅也。	10.3
		匹夫不可夺志也。	10.3
		临大节而不可夺也。	10.4
		君子人与？君子人也。	10.4
		不患人之不己知，患不知人也。	11.2
		不病人之不己知也。	11.3
		四海之内皆兄弟也。	11.5
		朽木不可雕也。	13.1
		粪土之墙不可圬也。	13.1
		未可也。	13.2
		其知可及也，其愚不可及也。	14.3
		邦有道，贫且贱焉，耻也。	14.4
		邦无道，富且贵焉，耻也。	14.4
		小人哉，樊须也！	15.2
		政者正也。	18.1
	吧、呢	衣敝缊袍，与衣狐貉者立，而不耻者，其由也与？	9.4
		君子何患乎无兄弟也？	11.5
		无为而治者，其舜也与？	16.2
		“举直错诸枉，能使枉者直。”何谓也？	19.2
	(used to pause, and for emphasis)	今也则亡。	2.2
		女与回也孰愈？	4.2
		赐也何敢望回？	4.2
		回也闻一以知十。	4.2
		赐也闻一以知二。	4.2
		赐也！始可与言《诗》已矣。	4.3
		其为人也，发愤忘食。	5.4
		人不堪其忧，回也不改其乐。	5.5
		其为人也孝弟。	6.1
		孝弟也者，其为仁之本欤！	6.1
		君子之过也，如日月之食焉。	5.5
		过也，人皆见之。	8.5
		更也，人皆仰之。	8.5
		小人之过也必文。	8.6

Word		Meaning/ Function	Example Sentences	Passage
			始吾于人也，听其言而信其行。	13.1
			今吾于人也，听其言而观其行。	13.1
			必也临事而惧，好谋而成者也。	13.5
			耕也，馁在其中矣。	15.1
			学也，禄在其中矣。	15.1
			乡也，吾见于夫子而问知。	19.2
			居是邦也，事其大夫之贤者，友其士之仁者。	19.3
			丘也闻有国有家者，不患贫而患不均，不患寡而患不安。	20.3
以	yǐ	用、拿	百工居肆以成其事。	1.2
			君子学以致其道。	1.2
			以能问于不能，以多问于寡。	3.4
			举一隅不以三隅反，则不复也。	4.1
			为政以德。	16.1
			道之以政，齐之以刑，民免而无耻。	16.3
			道之以德，齐之以礼，有耻且格。	16.3
			君使臣以礼，臣事君以忠。	17.2
			子帅以正，孰敢不正？	18.1
		根据	君子不以言举人，不以人废言。	13.4
			使民以时。	17.3
		而	回也闻一以知十。	4.2
			赐也闻一以知二。	4.2
			乐以忘忧。	5.4
			无求生以害仁。	10.1
			有杀身以成仁。	10.2
以为	yǐwéi	作为	曾是以为孝乎？	6.3
			仁以为己任，不亦重乎。	10.1
已	yǐ	了、啊	可谓好学也已。	2.3
			可谓好学也已矣。	2.4
			赐也！始可与言《诗》已矣。	4.3

Word		Meaning/ Function	Example Sentences	Passage
矣	yǐ	了、啊	仁在其中矣。	1.3
			不幸短命死矣。	2.2
			可谓好学也已矣。	2.4
			温故而知新，可以为师矣。	2.5
			昔者吾友尝从事于斯矣。	3.4
			赐也！始可与言《诗》已矣。	4.3
			乐亦在其中矣。	5.3
			其为人也孝弟，而好犯上者，鲜矣。	6.1
			过而不改，是谓过矣。	8.4
			小人穷斯滥矣。	9.1
			躬自厚，而薄责于人，则远怨矣。	11.4
			商闻之矣。	11.5
			友直，友谅，友多闻；益矣。	12.1
			友便辟，友善柔，友便佞，损矣。	12.1
			乐节礼乐，乐道人之善，乐多贤友，益矣。	12.2
			乐骄乐，乐佚游，乐宴乐，损矣。	12.2
			群居终日，言不及义，好行小慧，难矣！	12.3
			耕也，馁在其中矣。	15.1
			学也，禄在其中矣。	15.1
			夫如是，则四方之民襁负其子而至矣，焉用稼？	15.2
			夫何为哉？恭己正南面而已矣。	16.2
			苟正其身矣，于从政何有乎？	18.3
			舜有天下，选于众，举皋陶，仁者远矣。	19.2
			汤有天下，选于众，举伊尹，不仁者远矣。	19.2
			庶矣哉！	20.1
			既庶矣，又何加焉？	20.1
			既富矣，又何加焉？	20.1
亦	yì	也	学而时习之，不亦说乎？	1.1

Word		Meaning/ Function	Example Sentences	Passage
			有朋自远方来，不亦乐乎？	1.1
			人不知而不愠，不亦君子乎？	1.1
			乐亦在其中矣。	5.3
			君子亦有穷乎？	9.1
			仁以为己任，不亦重乎。	10.1
			死而后已，不亦远乎。	10.1
犹	yóu	还	二，吾犹不足，如之何其彻也	20.2
有	yǒu	(to initiate a sentence)	有杀身以成仁。	10.2
于	yú	在	昔者吾友尝从事于斯矣。	3.4
			士志于道，而耻恶衣恶食者，未足与议也。	9.3
			舜有天下，选于众，举皋陶，不仁者远矣。	19.2
			汤有天下，选于众，举伊尹，不仁者远矣。	19.2
		对于	敏于事而慎于言。	2.3
			何有于我哉？	5.2
			于我如浮云。	5.3
			君子喻于义，小人喻于利。	7.1
			躬自厚，而薄责于人。	11.4
			于予与何诛？	13.1
			始吾于人也，听其言而信其行。	13.1
			今吾于人也，听其言而观其行。	13.1
			于予与改是。	13.1
			苟正其身矣，于从政何有乎？	18.3
		向	以能问于不能，以多问于寡。	3.4
			叶公问孔子于子路。	5.4
			齐景公问政於孔子。	17.1
			季康子问政于孔子。	18.1
			季康子患盗，问于孔子。	18.4
			哀公问于有若曰："年饥，用不足，如之何？"	20.2
		被	乡也，吾见于夫子而问知。	19.2

Word		Meaning/ Function	Example Sentences	Passage
		给	己所不欲，勿施于人。	12.4
与	yú	吧	其斯之谓与？	4.3
			衣敝缊袍，与衣狐貉者立，而不耻者，其由也与？	9.4
			君子人与？君子人也。	10.4
			无为而治者，其舜也与？	16.2
		啊	孝弟也者，其为仁之本与！	6.1
			于予与何诛？	13.1
			于予与改是。	13.1
与	yǔ	和	女与回也孰愈？	4.2
			士志于道，而耻恶衣恶食者，未足与议也。	9.3
			君子敬而无失，与人恭而有礼。	11.5
			子行三军，则谁与？	13.4
			惟我与尔有是夫。	14.1
云尔	yúněr	等等	不知老之将至云尔。	5.4
哉	zāi	啊	贤哉，回也！	5.5
			小人哉，樊须也！	15.2
			善哉！信如君不君，臣不臣，父不父，子不子，虽有粟，吾得而食诸？	17.1
			富哉言乎！	19.2
			庶矣哉！	20.1
		呢	何有于我哉？	5.2
			夫何为哉？恭己正南面而已矣。	16.2
在	zài	在	仁在其中矣。	1.3
			一箪食，一瓢饮，在陋巷。	5.5
			在陈绝粮。	9.1
			死生有命，富贵在天。	11.5
则	zé	就	今也则亡，未闻好学者也。	2.2
			举一隅不以三隅反，则不复也。	4.1

Word		Meaning/ Function	Example Sentences	Passage
			弟子入则孝，出则弟。	6.2
			行有余力，则以学文。	6.2
			子行三军，则谁与？	13.4
			用之则行，舍之则藏。	14.1
			邦有道则知，邦无道则愚。	14.3
			天下有道则见，无道则隐。	14.4
			夫如是，则四方之民襁负其子而至矣，焉用稼？	15.2
			多闻阙疑，慎言其馀，则寡尤。	15.3
			多见阙殆，慎行其馀，则寡悔。	15.3
			何为则民服？	19.1
			举直错诸枉，则民服。	19.1
			举枉错诸直，则民不服。	19.1
曾是	zēngshì	竟然	曾是以为孝乎？	6.3
者	zhě	（的）人	十室之邑，必有忠信如丘者焉。	2.1
			有颜回者好学。	2.2
			未闻好学者也。	2.2
			盖有不知而作之者。	3.2
			未若贫而乐道，富而好礼者也。	4.3
			知之者不如好之者。	5.1
			好之者不如乐之者。	5.1
			其为人也孝弟，而好犯上者，鲜矣。	6.1
			不好犯上，而好作乱者，未之有也。	6.1
			从者病，莫能兴。	9.1
			士志于道，而耻恶衣恶食者，未足与议也。	9.3
			衣敝缊袍，与衣狐貉者立，而不耻者，其由也与？	9.4
			不如乡人之善者好之，其不善者恶之。	13.3
			暴虎冯河，死而不悔者，吾不与也。	13.4
			必也临事而惧，好谋而成者也。	13.5
			无为而治者，其舜也与？	16.2
			举直错诸枉，能使枉者直。	19.2

Word		Meaning/ Function	Example Sentences	Passage
			舜有天下，选于众，举皋陶，不仁者远矣。	19.2
			汤有天下，选于众，举伊尹，不仁者远矣。	19.2
			居是邦也，事其大夫之贤者，友其士之仁者。	19.3
			丘也闻有国有家者，不患贫而患不均，不患寡而患不安。	20.3
		（的）事	告诸往而知来者	4.3
			择其善者而从之，其不善者而改之。	8.2
		(used to pause, and for emphasis)	昔者吾友尝从事于斯矣。	3.4
			孝弟也者，其为仁之本欤！	6.1
			君子道者三。	7.6
			益者三友，损者三友。	12.1
			益者三乐，损者三乐。	12.2
			政者正也。	18.1
		吗	有一言而可以终身行之者乎？	12.4
之	zhī	他（们）、它（们）	学而时习之，不亦说乎？	1.1
			知之者不如好之者。	5.1
			好之者不如乐之者。	5.1
			默而识之。	5.2
			曲肱而枕之。	5.3
			择其善者而从之，其不善者而改之。	8.2
			过也，人皆见之。	8.5
			更也，人皆仰之。	8.5
			商闻之矣。	11.5
			有一言而可以终身行之者乎？	12.4
			众恶之，必察焉。	13.2
			众好之，必察焉。	13.2
			乡人皆好之，何如？	13.3
			乡人皆恶之，何如？	13.3
			不如乡人之善者好之，其不善者恶之。	13.3
			居其所而众星共之。	16.1

Word		*Meaning/ Function*	*Example Sentences*	*Passage*
			道之以政，齐之以刑，民免而无耻。	16.3
			道之以德，齐之以礼，有耻且格。	16.3
			先之，劳之。	18.5
			富之。	20.1
			教之。	20.1
		的	十室之邑，必有忠信如丘者焉。	2.1
			不如丘之好学也。	2.1
			盖有不知而作之者。	3.2
			不知老之将至云尔。	5.4
			君子成人之美，不成人之恶。	7.4
			君子之过也，如日月之食焉。	8.5
			小人之过也必文。	8.6
			岁寒然后知松柏之后凋也。	9.2
			可以托六尺之孤。	10.4
			可以寄百里之命。	10.4
			不患人之不己知。	11.2
			不病人之不己知也。	11.3
			乐道人之善。	12.2
			不如乡人之善者好之。	13.3
			夫如是，则四方之民襁负其子而至矣，焉用稼？	15.2
			道千乘之国。	17.3
			居是邦也，事其大夫之贤者，友其士之仁者。	19.3
		(used to add emphasis)	诲女知之乎！	3.1
			知之为知之。	3.1
			其斯之谓与？	4.3
			不好犯上，而好作乱者，未之有也。	6.1
			君子居之，何陋之有！	9.5
			用之则行，舍之则藏。	14.1
			苟子之不欲，虽赏之不窃。	18.4
诸	zhū	之	告诸往而知来者。	4.3

Word		Meaning/ Function	Example Sentences	Passage
		之于	君子求诸己，小人求诸人。	11.5
			举直错诸枉，则民服。	19.1
			举枉错诸直，则民不服。	19.1
			举直错诸枉，能使枉者直。	19.2
		之乎	信如君不君，臣不臣，父不父，子不子，虽有粟，吾得而食诸？	17.1
自	zì	从	有朋自远方来，不亦乐乎？	1.1

Idiom Index 成语索引

Vocabulary Expansion Index 词汇扩展索引